Creating Instructional Multimedia Solutions: Practical Guidelines for the Real World

Peter Fenrich
British Columbia Institute of Technology

Creating Instructional Multimedia Solutions: Practical Guidelines for the Real World

Mail requests for permission to make copies of any part of the work to:
Peter Fenrich
8223 Woodlake Court
Burnaby, BC
Canada
V5A 3P3

ISBN: 83-922337-1-9

Published by

Informing Science Press
Publishing arm of the Informing Science Institute:
131 Brookhill Court
Santa Rosa
California
95409
USA
Phone: +1 707 531 4925
Fax: +1 480 247 5724
ISPress.org
InformingScience.org

Printed in the US, Canada, the Netherlands, United Kingdom, and Australia

With appreciation of the patience needed while I wrote this book, I dedicate this book to Jayne, Shannon, Alexander, David, and Kim. May you always keep your sense of humor and stay forever young.

Acknowledgements

This book has evolved with the advice and feedback of many people. I greatly appreciate the numerous reviewers for their perceptive analysis. In particular, I would like to acknowledge:
- John Blackwell, Douglas College
- Eli B. Cohen, Informing Science Institute
- Mark Eisley, Boise State University
- Edward Forrest, Florida State University
- Liz Hammond-Kaarremaa, Malaspina University-College
- Patrick O'Brien, University-College of the Fraser Valley
- Leah Pietron, University of Nebraska-Omaha
- Sorel Riesman, California State University
- Edward Stohr, New York University
- Robert Watts, Idaho State University

My students have also been invaluable for their encouragement, ideas, and candid comments.

I wish to acknowledge the 'SAGE for Learning' research project, funded by the Social Sciences Research Council of Canada (SSHRC), for financial support and for providing opportunities for learning that found their way into this book.

I would particularly like to thank those who have supported both my career and me:
- Jayne (my wife)
- David Kaufman (a friend and colleague of many years for whom I have the utmost respect)
- Krishna Alluri (who has helped and continues to help me achieve a personal goal of supporting developing countries and their endeavors with instructional technology)
- Paul Thiel and Michael Hrybyk (managers who have supported and encouraged me to take on challenging projects that have pushed the boundaries of what can be taught effectively with instructional multimedia technology)
- Joey Dabell (a team member whose programming and other talents make new ideas succeed)

Thanks also to:
- Elena Underhill for the design of the front cover.
- Donna Smith who rescued me with her exceptional word-processing skills.

Preface

This book is intended for students, instructional designers, professors, instructors, teachers, trainers, software developers, and development team leaders who:
- are taking a course on creating instructional multimedia applications
- are or will be working on an instructional multimedia design and development team
- need to expand their skills into the multimedia technology field
- are excited about the possibilities of teaching with multimedia
- have worked on their own and unsuccessfully tried to do it all
- may have created mediocre multimedia courseware
- want to do it right the first time
- need a practical reference
- need practical guidelines for creating computer-managed presentations

This book focuses on the practical aspects of creating instructional multimedia applications and computer-managed presentations. In instructional multimedia applications, the computer assumes the teaching role. In computer-managed presentations, you maintain the responsibility for teaching the learners. In a sense, computer-managed presentations are a subset of instructional multimedia applications. Their differences will be highlighted throughout the book.

This book will not make you an instructional multimedia expert. Expertise comes through years of experience and continual learning. However, this book will provide you with the foundations for creating professional and effective products.

To gain support for your instructional multimedia applications and computer-managed presentations as well as to silence the critics, it is important to create excellent products. People will notice quality much more than quantity. This is especially true for your first project. This book, with its numerous practical hints, will help you do it right from your first project onwards.

Since creating instructional multimedia applications requires numerous different skills than traditional methods (e.g., lecture, discussions, print materials...), you should, if possible, involve instructional multimedia specialists in order to do it right. Instructional multimedia productions usually require the combined expertise found in a team of highly-skilled professionals such as instructional designers, subject-matter experts, programmers, and media specialists. However, your reality may be that there are minimal, if any, other resources available to you. Consequently, it may be wise for you to start by creating computer-managed presentations, as they are much simpler to produce. This book provides guidelines that can enable you to create both effective instructional multimedia products and computer-managed presentations.

Perhaps the biggest challenge in writing this book is teaching about multimedia with only text and visuals. Ideally, you should use this book in a setting where you can see numerous instructional multimedia examples and you can put the book's guidelines into practice. Since the principles presented (e.g., those for instructional design and screen design) are fundamental guidelines, the principles apply to all computer platforms and software development tools that currently exist and those that will be developed. In other words, the principles presented are independent of the technology being used. Note that some of the included references are dated from the 1980's and even 1970's. The principles provided by these researchers (e.g., in writing objectives, working with teams, using color...) are still valid today and will continue to be valuable in the future.

Specific hardware and software tools are not formally addressed in this book. Given that entire books have been written on them, it is not possible to give the tools justice within this book.

If you are an instructor teaching an instructional multimedia course and are using this book as a reference, it may not be necessary to teach all of the sections in the book. Some learners will have strong backgrounds in some areas. Adapt this book to the audience and time available. Note that there is no guarantee that a learner who has experience in a related area can proficiently do the skills needed for instructional multimedia applications. One reason for this is that it is fundamentally different to teach with a computer than with traditional methods. Nonetheless, the skills can be learned.

For brevity, this book only refers to instructors rather than professors, instructors, teachers, trainers, and facilitators. The presented principles apply equally well to anyone who teaches or trains students. In general, no distinction is made between teaching and training.

Constructive feedback is an important component of creating instructional multimedia applications. Similarly, constructive feedback can also improve print materials. I welcome any ideas that can strengthen this book.

Peter Fenrich

Contents

Instructional Multimedia Basics

There are many things you need to address before undertaking an instructional multimedia development project. First and foremost, you should determine the benefits, costs, and issues surrounding the multimedia production. You should also consider the factors necessary for successfully implementing your product. Once you decide you will undertake an instructional multimedia production, create a team and select an authoring tool that will enable you to efficiently produce high-quality materials. This section will help you make appropriate decisions before you develop an instructional multimedia application.

Chapter 1:
Introduction to Instructional Multimedia

Learning Outcomes

After completing this chapter, you should be able to:
- define the term multimedia
- describe an easy way to get involved with multimedia
- list the potential benefits students, instructors, and managers can receive from multimedia instruction
- list the potential benefits of individualized instruction
- estimate the costs of developing an instructional multimedia application
- state how to reduce costs
- explain why issues must be addressed
- discuss issues in multimedia that concern learners, instructors, and managers
- describe the copyright act
- discuss factors contributing to successful multimedia implementation

Introduction

Multimedia is the exciting combination of hardware and software that allows you to integrate different media such as video, animation, audio, visuals, and text on new or old personal computers as shown in Figure 1.1. "Multi" equates to many or more than one while "media," such as video, visuals, animations, audio, and text, are what transmit or carry messages. You can use multimedia to provide or enhance instruction (which this book will help you to do), entertain, persuade, inform, sell... Instructional multimedia applications are also known as computer-based training programs. Note that "new media" and "eLearning" are more recent terms for multimedia.

For instructional purposes, multimedia authoring tools, such as Macromedia Director® and PowerPoint®, can make it easy for you to incorporate different media into interactive presentations (e.g., by telling the computer to play a video file, showing the visuals and text for a question, providing feedback when a button is clicked...). Although instructional multimedia applications may require specialized tools (e.g., video cameras) and software to develop, multimedia applications can be presented on minimal hardware systems.

This chapter focuses on the potential of multimedia technology and differentiates between instructional multimedia applications and computer-managed presentations. The benefits, costs, and issues involved in developing instructional multimedia applications are presented to help you and others involved make informed decisions about whether to proceed with creating an instructional multimedia solution.

1.1　Instructional Multimedia Technology

Instructional multimedia technology offers you the potential to teach in ways that are not possible with traditional methods. For example, you can teach students how to manage the finances of a bank through a simulation that allows students to experience the consequences of their actions. The potential of instructional multimedia is limitless. There is, however, a danger with all this potential. For example, some people use media, such as sound effects, simply because the capability exists. It can be a costly mistake to do so. You should only use each medium if it cost-effectively enhances learning. The success of your multimedia projects depends more on the instructional design than the media or technology you choose.

Figure 1.1 – Multimedia computer

Practical Guideline:

Your instructional multimedia projects will succeed because of the instructional design, not the media or technology you choose.

Although instructional multimedia applications can entirely replace instructors, it is often not done since these applications can take significant skills and resources to create. Another factor is that many things are already taught efficiently and effectively with traditional methods. It is usually wiser to solve specific instructional problems and use the technology to complement and supplement traditional instruction. Rather than undertaking a full-scale instructional multimedia production, a less expensive and easy way for you to become involved in instructional multimedia is to create computer-managed presentations (CMP).

CMP are used to control the display of digital text, audio, visuals, animations, and video to audiences. CMP can also be used to link to data stored in other applications such as spreadsheets. A CMP screen is shown in figure 1.2.

Compared to instructional multimedia applications where the computer assumes the teaching role, CMP take only a small amount of time to create since the instructor is still responsible for teaching the students. For instructional purposes, you can use a CMP to help present engaging multimedia presentations that include colorful images, video, and audio. For example, imagine teaching students interpersonal skills with a library of short video vignettes accessed by your computer. You control when the CMP presents supportive multimedia information as you teach the material. Since CMP can be non-linear, you can have the students explore and discover as you teach.

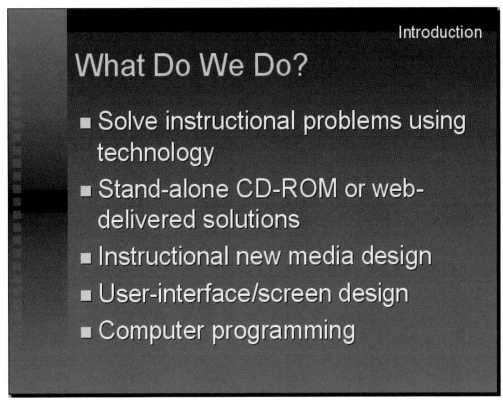

Figure 1.2 – Computer-managed presentation screen

CMP also have many uses in the business environment. For example, CMP can be used to effectively and vividly communicate:

- by marketers and sales people as a part of a multimedia sales portfolio
    - Imagine how much more a colorful video clip, photograph, or an animation would impress than a black and white illustration. Video demonstrations of how a product works can also impress clients.
    - If connected to the Internet or an intranet, there can be instant access to specifications, inventory, delivery schedules, current prices...
- in information kiosks
    - Applications range widely from advertising travel destinations to demonstrating products to presenting a company or school image.
    - Video can be very effective in kiosk applications.
- in formal presentations
    - Presentations can access current corporate information and present the data in charts and graphs.
    - CMP can even display live broadcasts such as news items or videoconferences.

1.2   Benefits of Multimedia Technology

Compared to traditional teaching methods, research generally supports teaching with multimedia technology. One problem with some of the comparative research is that excellent regular instruction is usually not compared to excellent multimedia instruction. If the regular instructional method is excellent, there is less need for a multimedia solution. So, fair comparisons are not done in some of the research.

Instructional multimedia applications offer many benefits to students, instructors, and administrators. However, depending on the problem being solved, the solution can range from being very cost-effective and even essential to being a waste of time and money. You should determine the benefits of an instructional multimedia production in order to justify the effort. Justify the production from a student's, an instructor's, and an administrator's perspective to help convince others to give their support. The support of stakeholders is critical for success.

> **Practical Guideline:**
>
> Be sure the benefits of an instructional production are significant before you develop the product.

1.2-1   Learner Benefits

A major benefit of instructional multimedia solutions you can provide learners with includes individualized instruction. With individualized instruction, students can:
- work at their own pace, proceed when they are ready, control their own learning path, and review as often as they want
- experience an infinitely patient tutor (reducing intimidation and frustration) that can adapt to their abilities and backgrounds and present information in different ways
- be actively involved in their learning and have immediate feedback
- be objectively evaluated (i.e., tests are based on specified criteria)
- have privacy (e.g., no embarrassment from making a mistake)
- learn when there is a need ("just-in-time" learning)
- learn when they want at any time of the day or night (if the equipment and facilities are available).

Practical benefits that students can receive include:
- increased learning and retention (increases up to 50% are commonly reported)
  - Major reasons for this include the benefits of individualized lessons listed above.
  - Multimedia instruction tends to lead to increased success rates.
- decreased learning time (time savings between 40% and 60% are typical)
  - Significant reasons for this include the benefits of individualized lessons listed above.
  - Students tend to be more attentive and spend more time on-task.
- participating in instructional strategies that are not possible in traditional settings
  - For example, this can be done in simulations where learners can manipulate representations of equipment and see consequences of their actions.
- an alternative method to learn skills
  - This can be very useful for students who are unsuccessful with the currently available methods.
- more interaction (when designed well) than in traditional settings
  - Active involvement in the learning process is critical and can be easily accommodated by a number of methods that includes asking questions regularly.
  - This can also be achieved by having students work in pairs or even in groups of three. This often leads to excellent discussions especially when the computer asks students to share life experiences, summarize concepts, and/or explain concepts to each other.

Other benefits that students can have include:
- minimal peer competition
  - There is more emphasis on the joy of learning.
  - Scores are usually private.
- higher motivation and more positive attitudes
  - Students tend to enjoy multimedia instruction.
  - Student attitudes towards instructional multimedia applications are generally positive if only because the computer offers a different approach than the typical teaching method they experience. Positive attitudes are usually initially high but tend to decrease over time (perhaps as the novelty effect wears off).
  - Positive attitudes are important for effective learning.

Practical Guideline:

Ensure there will be many potential benefits for students through learning from instructional multimedia technology. These benefits may be individualized instruction, increased learning and retention, decreased learning time, alternative instructional strategies, and more interaction.

Advantages of computer-managed presentations (CMP) over traditional methods include students tending to have positive attitudes towards CMP (if done well and not overused), students feeling that CMP are beneficial, and the potential for increasing learning.

1.2-2 Instructor Benefits

Benefits of instructional multimedia solutions instructors, facilitators, and supervisors can receive include:
- replacing learning activities with simulations, animations, and games when traditional teaching methods do not work (e.g., the topic cannot be effectively taught) or are too dangerous or costly
- saving time through reduced teaching, marking, and preparation time
  - Time savings can be used to save money, increase student contact time, allow a higher instructor to student ratio, or give instructors time to stay abreast of changes.
- being free to teach material that continually changes
  - Multimedia technology can be used to teach many mundane or routine topics.
- learning a new set of skills
  - This can be particularly beneficial if the instructor will be involved in subsequent projects.
- doing something exciting, innovative, and different
  - Many instructors look forward to a change in the routine.
  - This can help renew and energize instructors.

Practical Guideline:

Check that there will be benefits for instructors when instructional multimedia applications are developed. There could be potential for providing effective alternatives to skills that are hard to teach, saving time, having their time used more effectively, learning new skills, and doing something different.

Note that instructors, who are subject-matter experts for instructional multimedia applications, often increase their knowledge to a new height as they usually develop the content with a higher level of detail than traditional delivery methods.

Advantages for instructors of CMP over traditional methods include the ease of incorporating different media, the ease of editing materials, positive student attitudes, and impressing people.

1.2-3 Administrative Benefits

The major benefit of instructional multimedia solutions for administrators is cost savings. Cost savings can be through reducing instructor time, the time employees are away from the job, travel and accommodation expenses (e.g., when employees are located at distant sites), fees (e.g., tuitions), and costs of using needed equipment for training instead of generating income (e.g., airplanes used for training cannot make money by transporting passengers). As a rule of thumb, it can require 200 to 300 employees to learn from a multimedia tutorial before development costs are offset by savings.

Other important benefits to administrators can include:
- preserving expertise
  - This can be important when certain experts may not remain as employees. For example, they may be on a temporary contract or planning to retire.
- making expertise available
  - This can be a factor if the instructor or expert has limited time available to provide training or if other logistics make "live instruction" impractical.
  - This can be critical for keeping or getting employees up-to-date.
- students receiving consistent instruction
  - This can be particularly important when reliable high-quality instruction cannot be guaranteed.
- training internal multimedia experts
  - These skills can be used on future projects.

The costs of an instructional multimedia project can be offset by:
- selling the product
  - Profits can be made if the product is needed by others. It may be safe to assume that if your company has difficulties training certain skills, other companies will also have the same problem.
- using the developed software for other applications
  - Remember to ensure that you retain the rights to reuse the programming code if someone else is paying for the product. You should specify this in the contract.

Practical Guideline:

Determine if there will be benefits for administrators when instructional multimedia applications are developed. Administrators can be motivated by reducing costs, preserving expertise, making expertise available, providing consistent instruction, and developing internal expertise.

Advantages for administrators of CMP over traditional methods include the relatively low cost of involvement and positive student attitudes.

1.3 Costs of Multimedia Technology

Costs for developing instructional multimedia applications can range from being virtually free to millions of dollars. Each project tends to have vastly different costs. There are a number of factors (as described below) that influence costs. Computer-managed presentations can have minimal "hard" costs if you develop the presentations on your own time.

1.3-1   Development Costs

Development costs for instructional multimedia applications include team member salaries (and benefits), training costs, money for hardware and software, one-time costs, marketing and distribution, and product maintenance.

It is very difficult to estimate the costs of multimedia projects. Until you know the exact requirements and how you will solve the problem, cost estimates are really hopeful guesses. You cannot be too accurate until you know the instructional strategy and have selected the necessary media. For example, the costs can vary dramatically between needing professional video or not, being able to photograph the needed images rather than having an artist create them, whether you need 10 or 100 images created by graphic artists, and whether it is a simulation or a drill and practice exercise. Consider hiring an external consultant to give a cost estimate or asking others about the costs incurred for similar projects.

> **Practical Guideline:**
>
> Until you have all of the details, it is extremely difficult to give an accurate cost estimate.

Team member salaries and benefits can be substantial and often comprise the most significant cost in multimedia projects. Instructional multimedia projects can require from 100 to 300 hours total development time per hour of student time. This tends to be higher than for developing traditional instructor-led materials. Development time depends on the design difficulty, the team's expertise, the authoring tool's efficiency, whether materials, notes, design templates, and programming sub-routines already exist, and the amount of video, images, and other media needed. As a starting guideline, until more details have been determined, the salary budget can be divided as follows: 25% for instructional design, 20% for subject-matter expertise, 35% for programming, 10% for producing visuals, and 10% for other tasks. Compared to developing traditional materials, the main additional cost of developing multimedia materials is the programming time. Remember that the labor costs for computer-managed presentations can be minimal or even free (especially if you volunteer your labor).

You can reduce labor costs through using design templates, programming sub-routines, voluntary labor, and existing materials. Note that using templates can reduce design flexibility and creativity. Voluntary labor can affect scheduling since this labor may not be available on a full-time basis or when you need it. It can be cost-effective to use existing materials even if they are not exactly as needed. The decision to use existing materials or not is to determine whether using the existing materials will compromise learning in any way.

> **Practical Guideline:**
>
> Use existing materials unless learning will be compromised.

Labor costs are also affected by whether external specialists are hired. Although multimedia specialists are typically more expensive than in-house staff, in-house multimedia development staff can be expensive if there is not a continuous flow of work to be done.

Hiring external multimedia specialists can help:
- increase organizational flexibility
  - Some projects would not be possible without external help. For example, the skills may not be present or available.
- increase efficiency
  - Specialists can work much more efficiently than novices.
- gain temporarily needed skills
  - In many instances, a full-time position cannot be justified. It can be more cost-effective to hire for specialty skills, as they are needed.
- gain new ideas and approaches
  - New people can bring new insights into projects.

Before hiring external resources, verify that they can do the work in the time frame you need and within budget. View samples of their work to ensure that they really can produce high-quality materials. The reality is that many interactive multimedia productions are only marginally better than paper-based materials. Many could be called "glorified page-turners".

Training costs can be avoided but this can adversely affect the product's quality. Determine the quality level needed and match this to the team members' abilities. This comparison can be used as a guideline for determining if and how much training is needed. For safety, assume that some training will be needed when an individual is asked to work with a new technology. Do **not** assume that your production will be of high quality without training the team members. It would be safer to assume your production will be mediocre at best.

Practical Guideline:

Without training novice team members, assume your production will be mediocre at best.

If you have relatively modern computers, your hardware costs can be minimal as most modern computers are fast enough and have enough hard drive space to handle most applications. Consumer-level video cameras and digital cameras are affordable and adequate for many applications. You will also likely have some software costs such as purchasing an authoring tool, video-editing software, and photo-editing software. These also tend to be affordable, especially if you complete a number of products. Remember that the cost of creating quality instructional software right goes well beyond simply buying the hardware and software.

Practical Guideline:

Remember that you need a lot more than hardware and software to create effective products.

Although it is not common, there may also be costs for distributing the software needed to run the program (e.g., licensing fees or royalties for special fonts or video compression technology). You may also have some one-time costs that can include artwork, packaging of the final product, and making copies of the discs. Direct marketing and distribution costs (e.g., creating, printing, and mailing brochures, attending trade shows, long-distance phone calls...) largely depend on whether marketing and distribution is done internally or externally. External marketing and distribution costs are often covered through a royalty percentage.

Product maintenance can require some funding over time. Some "finished" products need periodic modifications, such as content updates.

Simple multimedia projects, such as computer-managed presentations, drill and practice programs, and visual databases, can be quick, easy, and inexpensive to create. You can often produce these projects with enthusiasm, low-level equipment, and minimal funding. Projects requiring specialized skills, such as instructional design, programming, video production, and animation, are much more costly to produce.

In summary, to quickly estimate the rough costs for your project:
1) Estimate the labor cost.
   a) Determine the number of days, including training time, each team member will work on the project. This is the hardest number to determine. As you get more details, your estimate can become more accurate.
   b) Multiply this by their salary per day. Salary per day equals the individual's total salary divided by their total number of days available for work. An employee's total salary equals their gross salary plus the value of benefits plus any expected bonuses. Total days available for work equals 365 less 104 for weekends less days of statutory holidays less days of vacation less days of

professional development. (You could also consider factoring in an average number of sick days per year.)

2) Determine all hardware costs such as new computers or video equipment.
3) Determine all software costs such as authoring tools and graphic packages.
4) Estimate all of the one-time costs.
5) Total all of these costs.

1.3-2 Comparing to Traditional Training

Occasionally, you will be asked to compare traditional instruction to multimedia instruction. Compared to traditional instructor-led training, instructional multimedia solutions tend to:

- have higher developmental costs
    - Labor costs can be substantial.
- have lower delivery costs
    - Savings can often be gained through reduced labor, travel, accommodation, tuition, as well as other costs.
- take longer to produce
    - Instructional multimedia applications often take months to produce.
    - After the initial (relatively small) learning curve, computer-managed presentations can be created in about the same amount of time as traditional instructor-led training.
- require more computer literacy
    - This is usually only a short-term concern that has long-term benefits.
- have more sales potential
    - Product sales can recoup partial or total costs. Ideal projects meet the needs of both internal and external clients.

1.3-3 Cost Effectiveness

Gaining approval often depends on whether the instructional multimedia solution will be cost-effective. Cost-effectiveness increases when:

- there are larger numbers of learners
    - This decreases the cost per student.
- the instruction must be offered many times
    - This decreases the cost per student.
- learners and instructors are widely scattered geographically
    - It costs time and money for instructors and/or students to travel.
- the material is stable with respect to content
    - Cost-effectiveness increases if the product can be used both now and in the future.
    - Seriously consider whether instructional multimedia solutions will be cost-effective if the content changes quickly. The problem of quickly changing content can be minimized if your design can allow for the content to be updated through the Internet.
- the materials can be inexpensively distributed
    - Consider using the Internet to distribute materials.
- you form collaborations
    - Some projects become possible if others provide in-kind labor or cash contributions. For example, you may obtain some in-kind labor or funding from organizations who want to have their products advertised (i.e., seen in photographs or video clips) or from others in exchange for marketing rights.

You can often save money by buying existing materials. However, these savings are reduced if modifications must be made or supplementary materials must be created.

> **Practical Guideline:**
>
> Buying existing materials can be significantly cheaper than developing materials.

Through experience and skill development, future projects are often more cost-effective. For example, future costs can be reduced when there is more internal expertise, set procedures, set standards (e.g., screen design and colors), and programming sub-routines. These potential savings are sometimes offset by taking subsequent projects to new heights.

Remember that all costs must be justified. You should only use expensive media to teach a skill if less expensive media are not effective. Do **not** create flashy or expensive materials simply because the capability exists. If extra funds exist, use the money towards creating more products rather than wasting the money on frills.

> **Practical Guideline:**
>
> Justify all costs!

1.3-4   The Internet

Costs for instructional multimedia applications can be reduced through using the Internet to:
* find, retrieve, and update existing materials
* get or provide expert advice
* deliver courses
* distribute your materials

Finding, Retrieving, and Updating Existing Materials

Through the Internet, computers have also become tools for sharing information. You can find information on almost any topic. Resources include software, visuals, video, audio, books, journals, magazines, newspapers, library catalogues, archives, special interest groups, and bulletin boards. The amount of information is vast and is continually growing. Software tools or browsers make it simple for you to locate and access specific information. Will the available information become so vast that searching for specific information will become hopeless? How will you or your learners know whether the content found is accurate?

By searching through databases, you can research content and obtain (sometimes for a fee) an increasing amount of existing materials (e.g., video clips, photographs, visual images, and audio) rather than creating original materials. This can affect team member requirements such as the need for a media specialist. (Read the Team approach chapter for more information about teams.) There may be fees associated with using existing materials but it can be much cheaper and faster than creating the materials yourself.

You can also use the Internet to update your own materials. This can be important when information changes frequently.

Getting or Providing Expert Advice

The Internet is an excellent tool for tapping into expertise found around the world. This can be very useful for solving problems. For example, when you are learning about an authoring tool, you will inevitably run into an obstacle. Rather than wasting hours trying to solve the problem, you can use the Internet to communicate with the software vendors to get solutions or with user groups who also use the tool. This can ultimately save you time and money.

You can also use the Internet to provide advice. One advantage of traditional "live" training is that experts can answer the learners' questions. For an instructional multimedia application, there may not be an instructor directly present. However, you can provide the resources of an expert through a variety of means such as videoconferencing, email messaging, or simply the telephone.

Delivering Courses

Through the numerous available tools, you can teach students through sending digital information over the Internet. The information sent can include digital video, audio, visuals, animations, text, and data (e.g., for simulations). Learning can be interactive, collaborative, in groups, individual... The Internet also contains a video conferencing system that allows users to see and hear each other on their computer systems. Note that video conferencing requires a significant amount of resources and extensive usage can slow down the system for other users.

It can be impractical to send and retrieve large amounts of multimedia data on the Internet. As an example, with a 56K modem, it can take minutes to download a one-megabyte video file. High-bandwidth connections and technological advancements (e.g., in compression techniques) help to minimize this problem.

Distributing Your Software

The Internet can be used to distribute your software free of charge. This can save handling and shipping costs. Note that some users do not have a fast enough connection to retrieve large amounts of data.

1.4   Issues Surrounding Multimedia Technology

It is important for you to deal with issues affecting students, instructors, and managers even if an individual's issues or concerns are unreasonable. Although individuals may not be rational when discussing issues, it is critical that affected individuals accept the concept of instructional multimedia solutions if the project is to succeed. Prepare answers to the following questions in order to be able to comfortably respond to the opponent's arguments. There are no set answers to the questions.

> **Practical Guideline:**
>
> Deal with issues affecting students, instructors, and managers even if their issues are unreasonable.

1.4-1 Issues Concerning Learners

For issues concerning learners, be prepared to answer the following questions:
- Will students accept change?
    - Are there past experiences, such as poor quality packages, affecting attitudes?
    - What should be done about students (e.g., extroverts) who have trouble working alone?
- Will there be role changes for learners?
    - Will students have to be active receivers of information rather than passive receivers?
    - Will students need to become proficient information researchers, problem-solvers, and strategists?
    - Will students have to rely on technology rather than instructors for obtaining specific information?

- Will students have enough time to deal with the technology?
  - Will the Internet become the most efficient information resource?
  - Is there a widening gap between what students need to know and what they can be formally taught?
  - Without instructional technology tools, will students be able to keep up with and find the information they need in their fields?
  - Will the available information become so vast that searching for specific information will become hopeless?
  - Will there be enough hardware?
- Do multimedia packages inhibit student creativity, communication skills, or social skills?
  - Will students believe information simply because it is on a computer?
  - Do multimedia packages generally focus on low-level skills rather than high-level skills?
  - Will computers impersonalize education? Conversely, is learning in a traditional prescribed order impersonal?
  - Do multimedia input devices inhibit some forms of communication? (For example, a mouse may be the only form of input.)
- Should access to some digital information be restricted? (For example, there can be problems with the pornography that is available on the Internet.)
  - How can decision makers reach agreements on what is unacceptable?
  - Will hackers be able to bypass access restrictions?
  - Who should be responsible for a student's actions?

1.4-2 Issues Concerning Instructors

For issues concerning instructors, be prepared to answer the following questions:
- Will instructors be replaced by the developed products?
  - Will instructors support the development if they have a fear of losing their jobs?
- Will there be role changes for instructors?
  - With digital information so readily available, will instructors be facilitators rather than lecturers?
  - Is it better to help students find information rather than produce information?
  - Will instructors have greater interdisciplinary roles rather than being responsible for knowing all of the content?
  - Will instructors be present to answer questions or will students be on their own? Is the cost of having an instructor present worth the amount an instructor can enhance a student's learning (e.g., through answering questions, providing feedback, guiding learners, initiating discussions, and humanizing the learning)?
- Will instructors accept change?
  - Do past experiences affect attitudes?
  - Do all affected instructors perceive a need for change?
  - Will poor instructor attitudes lead to sabotaging multimedia-based learning projects? (This has happened in the past.)
  - Will instructors fear that their lack of participation will negatively influence their chances for promotion or acceptance by their peers?
  - Although many instructors will need to adapt to new technologies, remember that new technologies can be used to simply enhance an instructor's teaching. For example, computer-managed presentations allow instructors to instantly show video clips when video is needed for effective learning. These simple non-threatening changes can be easily accepted by instructors.
- Are instructors too busy to change approaches?
  - Given an instructor's limited time, is creating instructional multimedia applications the best use of an instructor's time?
  - What will be neglected if time is spent on multimedia projects?
  - Will instructors want to wait for the next technological advances before starting a project?

- Will enough resources be provided to make the effort successful?
    - Will time be provided for training? Will instructors not want to be involved because they feel they are too far behind or have too much to learn? Will instructors need time to "feel" comfortable using different application programs, not having tangible (i.e., paper) products right away, and learning new roles?
    - Will enough time be provided to develop high-quality materials?
    - Given instructor release time is critical, will replacements be hired for released instructors?
    - Will the needed hardware and software be available for classroom use (e.g., for demonstrations and presentations) and for development?

1.4-3 Issues Concerning Administrators

For issues concerning administrators, be prepared to answer the following questions:
- Will administrators accept change?
    - What is the vision, if any, for instructional technology? What are the assumptions, if any, for this vision? Are these assumptions reasonable?
    - Do past experiences affect attitudes?
    - Do all of the affected administrators perceive a need for change?
- Are the costs associated with instructional multimedia support justified?
    - Should funding for instructional multimedia support only be given when there is a demand for the resources? Will there be significant demand if resources are not initially provided?
    - What are the costs of ignoring multimedia instruction? It can be prestigious to adopt technology.
    - What are the costs of trying to adopt all new technologies? As Will Rogers said, "Even if you are on the right track, you'll get run over if you just sit there."
    - How does the potential of a new system compare to the realities (and perhaps the security) of the current system? How will success be measured?
    - Will multimedia instruction be a passing educational fad? Television was falsely proclaimed to be the educational tool of the century.
- With digital information so readily available, will course goals and learning outcomes change?
    - Will new technology simply allow educators to do things differently or change what is taught?
    - Will students need to become problem-solvers and information researchers and focus less on learning facts?
- Should material be bought or created?
    - Are purchased packages of a high quality and at the right level?
    - Who should pay for the material?
    - Will the material be accepted if it is produced by someone else?
    - Is it more cost-effective to buy or produce the material?
    - If the material is created, who will pay the costs of training subject-matter experts and other team members?
    - If the product is created and sold, who gets the profits?
    - Is there a general belief that multimedia instruction is not cost-effective?
    - Is it really important to become a developer?
- How are team members and projects chosen?
    - Will the chosen team members have credibility?
    - Will a collective agreement force the acceptance of poorly qualified team members?
    - What are the guidelines for accepting proposals?
    - What should be done with enthusiastic people who do not have an ideal project proposal?
    - Is cost-recovery a criterion? If so, can the time frame be over a few years and who will market the product?
- Should standards be created or followed such as in screen design, help, buttons, quality, maintenance, updates...?
    - What are the standards?
    - Are the standards only internal or also in industry?

- What are some legal issues that should be considered?
  - Are there any concerns regarding intellectual property?
  - Is a waiver needed for an individual's moral rights? Moral rights are an individual's rights to the integrity of work or association with the work. For example, artwork created for the intention of promoting peace could not be used, without a signed waiver, for advocating racism or war.
  - Are patent rights needed for any software or hardware?
  - Is there any information that must be kept confidential? What obligations will team members (both internal and external) have regarding confidentiality?
  - How will future versions or updates affect prior legal issues?
  - Are there any reversion rights? (For example, if a partner has failed to meet contractual obligations, will certain rights be taken away?)
  - Will there be clearance to distribute the product in a variety of formats (e.g., DVD-ROM or Internet if the original content was in print)?
  - These issues should be settled as early as possible. The potential for earning money can adversely affect the most sincere intentions.
- What are the problems associated with determining product ownership?
  - What if it is a collaboration?
  - Who will have the honor and recognition of being an author? (Authors may receive future benefits such as honorariums from presenting at conferences.)
  - What if an instructor's notes are used as a starting point?
  - What if some work is done at home on the subject-matter expert's time?
  - What if instructors do some work on company hardware and software and some work on their own time?
  - How will royalties or profits be distributed? Should instructors receive royalties or profits for their ideas? How will this decision affect their motivation? How can all team members be compensated fairly?
  - The ultimate owner(s) must be specified. The product should be completely defined. This can include materials or products, functional and technical specifications, ideas and concepts, as well as the "look and feel".

Practical Guideline:

Solve ownership and revenue distribution issues before significant money is involved.

- What are the hardware issues?
  - What hardware and software is needed for development?
  - What hardware and software is needed by the learners?
  - Is the hardware compatible with other hardware and software?
  - Is the hardware compatible with existing standards?
  - Are computers too expensive?
  - Is the bulk hardware deal offered because production will end?
  - Will the hardware be outdated soon?
  - Will there be support for outdated hardware?
  - Should you wait for the perfect hardware and software solution? Would you wait forever?

1.4-4 Copyright

Copyright is the exclusive privilege that only allows authors or assignees (e.g., publishers) the right to copy, sell, and/or transmit their own original work. Original work does not have to be complete or "polished" but must be more than an idea. Generally, a work is "fixed" when it can be reproduced, communicated, or perceived. In many countries, copyright protection is automatic once the original work is created.

Registering a copyright is not required but can be useful for proving ownership. Whether or not the material has commercial value, copyright applies to original works that are:
- literary (i.e., text, computer programs, databases...)
- artistic (i.e., visuals, photographs, drawings...)
- dramatic (i.e., films, videos, scripts...)
- musical (i.e., music or words and music)

Without copyright clearance, copyright laws are infringed if the work of others is included in your productions. For example, you cannot change the medium (e.g., digitize a still image from a video clip), scan and then alter an image, or simply translate the material and then distribute the work in your production. For example, look at figures 1.3 and 1.4. The photograph in figure 1.3 is copyrighted to Peter Fenrich. If you modified the photograph to create figure 1.4, would you own the rights to the modified image or would Peter Fenrich?

Figure 1.3 – Original photograph

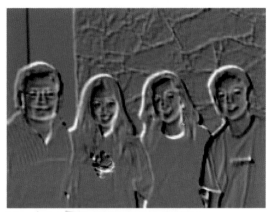

Figure 1.4 – Modified photograph

No, you would **not** own the rights to the modified image. Even if you received copyright permission to publish the original image, you would not be allowed, without further permission, to publish the modified image. A guideline for determining how much you could be sued for infringing on copyright is how much your use of the material will cost the copyright holder profit or value. Punitive damages would be an additional fine.

Note that just because you pay someone to create some material for you, there is no guarantee that you have the right to reproduce and market the material. It is safer to assume that you do not have these rights. Whenever, you hire out some work, be sure that you negotiate a contract that specifies who has the rights to the material.

Although an idea is not necessarily protected by copyright, a series of ideas can have copyright protection. A series of ideas could be a part of a software program's "look and feel". Although a program's entire "look and feel" may be too broad from a legal perspective, certain aspects of a program (e.g., distinctive menu structures or mouse click sequences) may be significant enough to be protected by copyright or by a design patent.

In general, you need copyright clearance **in writing** from the author(s) or copyright holder(s) for all materials (e.g., print, visuals, video, software...) that you use that were created by others. Remember that copyright also applies to derivatives or transformations of the original work. Determine whether the individual is the original author, the individual owns the work, and others own the work. For your safety, the copyright holder should be told exactly what you plan to do with the work and how the material might be modified and distributed. Many copyright holders will freely give you the right to use their work if no money is to be made. Conversely, they will often want some money or you are planning to earn money.

> **Practical Guideline:**
>
> You need written copyright clearance from the author(s) or copyright holder(s) for all materials you use that are created by others.

In general, copyright clearance is not required for:
- materials indicating that copying is permitted
  - In some cases, copying is only permitted for non-profit ventures.
- materials in which the copyright has expired
- some government publications
- making copies for back-up purposes (e.g., computer software)
- copying minor excerpts of materials for "private study"
  - This can be for research, critical analysis, reviews, and summaries.

For software, the license often specifies the conditions under which the material can be used.

The international copyright conventions do **not** permit individuals to copy material for educational purposes. Remember that there is no guarantee of copyright clearance on material just because the material was given freely. For example, "owned" material is illegally available on computer bulletin boards.

Notes:
- Not all of the above issues regarding students, instructors, administrators, and copyright will be present in all settings.
- Many of these issues apply equally between the public and private sectors.
- Many of these issues will not apply to those creating computer-managed presentations.

1.5   Implementing Multimedia Technology Solutions

Even if you create an excellent product, there is no guarantee that you can successfully implement your instructional multimedia solution. Successful implementation entails cost-effectively solving important problems and gaining the support of affected people. Remember, you must start gaining support before a project begins and maintain that support throughout the project.

Implementation and the Problem Being Solved

Implementing your instructional multimedia solution is more likely to be successful when:
- important needs are being solved
  - It is generally wise to solve problems that affected people recognize and accept as being important.
- your product effectively and efficiently solves the defined problem
  - There should be expected cost savings or a good return on investment. There is a better return on investment when developed material can be used by many learners. Costs are more easily justified when the hardware needed to run the software is inexpensive or is already available.
- traditional methods are not effective
  - Sometimes, the material cannot be taught using traditional methods. For example, a simulation may be the best way to teach the concept.
- the computer teaches over mundane skills (e.g., through drill and practice exercises)

> **Practical Guideline:**
>
> Make implementation successful by solving important needs.

Implementation and Affected People

Affected people will more likely support your production if:

- they aid in development
  - This helps provide ownership.
- their jobs are not threatened
  - Most multimedia materials should support rather than replace people. Would you cooperate in creating materials that could eliminate your job?

Practical Guideline:

Multimedia implementation is more successful when you involve affected people in the production and do not threaten their jobs.

- they are prepared for change
  - People have a tendency to resist change.
  - A gradual or partial change may be easier to implement than a fast or total change.
  - Give presentations to generate ideas and interest. Remember that you will need to be enthusiastic and truly believe in what you are proposing.
- your multimedia package is easy to use, has complete documentation, and is easy to load
  - It is preferable if products only require simple or standard equipment.
  - If the package is hard to use or load, and this should not happen, then technical support and/or training should be provided. If the product will be sold externally, who will provide this support?
- your project receives administrative support
  - Support should come from all levels (especially from key players) and be a part of a long-term strategic plan.
  - Support is more than just providing money. Support also includes believing in the potential results and understanding what is needed for the process to be successful.
  - It is often safer to begin with a small project that can be completed in a short time span. Small projects are more likely to be successful.

Summary

Multimedia is the exciting combination of hardware and software that allows you to integrate different media such as video, animation, audio, visuals, and text on an affordable computer. Media should only be used to cost-effectively enhance learning.

Computer-managed presentations are used to control the display of digital text, audio, visuals, animations, and video to audiences as well as link to data stored in other applications. Compared to instructional multimedia applications where the computer assumes the teaching role, computer-managed presentations take a small amount of time to create since you are still responsible for teaching the students.

Benefits of instructional multimedia solutions learners can receive include individualized instruction, increased learning and retention, and decreased learning time. From a learning perspective, learners can participate in instructional strategies that are not possible in traditional settings, have an alternative method to learn skills, and have more interaction than in traditional settings.

The major benefit an instructional multimedia application offers instructors is a solution for an instructional problem that cannot be adequately addressed with traditional teaching methods.

Administrators can benefit from cost savings, preserving expertise, making expertise available, employees receiving consistent instruction, and gaining market potential.

To quickly estimate the rough costs for your project:
1) Estimate the labor cost.
   a) Determine the number of days each team member will need. (Include any training time needed.)
   b) Multiply this by their salary and benefits per day.
2) Determine all hardware costs such as new computers.
3) Determine all software costs such as authoring tools and graphic packages.
4) Estimate all of the one-time costs.
5) Total all of these costs.

Compared to traditional instructor-led training, multimedia solutions tend to have higher developmental costs, have lower delivery costs, provide more consistent instruction, take longer to produce, and have sales potential. Multimedia solutions tend to be more cost-effective when there are larger numbers of learners, the instruction must be offered many times, the learners are widely scattered geographically, the learners are distantly located from training sites, and the software can be inexpensively distributed.

The Internet can be used to reduce costs by allowing you to:
- find, retrieve, and update existing materials
- get and provide expert advice
- deliver courses
- distribute your materials

Issues affecting students, instructors, and administrators have to be dealt with even if the issues are unreasonable. Acceptance of instructional multimedia applications is critical for any project to succeed.

There are many issues concerning learners. Some of the questions that must be answered include:
- Will change be accepted by students?
- Will there be role changes for learners?
- Will students have enough time to use the technology?

There are also many issues concerning instructors. Some of the questions that must be answered include:
- Will instructors be replaced by the system?
- Will there be role changes for instructors?
- Will enough resources be provided to make the effort successful?

Similarly, there are many issues concerning administrators. Answer the following questions:
- Are the costs associated with multimedia support justified?
- Should material be bought or created?
- What are some legal issues that should be considered?

Copyright is the exclusive privilege that only allows authors or assignees the right to copy, sell, and/or transmit their own original work. In general, copyright clearance is required **in writing** from the author or copyright holder for all materials created by others.

Even if you create an excellent product, there is no guarantee that you can successfully implement your instructional multimedia solution. Successful implementation entails cost-effectively solving important problems and gaining the support of affected people.

Application Exercises

1) Are books that contain both text and visuals considered multimedia products? Justify your answer.
2) Imagine that your boss has a negative attitude towards multimedia products. What could you say to him to help change his attitude?
3) If a manager claims that students will not like multimedia lessons, how would you refute this claim?
4) Describe how the costs of a second comparable project can be lower than the first project.
5) It currently costs $500 per employee for a traditional one-day training course. If a multimedia lesson were developed, the estimated cost per employee would be $200. The lesson will require 600 hours of development time at an average labor cost of $40 per hour. How many employees would need to take the multimedia training to justify the developmental costs?
6) It currently costs $700 per employee for a traditional one-day training course. If a multimedia lesson were developed, the estimated cost per employee would be $250. The lesson will require 500 hours of development time at an average labor cost of $50 per hour. There will be additional fixed costs of 10,000 for hardware, software, and one-time costs. How many employees would need to take the multimedia training to justify the developmental costs?

Case Study

Six instructors were on a four-week professional development leave from their regular duties. During this time, the instructors participated in a workshop on creating instructional multimedia applications. In the first three weeks, the mornings were devoted to learning the principles and guidelines of creating instructional multimedia applications. During the afternoons of the first week, two instructors evaluated authoring tools, another learned a graphics package, and the other three evaluated sample courseware. In the afternoons of the second and third weeks and throughout the fourth week, the instructors put the principles and guidelines learned into practice by creating an instructional multimedia tutorial.

Case Study Questions

1) What were the potential benefits gained by the employer, instructors, and students?
2) Based on salaries from your own organization, estimate the costs for this or a comparable project?
3) How would the costs have differed if external personnel were hired?
4) What are some issues that would have had to be resolved?

References

3M. (1993). Brilliant meetings: The art of effective visual presentations. Austin, TX: 3M Austin Center.

Adams, N. (1993, May). CBT or not CBT. Training, 30(5), 73-75.

Blaize, S. (1994, November). Who owns Rita Hayworth? Multimedia copyrights: Your rights and theirs. Digital Video Magazine, 2(10), 62-66.

Card, D. (1992, April). Lotus Development v. Borland International. Canadian Computer Law Reporter. 9(4), 51-53.

Feifer, R., & Allender, L. (1994). It's not how multi the media, it's how the media is used. Proceedings of the ED-MEDIA 94 World Conference on Educational Multimedia and Hypermedia.

Hannafin, M., Dalton, D., & Hooper, S. (1987, October). Computers in education: Ten myths and ten needs. Educational Technology, 27(10), 8-14.

Hofstetter, F. (1994). Multimedia presentation technology. Belmont, CA: Wadsworth Publishing Company.

Huntley, J., & Easley, G. (1994). The brown book of multimedia. Dubuque, IA: Wm. C. Brown Communications.

Ives, B., & Forman, D. (1991). Calculating competitive advantage. Multimedia Solutions, 1(6), 32-37.

Janniro, M. (1993, Spring). Effects of computer-based instruction on student learning of psychophysiological detection of deception test question formulation. Journal of Computer-Based Instruction, 20(2), 58-62.

Maddux, C. (1994, September). The Internet: Educational prospects and problems. Educational Technology, 34(7), 37-42.

Pearlstein, R. (1993, November/December). Keep-your-distance learning. Performance and Instruction, 32(10), 8-9.

Romiszowski, A. (1988). The selection and use of instructional media: For improved classroom teaching and for interactive, individual instruction (2nd ed.). New York, NY: Nichols Publishing.

Rosenborg, V., Green, B., Hester, J., Knowles, W., & Wirsching, M. (1993). A guide to multimedia. Carmel, IN: New Riders Publishing.

Sherman, G., & Klein, J. (1995). The effects of cued interaction and ability grouping during cooperative computer-based science instruction. Educational Technology Research and Development, 43(4), 5-24.

Siegel, M., & Sousa, G. (1994, September). Inventing the virtual textbook: Changing the nature of schooling. Educational Technology, 34(7), 49-54.

Smith, L., & Renzulli, J. (1984, Winter). Learning style preferences: A practical approach for classroom teachers. Theory Into Practice, 23(1), 44-50.

Tuck, J. (1988, September). Professional development through learning centers. Training & Development Journal, 42(9), 76-79.

von Wodtke, M. (1993). Mind over media: Creative thinking skills for electronic media. New York, NY: McGraw-Hill.

Chapter 2: Team Approach

Learning Outcomes

After completing this chapter, you should be able to:
- explain why it is important to have a team
- list skills team members should possess
- describe characteristics team members should possess
- list commitments needed of team members
- express how to enhance communication among team members
- state how project managers can provide effective leadership
- describe the roles of the different team members

Introduction

You should use a team approach to develop instructional multimedia materials. If you work with a team, you can produce better products than if you work alone. This chapter focuses on reasons for using the team approach, team member requirements such as skills needed, characteristics of individuals, and commitments to the project, how to facilitate effective communication, and the critical roles each team member may assume. Team members can include project managers, instructional designers, subject-matter experts, programmers, media producers, photographers, graphic artists, editors, reviewers, and pilot students.

2.1 Rationale

There are many reasons why you should create a team to develop instructional multimedia materials. These reasons include:
- Very few people have all of the necessary skills.
    - Producing instructional multimedia materials is a complicated process. Multimedia production is well suited for the team approach. Typical skills needed include project management, instructional design, subject-matter expertise, programming, video production, graphic arts, and editing.
    - Even though you may be excellent at teaching in traditional ways, there is no guarantee that you can teach effectively with computers. Each team should include an instructional designer who specializes in instructional multimedia productions.
    - Like a stereo, instructional multimedia products can only be as good as the weakest link. A $2,000 amplifier has little value when connected to $5 speakers. The same idea applies to a multimedia production team. The powerful multimedia development tools that are available cannot compensate for a lack of talent.

> **Practical Guideline:**
>
> Do **not** assume that individuals who can teach well in traditional ways have the skills needed to create effective instructional multimedia applications!

- All work is done competently and efficiently when working with highly-qualified personnel.
    - Specialists can often reach greater heights than novices. For example, it is likely that a professional programmer can create more elegant features and more efficient sub-routines than non-professional programmers.
    - Since teaching with computers is very different than teaching with traditional methods (e.g., lectures, discussions, print materials, video tapes, audio tapes...), qualified personnel are needed to ensure all of the required skills are present for the project.
    - Training may be needed for some or all of the members. Providing training can increase morale since employees who receive training often feel valued.
    - Projects can be completed more quickly since many tasks can be done concurrently.
    - If possible, pay for the best. Experts are often able to foresee and solve difficulties before the problem can seriously affect the project. Hire for potential as well as for the required skills.
- The whole is greater than the sum of its parts.
    - More ideas arise from a team than from an individual.
    - Team members can provide different perspectives on problems.
    - All members should be encouraged to help generate creative solutions. It is not wise or reasonable to assume that the instructional designer will provide all of the creative ideas.
    - Team members can offer feedback during formative evaluations. This is very useful since evaluation should be on going throughout the development process.
- Many individuals will not have the interest or time to do all of the tasks.
    - As an example, many subject-matter experts do not like to do the programming.
    - Another problem is that working alone can be boring. Human interactions can make the development process fun.

Practical Guideline:

Teams create better instructional multimedia products than individuals!

Ideally, your organization should have a media centre that allows free access to all of the needed skills so that a team can be used for creating instructional multimedia products. Imagine how much easier it would be to develop a multimedia product if there is audio/visual support for planning and recording video and audio, technical support for setting up and using the developmental hardware and software, and specialists to advise on digitizing and compressing materials. However, the reality is that most organizations do not have these resources available. One solution is to create computer-managed presentations (CMP) where a team is helpful but not critical.

2.2   Team Member Requirements

There are a number of general skills, characteristics, and commitments that team members need in order to work effectively as a unit.

2.2-1   Skills

When selecting team members, you should ensure that they have:
- excellent people skills
    - Imagine working on an intense multimedia development project with people who cannot work effectively on a team.
- excellent communication skills
    - A lot of effort can be wasted if specifications are misinterpreted.

- a variety of talents to help other members in their roles
  - Team members should not be stereotyped into only performing certain skills or activities. Many people like and need to expand their horizons and learn new skills.
  - A "helping" atmosphere is facilitated if each team member appreciates the other team members' roles, skills, and constraints.
  - Depending on the skills of each member and the time and resources available, each member can take on a variety of roles and responsibilities.

Practical Guideline:

All team members need effective people and communication skills.

2.2-2 Characteristics

When selecting team members, you should ensure that they are:
- flexible
  - Team members are commonly asked to complete tasks that are outside of their area of expertise.
  - The multimedia field is constantly changing and evolving. Team members must often learn new techniques and how to work with changing hardware and software.
- innovative
  - Creative ideas can help change mediocrity into excellence.
  - The development area should encourage creativity, be safe (e.g., team members can make mistakes, offer suggestions, make changes...), and be fun.
- willing to learn and willing to accept constructive feedback
  - Formative evaluation is on going through a product's development. Feedback about changes and needed improvements are expected and inevitable.

2.2-3 Commitments

When selecting team members, you should ensure that they are:
- committed to working on the project
  - Enthusiasm, motivation, and perseverance keys to success.
- available to work on the project
  - Management support may be needed before team members can contribute to a project.
- committed to working on a team rather than individually
  - As stated above, the team approach is critical for making high-quality products.
- willing to occasionally perform above and beyond the call of duty
  - This is often required because of last minute changes, having to meet deadlines, having to quickly fix problems, and needing to work late (e.g., when the film crew is available).
- willing to give demonstrations and presentations
  - This is a critical component of implementation that generates enthusiasm for future projects.

2.3   Facilitating Effective Communication

If you create your project with a team then it is critical that every team member works well together (or at least as best as possible given the different personalities). A key factor in this is how well the team communicates together. Effective communication can help solve problems before problems become serious.

To help the team communicate effectively, you should:
- have excellent people and communication skills
- hold regular meetings
- set standards for working as a team
- delegate clearly by assigning roles and responsibilities
- make a visual timeline showing milestones
- create design documents

People and Communication Skills

Without excellent people and communication skills, there are more likely to be personality problems, misunderstandings, work efforts going "off-track"... Facilitate communication by writing clearly and concisely.

People skills include being receptive and available to team members. This helps set a positive atmosphere for the communication process. This can be facilitated by managing by "wandering around" (i.e., seeing and asking about what each team member is doing).

Hold Regular Meetings

Each meeting, often held on a weekly or biweekly basis, should have a purpose, be worth the time, and follow an agenda. The agenda should be given in advance to allow individuals to come prepared. Each team member should provide a report of:
- what they have accomplished compared to what was intended
- activities planned until the next meeting
- constraints that may affect their ability to achieve the activities

Little things like providing drinks and treats at these meetings can help maintain a positive atmosphere. In a sense, this is only fair since team members typically "go beyond the call of duty" and the time spent in the meeting takes time away from working on their specific tasks.

Set Standards for Working as a Team

The standards you should set for working as a team include:
- ensuring that everyone is given courtesy and respect
- not interrupting individuals who are speaking
- keeping team problems within the team
- discussing and solving problems, without attributing a "right" or "wrong" judgment, as soon as possible
- actively listening and not making assumptions
- providing constructive feedback
- ensuring that sub-teams regularly report to the whole team

Delegate Clearly by Assigning Roles and Responsibilities

Roles and responsibilities should be determined and agreed to by both the individual and the team leader. It is safest to write down every team member's roles and responsibilities.

Make a Visual Timeline Showing Milestones

If the timeline is visual then there is less chance of having any misunderstandings. Timeline milestones can be set to the phases of the instructional development cycle or steps of the systematic instructional design process.

Status reports should be regularly written to inform all team members of the project's current status as compared to the timeline. Knowing that a task is behind schedule gives you the opportunity to decide whether or not to assign more resources to the task.

Create Design Documents

Design documents should include details on:
- technical requirements
- technical details (e.g., hardware and software limitations)
- screen design, user-interface, and the use of color
- learner control
- feedback (e.g., level of detail, standards for correct and incorrect answers)

Effective open communication is critical for team members to successfully work together. Effective communication is also needed to discuss and define, to each team member, their roles and responsibilities (as listed below).

2.4   Roles of Team Members

Instructional multimedia applications require numerous tasks to be performed. These tasks can be performed by a large number of different specialists, by a small group of individuals who assume more than one role, or by you. Depending on the skills needed and the availability of those skills, the tasks can be done by internal personnel, external consultants, or a combination of the two. From a practical perspective, if the task is done well and efficiently, it does not really matter who does it. The critical factor is that one or more people assume or are assigned responsibility for each of the following roles and tasks.

2.4-1 Project Managers

Project managers are responsible for managing the project. This includes:
- holding the bottom-line responsibilities
- making budgetary decisions
- coordinating data gathering (e.g., for needs analysis questionnaires or formative evaluations)
- creating a project plan by setting milestones and completion schedules
- providing management with progress reports
- performing managerial duties and providing some project coordination
- putting together teams and assigning tasks
- arranging for facilities (e.g., rooms, furniture, hardware...)
- providing effective leadership through:
    - being involved
    - challenging the status quo
    - taking risks
    - inspiring and sharing a vision
    - building and maintaining morale
    - enlisting support
    - enabling others to act (e.g., sharing power)
    - fostering collaboration rather than competition
    - mediating problems
    - recognizing individual contributions
    - setting an example
    - planning small wins
    - celebrating accomplishments

2.4-2 Instructional Designers

Typical tasks instructional designers have responsibility for include:
- identifying instructional goals
- conducting goal analyses
- conducting subordinate skills analyses
- identifying entry skills and characteristics
- writing learning outcomes
- developing test items
- proofing test and exercise questions
- designing and developing effective instructional strategies
- selecting the media
- searching for and evaluating suitable existing courseware
- creating effective screen designs
- helping to write storyboards
- writing down all branching and sequencing information
- designing and conducting formative evaluations
- linking the educational and computer technologies together
- providing a link between all of the team members and clients
- writing documentation (e.g., instructional strategy flow charts)

(See the Instructional design chapter for more details.)

2.4-3 Subject-Matter Experts

Subject-matter experts (also called content experts) are often responsible for:
- providing the project's purpose
- writing the content
- providing ideas
- reviewing existing materials
- supplying test and exercise questions
- writing storyboards based on the determined design
- participating in formative evaluations

Subject-matter experts sometimes take on acting roles. Depending on the individual, these roles can be major or minor. In many cases, subject-matter experts simply perform tasks that they normally would do. In these cases, scripts are usually not memorized but are what one would normally say to their students.

If subject-matter experts have concurrent responsibilities, management should:
- hold weekly team meetings
- get support from their boss
- make the project a part of their performance review
- make a visual schedule
- provide rewards

2.4-4 Programmers

Typical responsibilities of programmers include:
- identifying the hardware and software capabilities and limitations
- providing technical advice
- critically examining the design specifications to determine whether the specifications can be achieved

- creating sub-routines that can be easily edited
- transferring storyboards to the computer using the specified authoring tools
- creating some visuals (especially non-artistic requirements)
- digitizing, manipulating, and/or reformatting media
- testing and debugging programs
- developing and maintaining necessary databases
- transferring courseware to other platforms
- writing documentation (e.g., program coding flowcharts and hardware and software specifications)
- installing and maintaining computer hardware and software
- regularly backing-up software

2.4-5   Media Producers

Media producers often have a variety of responsibilities including:
- hiring or assuming the roles of a scriptwriter, camera operator, sound technician, and light technician
- helping select media for course segments
- proofing final video and audio scripts
- scheduling production
- filming and logging video and audio
- editing the final material
- backing-up the material both during and after the project
- finding existing media materials

Based on the resources available and skills of each individual, these tasks can be performed by one person or a team of professionals.

2.4-6   Photographers

Photographers are often responsible for:
- helping to select media for course segments
- setting up the lighting and backdrop for photographs
- ensuring that the photograph has artistic flair
- consulting with subject-matter experts to confirm accuracy
- editing images (e.g., making changes, sizing, and cropping)
- transferring images between formats
- performing back-ups

2.4-7   Graphic Artists

Graphic artists can be responsible for:
- helping to select media for course segments
- creating visuals that are too difficult for the programmer to do
- creating animations
- helping with screen design guidelines
- creating visual templates for consistency and speed
- consulting with subject-matter experts to confirm accuracy
- editing images (e.g., making changes, sizing, and cropping)
- transferring images between formats
- performing back-ups

Note that it is generally faster to take photographs than to create images. Consequently, you will likely use more photographs than graphic images in your multimedia productions.

2.4-8 Editors

Responsibilities of editors include checking for:
- basics (e.g., spelling, grammar, punctuation, misused words...)
- essentials (e.g., continuity between sentences, awkward sentences, starting paragraphs with the main point, smooth transitions between paragraphs, structural problems, inconsistencies...)
- writing style consistency
- factual errors

Instructional designers and subject-matter experts often edit the material.

2.4-9 Reviewers

Reviewers are critical for providing formative feedback on the content. To ensure the reviewer checks for what is needed:
- provide a list with specific questions and ideas
- ask them to make numerous passes through the material
  - It is too hard for reviewers to focus on too many points through any single pass. If there are too many things to focus on, some will be forgotten once in a while.

Request reviewers to write down all of their thoughts. Little details may be more important than expected and can add up to be significant.

2.4-10 Pilot Students

Pilot students must provide formative feedback on all aspects of the program. Pilot students are essential for determining whether the program actually teaches. Since students are often in a "rush," encourage them to evaluate the program thoroughly. Another potential problem is that volunteer students sometimes miss showing up for the evaluation.

Summary

The team approach is used to develop better instructional multimedia materials than can be created through individual efforts.

Reasons for creating a team to develop instructional multimedia materials include very few people having all of the necessary skills, work being done competently and efficiently, projects being completed more quickly, and most individuals do not have the interest or time to do all of the tasks.

There are many skills, characteristics, and commitments that team members need in order to work well as a unit. Team members should have excellent people and communication skills and a variety of talents. They should be flexible, innovative, enthusiastic, and willing to learn and accept constructive feedback. Team members should be committed to the project, available to work, and willing to work on a team.

Communication plays a key role in attaining and maintaining an effective team. To facilitate communication, you should be receptive and available, be involved, hold regular meetings, set standards for working as a team, delegate roles and responsibilities, make a timeline, write status reports, and create design documents.

Depending on the skills of each member and the time and resources available, each member can take on a variety of roles and responsibilities. Multimedia projects can include team members such as project managers, instructional designers, subject-matter experts, programmers, media producers, photographers, graphic artists, editors, reviewers, and pilot students.

Application Exercises

1) If a project manager has poor communication skills, how might this affect the project?
2) Would you hire a subject-matter expert who is an excellent teacher, has successful multimedia development experience, and insists on doing things his way? Explain your answer.
3) Assume that your boss agrees that an instructional multimedia solution is needed. However, he feels that you should do it by yourself even though you do not have any previous experience. What could you say to him to argue the point that a team would be more effective?
4) Assume that you are able to hire some people to develop an instructional multimedia application. Aside from the specific skills, such as programming, what characteristics should the person have to work on your team?
5) If you are the team leader, what should you do to help the team communicate effectively?

Case Study

Six instructors were on a four-week professional development leave from their regular duties. During this time, the instructors participated in a workshop on creating instructional multimedia applications. In the first three weeks, the mornings were devoted to learning the principles and guidelines of creating instructional multimedia applications. Based on personal interests, skills, and available time, each instructor chose the role of subject-matter expert, programmer, or graphic artist. The workshop leader provided instructional design expertise. During the afternoons of the first three weeks, the "programmers" evaluated authoring tools, selected a tool, and learned to use the tool. The "graphic artist" learned a graphics package and created some sample images. The subject-matter experts evaluated sample instructional multimedia applications, worked through the instructional design process, and created a "paper" version of the materials. In the fourth week, the "paper" version was evaluated and revised, and then the programmers started transferring the material to the computer.

Case Study Questions

1) What were potential consequences of working with instructors who did not have programming skills?
2) Was the "team approach" adequately followed? Justify your answer.
3) If you wanted to build some multimedia expertise within your own organization, what would you do differently? What would be the costs and benefits of your approach?

References

Agnew, B. (1994). Communication and the collaborative process. Proceedings of the Multicomm '94 Conference on Multimedia Solutions for Business and Education.

Dick, W., & Carey, L. (1990). The systematic design of instruction (3rd ed.). Glenville, IL: Harper Collins Publishers.

Kouzes, J., & Posner, B. (1987). The leadership challenge: How to get extraordinary things done in an organization. San Francisco, CA: Jossey-Bass Publishers.

Rosebush, J. (1995, July). A guide to multimedia production staffing. CD-ROM Professional, 8(7), 32-43.

Sukhoo, A., Barnard, A., Eloff, M., Van der Poll, J., & Motah, M. (2005). Accommodating Soft Skills in Software Project Management. The Journal of Issues in Informing Science and Information Technology, 2, 691-703.

Chapter 3: Authoring Tools

After completing this chapter, you should be able to:
* define authoring
* compare and contrast the different categories of authoring tools
* evaluate authoring tools
* choose an appropriate authoring tool for specified needs

Introduction

Authoring is the process of issuing, testing, and revising instructions for presenting materials on a computer system. There are many tools available to help you author efficiently. These authoring tools will be classified as being authoring systems, object-based systems, or programming languages. The advantages and disadvantages of each tool classification will be compared and contrasted. This chapter also provides an extensive list for evaluating authoring tools to help you determine which tool best suits your expected present and future needs. The authoring tool(s) you choose can greatly increase the potential, development speed, and effectiveness of your instructional multimedia production.

3.1   Comparing and Contrasting Authoring Tools

It is difficult to slot authoring tools into specific categories since each tool can have features or limitations that are found in other categories. This difficulty is further enhanced through product changes and upgrades. For these reasons specific product names are not mentioned for each category. The categories below are provided for illustrative purposes rather than concise delineators of tools.

3.1-1 Authoring Systems

Authoring systems tend to be menu driven. You are specifically prompted for information or information is slotted into available locations. For example, on a multiple-choice question, you could be prompted for the text, then the possible answers, then which answer is correct, then the feedback for correct answers, then the feedback for each incorrect answer... In general:
* Authoring systems tend to be easy and quick to learn and use.
* An inherent problem with authoring systems is that some skills cannot be taught if the system does not have the capability built into it. For example, simulations requiring complex variable manipulation tend to be impossible within authoring systems.
* Authoring systems may be unsuitable for general developers since the tools are often designed for specific tasks.

3.1-2 Object-Based Systems

Object-based systems are very common and popular. These systems contain some pre-defined objects that can be programmed to do things. For example, some objects such as buttons are defined within the system. The button can be programmed to branch the learner to a new screen when the button is clicked. Other objects, such as video clips or visuals, can be imported into the application and be given programming commands. For simplicity, this category includes authoring tools that use metaphors representing a time-base system, cards, or flowcharts. A sample screen of a time-based authoring system is shown in figure 3.1.

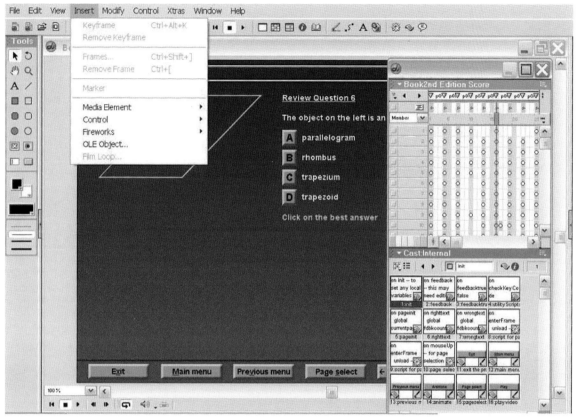

Figure 3.1 – Time-based authoring system screen capture   Used by permission of Macromedia, Inc.

In general, for object-based systems:
- Learning and authoring time can range from fast to slow.
- Authoring time can be very efficient if you create programming sub-routines for tasks that will be done repeatedly. For example, create a sub-routine for multiple-choice questions. After this investment, new questions can be quickly added by loading the new material (e.g., visual name or text) into variables, specifying the correct answer, and then calling up the sub-routine. The screen layout, answer judging, feedback, branching... will be done by the sub-routine.
- Most object-based systems have at least a limited command set available for programming (or scripting). Other systems have extensive command sets available. The extent of the command set affects the system's teaching capabilities and the time needed to learn the tool. Difficult applications usually require professional programming with the command set.
- The number of available programmers proficient with a specific object-based system tends to be small.
- Software costs range from expensive (e.g., $5,000) to a few hundred dollars. Price is not always an indicator of the product's usefulness. Some inexpensive tools have excellent capabilities.

3.1-3 Programming Languages

Programming languages (e.g., C, C++, Visual BASIC, and Java) have an extensive command set available. However, these commands are generalized for any application. Specific routines for teaching with computers (e.g., answer judging) must be developed. In general, for programming languages:
- Learning time is typically slow.

- Authoring time is slower than with the other tools but can be reasonable if sub-routines are created and used. Justify using a programming language since authoring time is a significant production cost.
- Teaching capabilities are extensive.
- The available workforce of programmers proficient with a specific programming language tends to be large. This can be particularly important when programming help is needed in a hurry and there is little or no training time available.
- Programs written with programming languages tend to execute quickly and run on minimal computer platforms.
- Software costs tend to be inexpensive (e.g., a few hundred dollars).

Practical Guideline:

Before developing an instructional multimedia application with a programming language, justify why it would be better than an object-based system.

3.1-4   Computer-Managed Presentations

Computer-managed presentations (CMP) can be created with the above tools but are often created with tools (e.g., PowerPoint™) that are easier to learn and quicker to use. These tools are the easiest way for you to get started with developing instructional multimedia applications. Carefully evaluate the CMP tool to ensure that the tool can do all that you need. Some desirable features, that go beyond simply incorporating different media, include pre-designed templates for common presentation formats, digital chalk (which lets you highlight, draw, or add information on the screen during a presentation), linking to static or dynamic data from other applications (such as spreadsheets), generating charts and graphs, special effects such as wipes and animated text, running other programs from within itself, branching from menus without having to do programming, showing multiple-choice questions and feedback for the different responses, and output capabilities including speaker notes, handouts, and slides.

3.1-5   Practical Considerations

There are many authoring tools available. Depending on each unique situation, some tools will be excellent while others will be poor. Evaluate the authoring tool thoroughly before you use it for a project.

Practical Guideline:

Due to varying strengths and weaknesses, evaluate an authoring tool thoroughly before you use it for a project.

As a general rule, tools that are easier to learn and use tend to have fewer capabilities (and vice versa). For major projects requiring difficult teaching strategies, consider using a high-end object-based system. However, difficult teaching strategies often require a programmer with the time, skills, and patience to learn the authoring tool and then do the programming. Would this be worthwhile for one project? For small straightforward projects and prototyping, low-end object-based tools and possibly authoring systems can work effectively.

Due to the extensive learning and authoring time needed, be sure you have a solid rationale for using a programming language. Programming languages are commonly used when unique features, unavailable on other tools, are needed.

By creating templates and sub-routines, which takes a significant amount of development time, programming languages can become fairly efficient. However, there is a danger with creating them. You may restrict your creativity by designing to the templates rather than designing the most effective way to teach. You can sometimes save time by obtaining templates and sub-routines from others. However, the templates and sub-routines may need to be modified to meet your needs.

> **Practical Guideline:**
>
> Create templates and sub-routines for authoring efficiency but design your applications without them in mind.

Efficiency can also be achieved with authoring tools that have cross-platform capabilities -- where the program or code can be transferred between computer platforms (e.g., between PCs and Macintosh®[1] computers). This can increase the number of computer stations that can run the software and also increase market potential. Note that the transfer may not be perfect due to inherent differences in the platforms. There can be differences leading to distorted visuals, color changes, and/or sizing and alignment irregularities in fonts. Distorted visuals can be a particular problem in applications such as those involving schematic diagrams. Problems caused by different fonts can be minimized by using cross-platform fonts, using tabs (rather than spaces) for alignment, and providing extra "white space" around text. In other words, do **not** constrain text to a minimal space. Transfer a prototype between platforms to determine specific differences before developing the entire program.

Since many authoring tools are designed for ease of use, there is the potential for you to complete all of the project tasks by yourself. A possible serious consequence is that the expertise found in the team approach can be lost. As musical instruments do not make professional musicians, authoring tools do not make professional multimedia designers. Aside from computer-managed presentations, a team is usually needed to efficiently create effective products. (See the Team approach chapter for details on the many advantages in working with teams.) Deciding on which authoring tool to use should be partially based on who will do the programming.

Some limitations of authoring systems and low-end object-based tools, such as the inability to teach some concepts (e.g., simulations requiring complicated variable control) and efficiencies (e.g., the inability to create some sub-routines), can be overcome by linking to routines created with programming languages. However, one reason for using an object-based tool or authoring system is to avoid working with a programming language.

Note that initial versions of authoring tools tend to be prone to errors. It is safer for you to use an authoring tool that has been on the market for a few years and has been developed by companies committed to improvement. However, if an authoring tool has unique features that are critical for development then a "young" product may be the best alternative regardless of the expected inherent difficulties.

> **Practical Guideline:**
>
> Avoid initial authoring tool releases.

Since different authoring tools have different strengths and weaknesses, consider using more than one authoring tool when numerous projects will be undertaken. However, there are costs to using too many authoring tools. Each authoring tool costs money to purchase and maintain such as updates. More significantly, costs arise from the time needed for evaluating, learning, and developing efficiencies for each tool. Time is also lost when a tool has not been used for a long time and the programmer needs to spend time becoming re-acquainted with the tool's idiosyncrasies. A reasonable solution is to use an excellent authoring tool for most needs and use one or two other tools for special needs. Remember that talent is more important than the tool being used.

> **Practical Guideline:**
>
> Powerful tools cannot counteract a lack of talent!

---

[1]Macintosh is a trademark of Apple Computer, Inc.

For multimedia development, other specialized software packages (e.g., for visuals, video editing, and sound editing) may also be needed.

3.2   Evaluating Authoring Tools

When evaluating an authoring tool, first create a list of your present and future needs. How can you select a tool if you do not know what you want to do with it? The evaluation is best done through actually working with the authoring tool and trying to solve a variety of your listed needs. Some evaluation information can be gained by questioning others who are using the tool and through published reports. Published reports can be based on thorough hands-on testing, biased, or written by the proprietary company itself.

When evaluating authoring tools to determine which tool best meets your needs, remember that it is unlikely that any one tool will meet all of your specified needs since the perfect authoring tool does **not** exist. However, the authoring tool you use can significantly influence the effectiveness of the multimedia production. Many potentially great projects have been mediocre because of an authoring tool's limitations.

> **Practical Guideline:**
>
> Although the perfect authoring tool does not exist, there is usually at least one tool, which can effectively handle your expected present and future needs.

For every authoring tool evaluated, record notes on each of the following items. Remember that most projects will only need a sub-set of the listed potential features. Note that many of the features listed below for evaluating an authoring tool's effectiveness in creating instructional multimedia applications also apply to evaluating computer-managed presentation tools.

3.2-1   General Information

General information is important for keeping records and following up with enquiries — especially when a few authoring tools are being evaluated. Note the:
- system name
- producer/vendor
- address
- phone and fax numbers
- date reviewed
- material reviewed (e.g., full system, demonstration disc, brochure...)
- reviewer's name
- reviewer's recommendation

3.2-2   Authoring Features

In general, you will need the following authoring features to ensure that authoring is efficient:
- The authoring tool should be easy to learn and use.
    - It can be advantageous if the tool has some menu driven features.
    - The time to learn should be minimal but proportional to its potential.
    - There should be a tutorial.
    - The help screens should be useful.
    - There should be a support group. Support groups can provide a wealth of information and help.

- It should be easy to set-up and operate the software.
  - Installation must be simple.
  - The program should boot quickly to save time.
  - The program should run with typical memory capacities.
  - Clear prompts should be given.
- The authoring tool should be efficient to use.
  - It must be easy to add and edit text, audio, visuals, video, animation, buttons, and background images. It should be easy to import the different common file formats.
  - It should be easy to set and change foreground and background colors.
  - It should be easy to create templates and sub-routines.
  - It must be easy to move to the next, previous, and other screens.
  - It must be easy to move and copy material.
  - It must be simple and easy to change the material's sequence.
  - The program should have fast execution from anywhere in the material's sequence. In other words, programmers should be able to quickly see what they have created.
  - The tool must have built-in error checking such as for non-existent branch locations.
  - If an error is found, the programmer should receive clear instructions on what caused the error and then have the option to immediately edit the error.
  - The author should be able to quit at any time rather than having to first back out of a series of menus. This feature should come with a warning if some changes have not been saved.
  - There should be an automatic routine for creating runtime (student playback) versions. This feature should coordinate the required external files (such as a media player) and create any directories as well as program groups and icons...
  - It is helpful if you can automatically generate a flowchart of the instructional sequence.
  - Printing options (e.g., code, flowchart, text, and visuals) are helpful.
  - It should be easy to add comments for later referencing.
- The authoring tool should allow for variable control.
  - Both global and local variables should be easy to declare and use. It is convenient if global variables only need to be declared in one initial location.
  - It must be possible to manipulate, store, and retrieve both strings (e.g., text characters) and numbers (integers and decimals). Data manipulation includes joining, moving, replacing, and resetting to empty or zero.
  - Both basic (e.g., addition, multiplication, exponents...) and advanced (e.g., sine, logarithms, rounding...) mathematical functions should be available.
  - Mathematical logical operators (e.g., equal, less than, and, or, not...) should be available.
  - It should be possible to branch to locations stored within variables.
  - It can be helpful to be able to transfer data between programs.
  - It should be possible to store data, such as marks, outside of the program. It is preferable that data storage is compliant with national or international standards.
  - You should be able to retrieve data from outside of the program such as from databases or get updated information from the Internet.
  - It should be possible to access system information such as time, date, available memory, computer speed, and screen size.
- It should be easy to call external routines such as calculators.
  - Execution must be quick.

3.2-3 Teaching Features

In general, you will need the subsequent teaching features to have the freedom to teach in any way that you determine to be effective:
- It should be possible to use a wide variety of instructional strategies.
  - These include tutorials, drill and practice programs, simulations, and educational games.

- It should be possible to incorporate a wide variety of question types.
  - Question types should include true-false, multiple choice, short answer, matching, selecting an image or part of an image, drag and drop items, and long answer/essay.
- There should be flexible answer judging.
  - More than one correct answer should be allowed.
  - It must be possible to provide specific feedback for any expected or unexpected right or wrong answers.
  - Spelling errors should be accommodated for keyboard input.
  - It must be possible to give different feedback for each answer and each attempt.
  - There must be the capability to control feedback with variables.
  - It must be possible to provide any amount of feedback.
  - It is critical that feedback can include all of the different media.
  - There must be the capability to control the number of attempts per question.
- There must be extensive branching capabilities.
  - It must be possible to branch a learner at any time (e.g., from menus and submenus), dependent on input, or conditionally based on scores, number of attempts, time...
  - For some applications, such as DVD-ROM (Digital Video Disc – Read Only Memory) and CD-ROM (Compact Disc – Read Only Memory) databases, students should be able to search (e.g., based on keywords) for specific information and be branched to those locations. From a practical perspective, consider a DVD-ROM to simply be a CD-ROM with much more capacity.
- Capabilities of random number insertion can be useful.
  - There should be the capability to generate random numbers (both integers and decimals) from within a maximum and minimum range.
- Capabilities of random question selection from a pool of questions can be useful.
  - This can enable students to receive unique questions and tests each time they run the program.
- There should be computer-managed learning features.
  - Important features can include student registration, data security, student/class scoring, records of the time a student spends on the system, analysis/report generation, and storing output in standardized formats (such as for word processors).

3.2-4   Student Features

In general, the following student features are needed to ensure that the program is user-friendly and students will not become frustrated. Student features include:
- easy set-up and operation
  - It should be quick and easy to boot up the program.
  - All prompts should be clear and easy to follow.
  - Runtime files should run from networks, hard drives, DVD-ROMs, CD-ROMs, and/or the Internet.
- quick, but preferably instant, screen displays
- immediate response time even on low-end hardware platforms
- student control
  - Students should be able to control their learning path through menus and submenus.
  - Students need paging control to freely move forward, backward, to the previous menu, to a glossary...
  - Students should be able to review at any time.
  - Students should be able to exit the program at any time.
  - It can be helpful if students can print screens and leave comments.
- error-free execution
  - The program should **not** crash (except when the programmer has made an error) on any system that has the specified minimum requirements.

3.2-5 Text

With respect to text, the authoring tool should allow you to:
- easily create and modify text
    - It should be easy to cut, copy, paste, and delete text.
    - It should be fast and simple to change colors and to highlight (e.g., bold, underline, Italics...).
    - There should be an automatic word wrap feature.
    - It should be easy to format text (e.g., left justification, centering, right justification, single and double-spacing...).
- easily import text from word processing files
    - The RTF (Rich Text Format) standard preserves formatting (e.g., bold, underlines...) but consequently uses a larger amount of storage space than text-only files. The RTF standard is compatible between the Macintosh® and PC platforms.
- use all standard keyboard characters
- use a variety of fonts and font sizes
- import or create special characters (e.g., math symbols)
- easily size fonts and special characters larger or smaller
- include superscripts and subscripts

3.2-6 Visuals

For visuals, the authoring tool should:
- have a built-in graphics (or paint) package
    - Object-oriented and/or vector-based graphics are preferred.
    - A screen capture feature is useful.
    - It can be helpful to be able to create icons.
    - It should be possible to generate graphs and charts based on static and dynamic data.
- be compatible with other formats
    - It should be easy to import visuals from other packages.
    - It should be easy to export visuals to other packages.
    - It should be possible to store externally-created visuals internally. This enables the authoring tool to find and display the visuals faster. As well, internal visuals are less easily used by others.
- support common screen sizes
- support and control common color palette standards
    - The default color palette should match any industry standards.
    - It should be easy to convert imported visuals to the color palette you are using in your program.
- be able to reference pixels
    - It should be easy to place items, such as text and visual images, anywhere on the screen. You may need to do this via variable control.
- allow for overlays
- allow for windows
- let you scale and rotate images

3.2-7 Animation

With respect to animations, the authoring tool should allow you to:
- easily create simple animations
    - There should be capabilities of moving objects around the screen and to also control the animation's speed.
    - There should be a tweening (in-betweening) feature that provides the capabilities of automatically creating a series of visual images between two previously placed images.
- easily "play" animations created with external animation tools

3.2-8 Audio

For audio, the authoring tool should allow you to:
- easily access and control audio
  - There should be compatibility with common file format standards (e.g., WAV, SND, MP3, and MIDI).
- easily play speech and sound files that were recorded with external tools
- generate beeps
  - It should be possible to control the beep's length and pitch.
- stream audio or enable links to tools that allow you to do so

3.2-9 Video

With respect to video, the authoring tool should allow you to:
- easily access and play common formats of video (e.g., WMV, QuickTime, MPEG-1, MPEG-2, MPEG-4, and AVI) from networks, hard drives, DVD-ROMs, and CD-ROMs
- control the video (e.g., pause, slow forward, fast forward, slow reverse, fast reverse)
- display the video at any screen location or size you choose
- stream video or enable links to tools that allow you to do so
- stream video at the different Internet connection speeds that learner's may have

3.2-10 Compatibility

Compatibility is necessary to ensure that both development and runtime hardware and software run without error on common platforms. Compatibility is also needed so that limitations that affect learning are not introduced. For example, if the analysis determines that high-bandwidth video is critical for learning then the system must be able to handle high-bandwidth video.
- Ensure that the final product is 100% compatible with the varying hardware standards of your learners' computers.
  - There should be high portability to differing hardware specifications.
  - It is sometimes preferable to use an authoring tool that can create cross-platform code.
- Learner input should be possible via mouse, touch screen, and keyboard.
  - Voice and keyboard input are often not critical for effective learning.
- The software should be able to determine characteristics of the computer on which the runtime software is running.
  - The user should receive a warning message if their system cannot adequately run the program.
  - If the program is to be run from a DVD-ROM or CD-ROM, it can be useful if the program can first search for data and updated information from an internal network or over the Internet.
  - If the authoring tool requires that some files be present on the hard drive then the installation should be as automatic as possible. The installation should preferably not affect the computer's start-up files. The tool should preferably provide an "uninstall" feature.
- The authoring tool should be able to launch other programs.
  - For example, the learner could work with a spreadsheet to generate data and then return to the program.
- There should be standard random access memory (RAM) requirements for both development and runtime software.
  - If the RAM requirements are excessive then you have to consider whether the extra costs for the development and/or runtime hardware are justified.
  - It can be helpful to control what information is kept in RAM. For example, specify that visuals or routines that will be used regularly remain in RAM while unneeded ones are immediately removed from RAM.
  - It can be useful if the software can pre-load information into RAM in order to speed up the runtime program.
  - Determine if the product's execution speed is acceptable on the student's hardware platforms and whether the minimum hardware configuration is acceptable.

- There should be minimal or reasonable hard disk storage requirements for both development and runtime software.
- It should be possible to run the runtime software from a network.
- It should be possible to stream the runtime software over the Internet.
- It should be possible to run the program through different web browsers.
- If it is a concern, the software should have an encryption feature that prevents unauthorized use of the runtime product.
- If it is a concern, the software should have a security feature that prevents others from copying the programming code.
  - This can help protect valuable work and ideas from being stolen.
  - It is preferred to have materials self-contained within the executable program. As well as making it more difficult to steal your material, internally-contained materials can reduce the trouble of remembering which files to include in run-time products.

3.2-11 Support

Support is necessary to help make your authoring efficient and to minimize your frustration. Support should include:
- a training tutorial
- vendor training
- technical advice
  - This can be through a free telephone hot-line.
- a user group
  - This can be through the Internet or bulletin board services.
- good documentation
  - There should be detailed well-indexed user manuals, a quick reference manual, context-sensitive help screens, technical manuals, and numerous practical examples.
- a warranty
  - A warranty can be particularly important when the software has "bugs".
  - Determine whether the company quickly fixes "bugs". This can be done by contacting other users.

3.2-12 Costs

Costs may not simply include the price of the basic authoring tool. There may also be additional costs for a presentation system (student runtime files), management system, drivers for peripherals, additional copies or a network price, distribution fees for each runtime program, license fees, and maintenance or update costs. Note that updates are needed in order to accommodate new hardware and software advances. Find out whether you can preview the authoring tool for evaluation purposes and whether there is a fee for previewing the software.

3.2-13 Contracts

Authoring tools come with a contract. Determine the impact of any contractual constraints or costs.
- Can you sell your product freely? This is preferred. If you have to pay the company a royalty for each product sold or user fees then consider purchasing a different authoring tool.
- What are the costs of updates or maintenance? Can you afford it?
- Can you copy or share the authoring tool with other employees?
  - Depending on your timelines and the available personnel, some projects could require simultaneous authoring.

Summary

Authoring is the process of issuing, testing, and revising instructions for presenting materials on a computer system. The tools available for authoring can be classified as being authoring systems, object-based systems, or programming languages.

As a general guideline:
- Authoring systems tend to be menu driven. You are specifically prompted for information or information is slotted into available locations.
- Object-based systems consist of objects that are programmed to do things. Most object-based systems have at least a limited command set available for programming.
- Programming languages have an extensive command set available. However, these commands are generalized for any application. Specific routines for teaching with computers must be developed.

In general:
- Authoring systems tend to be the easiest to learn and use.
- Programming languages have the best capabilities.
- Each tool has different strengths and weaknesses.
- The perfect authoring tool does **not** exist.

You must thoroughly analyze each authoring tool to determine if it meets your expected present and future needs. The analysis is best done by actually using the tool. When evaluating an authoring tool consider authoring features, teaching features, student features, text, visuals, animation, audio, video, compatibility, support, costs, contracts, and whether the product is mature or an initial release.

Application Exercises

1) If you are going to start multimedia development by creating a simple tutorial and your boss requests that you use the C++ programming language, what would you say to him?
2) What is the danger of working with a new authoring tool that has just been released?
3) As an authoring tool's capabilities increases, what tends to happen to the learning and authoring time?
4) What are the main advantages of using a computer-managed presentation tool?
5) True or false?
    a) Templates can be created to make programming very efficient.
    b) An authoring tool's selection should be based on present and future needs.
    c) A good authoring tool ensures a good product.
    d) New software developments have given rise to the perfect authoring tool.

Case Study

For the workshop on creating instructional multimedia applications, two instructors assumed the "programmer" role for creating a tutorial. Based on the provided parameters (e.g., for screen design, the user-interface, and expected simple animations), the short project timeline, the instructor's lack of programming expertise, and consultation with the instructional designer, two of the authoring tools were felt to be too difficult too learn. They then spent the afternoons of the first week evaluating two intermediate level authoring tools with the intention of selecting one tool to develop the tutorial. After working through the authoring tool's learning guides, the instructors chose one tool.

Case Study Questions

1) Was time allotted in the five afternoons enough to adequately evaluate the authoring tools? Why?
2) What other ways would you use to gather more information for evaluating the authoring tools?
3) If the tool will be used on a variety of future projects, what else would you do to evaluate the tool?

References

Joss, M. (1996, January). Multimedia presents! A look at high-powered interactive presentation software. CD-ROM Professional, 9(1), 62-72.

Karon, P. (1996, January, 22). Multimedia for the masses. Infoworld, 18(4), 64-79.

Livingston, D. (1994, January). Choosing an authoring system: Tips to guide your selection. CD-ROM Professional, 7(1), 83-90.

Strauss, R. (1995, February). The development tool fandango: Deciding the authoring system versus programming language question. CD-ROM Professional, 8(2), 47-55.

Section 1: Instructional Design

This section will help you define a problem and determine whether the problem should be solved through instructional multimedia. Once you decide to develop an instructional multimedia application, you must ensure that your efforts result in a product that effectively solves the defined problem. The instructional development cycle and instructional design process presented in this section are essential tools that can help you create effective products. Many projects have failed because these processes have not been followed.

Chapter 4:
Instructional Development Cycle

Learning Outcomes

After completing this chapter, you should be able to:
- describe the activities of each phase of the instructional development cycle
- follow the instructional development cycle when creating courseware

Introduction

The instructional development cycle is the systematic repetitive process of activities you need to do to solve an instructional problem.

This chapter describes the instructional development cycle and the potential problems with literally following the model. You will also be provided with details and practical guidelines for completing the tasks involved in the cycle's analysis, planning, design, development, implementation, evaluation, and revision phases.

4.1 Description

The purpose of following the instructional development cycle is to help ensure that your instructional multimedia project is a success. Many projects that have not followed this or a comparable process have failed or have had serious problems.

There are many instructional development models. Generally, most new models are based on previous ones, none are proven (most are PhD theses), and most include the same phases in one form or another. The instructional development cycle model, as seen in figure 4.1, is adapted from Spitzer (1991). This model represents what you should do in an ideal world. In practice, limited resources and time constraints dictate that you will do some steps superficially.

The instructional development cycle starts with the analysis phase and continues with the planning, design, development, and implementation phases. The evaluation and revision phase is ongoing throughout the development cycle. Each phase is a checkpoint. After each phase, evaluate the results, make revisions, and get approval to proceed. The instructional development cycle contains the systematic instructional design process. (See the Instructional design chapter for details.)

> **Practical Guideline:**
>
> Evaluate and revise throughout the development cycle!

[handwritten margin notes: 1. analysis / 2. planning / 3. design / 4. developm / 5. implem. / 7. dev. includes / 6. 7. evaluation + revision]

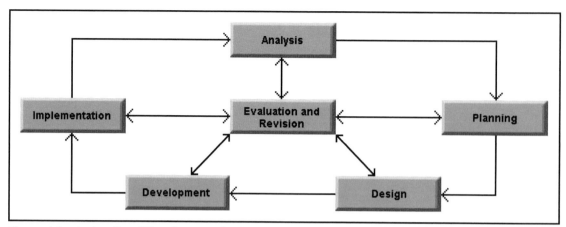

Figure 4.1 – Instructional Development Cycle

You may have some potential problems if you literally follow this model:
- There might not be enough resources to thoroughly complete all of the phases.
  - If resources are limited then consult with experienced instructional multimedia designers to determine how and when to "cut corners". For example, they may be able to determine that some low-end skills should be left as paper-based pre-requisite material while multimedia is used to teach the high-end skills. In particular, this would shorten the development phase.
  - If a part of a phase is omitted then it should be an informed decision rather than an oversight.
  - Try not to become overwhelmed with completing all of the tasks. As you become more experienced with the instructional development cycle, many of these decisions and ideas will become intuitive and only take a minimal amount of time to complete.
- The project may never end.
  - To counter this, each phase must be signed off (i.e., sign an agreement with management or the client) with the intention that the work in that phase has been completed to everyone's satisfaction given the restraints of the project.
- It can become very expensive to keep making changes.
  - Consider whether it is worthwhile to do minor revisions. There must be a balance between costs and the value gained. Is it reasonable to expect a perfect product?
  - Minor problems are likely to be continually found since evaluation is ongoing throughout the cycle.
- Some phases may need to be started before others are completed.
  - This should be expected and should not cause problems as long as the needed information is available to start the tasks early.
  - Time constraints and team member availability can affect starting times.

In general, both instructional multimedia applications and computer-managed presentations (CMP) should both equally follow the instructional development cycle. However, since CMP tend to be less formal and created with fewer resources, you can safely create a CMP with only superficially following the instructional development cycle.

4.2   Analysis Phase

The initial purpose of the analysis phase is for you to define the actual problem and then determine whether the problem needs an instructional multimedia solution. The analysis phase should provide you with a concise problem definition and initial cost estimates. Constraints should also be identified.

In the analysis phase:

a) Do the following steps, as described in the Instructional Design chapter:
   - Identify the instructional goal(s).
   - Conduct a goal analysis.
   - Conduct a subordinate skills analysis.   *(initial skills)*
   - Identify entry behaviors and characteristics.
   - Write learning outcomes. Learning outcomes form the basis of all of the subsequent steps.

Practical Guideline:

Learning outcomes are the foundation for all design and development.

---

b) Provide initial cost estimates as required.
   - As the analysis phase proceeds, more information becomes available for more accurate estimates.
   - It may be wise for you to inflate your initial cost estimates in order to be sure you can complete the project within your budget.
   - Since CMP are often made without a budget, you may be able to skip this step of the analysis phase.

c) Determine if there are funding and resource constraints.
   - Consider ranking the learning outcomes to determine which skills should be taught by a multimedia approach.

d) Conduct an evaluation and make revisions.

Do everything in the analysis phase thoroughly. If you spend more effort in this phase then less effort will be wasted in revisions and in the subsequent phases.

Practical Guideline:

The time invested in the analysis phase tends to save more time throughout the rest of the process.

4.3   Planning Phase

The planning phase helps your whole project proceed smoothly. A major component of the planning phase involves identifying and addressing potential problems. It is wiser for you to deal with problems before investment in design and development begin. Other major planning tasks include assembling the team and setting timelines.

a) identify possible problems
b) assembling the team
c) timelines

In the planning phase:

a) Anticipate and prevent potential problems.
   - Find out if there is acceptance and commitment at all levels. If not, be sure the project is clearly defined, ensure the project satisfies your organization's goals, provide a cost-benefit analysis to the stakeholders, and find some advocates. It can be beneficial to quickly create a simple prototype to help sell the idea. Do **not** begin a project unless you have authorization and support.
   - Finalize the budget and get approval for funding. This is crucial. For safety, retain a 10 to 20% contingency fund.
   - Determine potential implementation problems and solutions such as a need for hardware upgrades to run the product or a lack of time to learn from the instructional solution.
   - Determine time and other constraints (e.g., hardware and personnel availability).
   - Find out if the final product needs cross-platform compatibility. If so, choose an authoring tool that facilitates this development and do a few tests early on in order to determine if there will be any problems. Note that cross-platform compatibility increases the product's market potential.

- Create a plan for evaluating the product's effectiveness. You will need to try out the product or partial product at a site. As a part of the evaluation plan, determine if an external evaluation is needed, such as for credibility or to ensure accuracy.
- Maintain a record of costs, time, problems, and solutions to help plan future projects.
- Predict potential future problems including whether there will be a need for an updated version.

Practical Guideline:

Only begin a project if you have authorization and support.

- Start assembling the team. (See the Team Approach chapter for more details.)
  - Specify and assign members to the team. Consider how the project will affect staffing. Consider personality conflicts.
  - Determine the skills and roles of each team member.
  - Determine if other skills are needed. If so, determine whether to provide training or hire individuals. This decision can be based on whether the skills will be needed in the future. Remember that employees feel important if they receive training. Employee training can increase motivation and productivity.
  - Even though it is not ideal, CMP often have to be created by individuals.
- Start setting timelines.
  - Be realistic since projects often take longer than expected. Some managers ask for triple the time expected and barter for twice the amount while others simply plan for twice the expected time. Accurate time estimations come with experience but there are often uncontrollable factors such as strikes, illnesses, equipment delays, mistakes due to normal human errors, and unanticipated challenges such as in computer programming.
  - Start setting time frames for each team member to finish their tasks. Review these plans with each team member. There should be agreement that the plans are reasonable and can be achieved in the allotted time frames.
  - Consider using a computerized project management tool, especially for large or complex projects. Project management tools can help identify potential problems such as an individual having too much to do at one time.
  - Remember that documentation is an important but often unpopular and thus neglected component of the project.
  - This step of setting timelines might not be required for CMP.
- Conduct an evaluation and make revisions.

Practical Guideline:

It is safest to assume that a project will take longer than expected.

4.4   Design Phase

Based on your problem definition and the stated learning outcomes, the design phase leads you to creating the instructional strategy — what needs to be done to ensure that the students will effectively and efficiently learn. Another component of the design phase is to define the standards and needed utilities so that programming can begin. A last step is to finalize all of the resource requirements.

In the design phase:
- Develop the test questions. (See the Question Writing chapter and the Develop criterion-referenced test questions step of the Instructional Design chapter for more details.)
    - Determine whether testing is realistic enough and a true performance measure.
    - All difficulty levels must be considered. Many existing computer-based training packages are weak in that they only address low-level thinking skills.
    - For CMP, you can verbally present questions and interactive strategies.
- Develop an instructional strategy. (Read the Develop an instructional strategy step of the Instructional Design chapter for more information.)
- Select the media based on the instructional strategy. (The Media Selection chapter has more details.)
- Determine needed standards and utilities.
    - Locate any existing internal standards for multimedia applications.
    - Set standards for writing style, such as second person, and decide whether the tone will be friendly, formal, or something else. The writing style and tone should not necessarily be the same for every product and audience. For example, doctors would likely prefer a different style and tone than high school students.
    - Set or affirm screen design standards for orientation information, headings, prompt locations, prompt wording, error messages, navigation buttons, fonts, font sizes, color palettes, colors, and how to highlight. Note that within reason, standards should evolve as ideas and technology changes. Imagine the results if you followed the standards that were set for 1985 computer technology. (See the Screen Design section for more information.)
    - Set learner control and navigation standards.
    - Decide if input will be via mouse, keyboard, touch, or other device. If there will be keyboard input, state the specific function key roles. Determine if spelling is important for keyboard input.
    - State feedback formats such as having two tries per question, different feedback on each try, the amount of feedback... (See the Feedback chapter for more details.)
    - Determine scoring for tests and criteria for passing.
    - State what information, if any, will be recorded. This can include information such as the student name, student number, test results, and time on each lesson.
    - Determine if a note pad, paint package, spell checker, calculator, glossary, and/or program map (to allow a student to branch to any section) are necessary.
    - Remember that from a learning perspective, elegance and simplicity will win over flash and glitz.

Practical Guideline:

Enhance learning with elegance and simplicity rather than non-educational special effects.

- Have the programmer begin coding the above standards and utilities into templates and sub-routines.
    - This task can range from taking a few hours to hundreds of hours depending on the authoring tool, the standards, whether existing programming sub-routines exists, whether similar projects have been done, and the programmer's experience. The time spent will pay for itself in programming efficiency and design consistency.
    - These templates and sub-routines can also be used in future projects.
    - Test and validate the standards and utilities as they are developed so that problems are discovered when it is still early enough to easily make changes.
    - Creating CMP does not require programming and is usually done by the instructor.
- Finalize the resource requirements such as personnel, hardware, software, and specialty items such as a video camera, digital camera, and editing software.
- Conduct an evaluation and make revisions.

4.5   Development Phase

The development phase leads you through creating a storyboard of the instructional strategy, finalizing the media selection needed to teach the material, and then developing and programming the materials.

In the development phase:
- Create a storyboard based on the instructional strategy and design specifications created in the design phase. (Read the Instructional Design chapter for more details on creating storyboards.)
- Based on the storyboard, make final decisions about the media selection needed to effectively teach the material.
- Based on the storyboard, develop and select instructional materials. (Check the Develop and select instructional materials step of the Instructional Design chapter for more information.)
- Program the needed utilities and the storyboard.
- Conduct an evaluation and make revisions.

4.6   Implementation Phase

Implementation is the process you need to follow of trying out the system in the "real world" to find out what works and what needs revision. Evaluation is an integral component of implementation.

In the implementation phase:
- Plan to have the facilities, hardware, and software available.
  - Do a practice run in advance to be sure everything is working as needed.
  - Schedule learners in advance.
- First, implement a prototype.
  - Prototypes often work better in theory than in practice.
  - Changes made in the prototype, such as color standards, can apply to all future sections. This is easier and cheaper than later having to repeat the same changes in many completed sections of the program. Using templates and sub-routines can minimize the changes needed in that, if you make a change within them, the change is automatically applied throughout the entire program.
  - If you observe learners using the prototype, you can better appreciate the learners' needs.
  - Specifically ask learners about any concerns you have. If you do not ask, you may never find out if there is indeed a problem.

Practical Guideline:

To save time, implement a prototype before significant design and development is done.

- Consider factors that lead to successful multimedia implementation. (The Implementing multimedia solutions section in the Introduction to Instructional Multimedia chapter has more information.)
- Conduct an evaluation and make revisions.

4.7   Evaluation Phase

Evaluation is the systematic collection and analysis of information to aid in decision making and planning. Both the learner's hardware systems and the created software must be evaluated. Remember that evaluation is an on-going process throughout the instructional development cycle. (Check the "Conduct a formative evaluation step" of the Instructional Design chapter for essential details of how to evaluate the software and whether effective learning is taking place.)

The software should be tested on different computer systems with varying speeds, memory, screen resolutions, and monitors and possibly web browsers with varying Internet connection speeds. This should be done early in the process with initial prototypes.

4.8   Revision Phase

Base revisions on the evaluation feedback and data. Since evaluation is on going throughout the instructional development cycle, revisions are also on going.

If a first version of the software is released early to "beat the competition" and earn money, there will likely be errors. Is it worth the damage to the product's reputation?

If major revisions are required near the end of a project, (good analysis, planning, and on-going evaluations should prevent this), there may be problems in that some staff:
* are temporarily hired and have left the project
* will no longer be excited or interested in the project
* are busy with new projects

Note that it is basically impossible to create a perfect product. At some reasonable point (e.g., changes will no longer be cost-effective), there should be no further revisions. It is then time to celebrate a finished project. Remember that team members often go beyond the call of duty.

> **Practical Guideline:**
>
> Celebrate the completion of the project!

In the future, updates may need to be done. For example, this can stem from outdated content or data or from needing to add new information.

Summary

The instructional development cycle is the systematic repetitive process of activities, which includes the systematic instructional design process, you need to do to solve an instructional problem.

The instructional development cycle includes the analysis, planning, design, development, implementation, and evaluation and revision phases. After each phase, evaluate the results, make revisions, and get approval before proceeding.

The analysis phase includes identifying the instructional goal(s) and developing these goals through to writing learning outcomes. Other tasks include providing initial cost estimates and determining funding and resource constraints. Time invested in the analysis phase pays for itself in subsequent phases.

In the planning phase assemble the team, anticipate and prevent potential problems, and set timelines.

The design phase includes developing test questions and instructional strategies, selecting the media, determining needed standards and utilities, beginning the programming, and finalizing resource requirements. The computer programmer should create templates and sub-routines to save time.

The development phase entails creating a storyboard based on the instructional strategy. Subsequent steps include finalizing the media selection and developing and selecting instructional materials. Other steps include creating the needed utilities, and completing the programming.

The implementation phase involves planning to have the facilities, hardware, and software available, trying out the materials, evaluating the materials, and determining factors that will lead to successful implementation. To save time, implement a prototype before significant design and development is done.

The evaluation phase includes conducting a formative evaluation throughout each phase of the instructional development cycle and collecting and analyzing data.

The revision phase involves making changes based on the evaluation's results.

Application Exercises

1) Assume, in an instructional multimedia development project, the project leader planned for the evaluation phase to begin after the implementation phase. What is the weakness in this plan?
2) Your boss wants your instructional multimedia project to be perfect. What is wrong with this desire?
3) Your boss asked you to save money by minimizing the amount of time spent in the analysis phase. What is the danger in this request?
4) During the implementation phase, the software was thoroughly tested on your computer with a variety of different students. After the revisions were made, the final product was produced. What are two potential problems with this scenario?

Case Study

Six instructors were on a four-week professional development leave from their regular duties. One of the goals was to create a marketable product. The workshop leader was an experienced multimedia designer but none of the instructors had any experience in creating or programming instructional multimedia applications. In the first three weeks, the mornings were devoted to learning the principles and guidelines of creating instructional multimedia applications. During the afternoons of the first three weeks, the "programmers" evaluated authoring tools, selected a tool, and learned to use the tool. The "graphic artist" learned a graphics package and created some sample images. The subject-matter experts evaluated sample instructional multimedia applications, worked through the instructional development cycle, and created a storyboard. In the analysis phase, it was estimated that the "programmers" would have the basics of the authoring tool mastered by the end of the fourth week and they would each need at least one more week to transfer the storyboard to the computer.

Case Study Questions

1) What needed to be done in order to ensure that the project could be completed?
2) What activities would have been done in the different phases of the project?

References

Berge, Z., Collins, M., & Dougherty, K. (2000). Design guidelines for web-based courses. In Abbey, B. (Ed.), Instructional and cognitive impacts of web-based education. (pp. 32-40). Hershey, PA: Idea Group Publishing.

Gagne, R., Briggs, L., & Wager, W. (1988). Principles of instructional design (3rd ed.). New York, NY: Holt, Rinehart and Winston.

Gustafson, K. (1981). A survey of instructional development models. (ERIC Document Reproduction Service No. ED 305 921)

Spitzer, D. (1991). Introduction to instructional technology (2nd ed.). Boise, ID: Boise State University.

Chapter 5: Instructional Design

Learning Outcomes

After completing this chapter, you should be able to:
- describe the activities of each step of the instructional design process
- use the instructional design process to create courseware
- conduct a needs assessment
- state characteristics of students who are particularly suited for multimedia lessons
- write complete learning outcomes
- sequence learning outcomes to best facilitate learning
- decide when pre-tests should be used
- describe characteristics of effective post-tests
- motivate learners in multimedia lessons
- design lessons that include all of the instructional events
- estimate the amount of content needed per learning outcome
- describe characteristics, strengths, and weaknesses of the different types of instructional multimedia
- choose the appropriate type of instructional multimedia for a given scenario

Introduction

Instructional design is a systematic repetitive process of activities aimed at creating a solution for an instructional problem.

This chapter first describes the instructional design process. You will then be provided with details and practical guidelines for completing each step in the process. Within these steps you will also be presented with information on conducting a needs assessment, conducting a learner analysis, learning style research, motivating students, the instructional events, and the basic types of multimedia instruction.

5.1   Description

Instructional design is the systematic process of activities you need to do to solve an instructional problem. Use this process to help ensure that your final product is successful. As with the instructional development cycle, many projects that have not followed this or a comparable process have failed. The instructional design process steps are shown in figure 5.1. These steps, which are similar to other models, are adapted from Dick and Carey's (1990) model.

Like the instructional development cycle, the instructional design process can go on forever. Each step is a checkpoint and must be signed off with the general knowledge that the results are acceptable enough to continue forward in the project. However, subsequent evaluation feedback may indicate that changes must be made in previously signed-off steps. These changes sometimes result from not putting the necessary time and resources into each step.

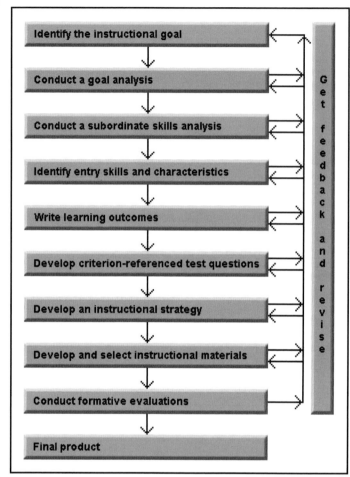

Figure 5.1 – Steps in the instructional design process

This model represents what should be done in an ideal situation. However, your reality of cost and time constraints will sometimes force you to make modifications. Safe modifications, such as omitting or minimizing steps, depend on the actual problem being solved, the information that is available, and your intuition or experience of knowing where it is safe to take "short cuts".

For high-end applications, the entire systematic instructional design process can take you from 100 to 300 hours of development time to complete one student instructional hour. Factors affecting the length of time include the project's complexity, authoring tool used, resources available such as instructor notes, team member experience, team dynamics, whether suitable design specifications exist, whether programming sub-routines exist... Computer-managed presentations can be completed in a fraction of this time.

Lessons developed for computer-managed presentations should also follow the systematic instructional design process. Some minor differences between computer-managed presentations and instructional multimedia applications have been included. You can find more tips for creating computer-managed presentations in Appendix I.

Systematic instructional design is an integral part of the instructional development cycle. (See the Instructional Development Cycle chapter for more information.)

5.2   Identify the Instructional Goal(s)

Instructional goals are general learning outcomes, such as being able to speak conversational French, that will later be broken down into specific measurable skills. Before identifying the instructional goal, you must first define the actual problem. Information for defining the problem and identifying the instructional goal is gathered through a needs assessment.

[handwritten margin note: → define the problem by making a needs assessment]

A needs assessment is a method:
- for determining the actual problem rather than symptoms of a problem
  - For example, the symptom may be refusal to use the computer system because the "program does not work" but the real problem is a fear of the technology.
- of gathering information ✓
- for understanding potential users ✓
- of consultation ✓
- that ensures involvement, ownership, and fewer surprises for all affected individuals ✓

> **Practical Guideline:**
>
> Be sure that you define the real problem rather than a symptom of the problem.

5.2-1   Needs Assessment Tools and Techniques

Needs assessment tools and techniques include interviews, observations, surveys, group meetings, and reviewing existing documentation. You will need to decide which is the best way to get accurate information, given limitations such as time or money.

Interviews

In interviews, consider asking people about problems they have experienced, to rank a list of skills that can make them more effective, about their feelings or impressions pertaining to certain skills, and/or to identify what they feel is the best solution to a problem.

In-person interviews are preferred since body language can provide critical information. Phone interviews can be convenient. However, it takes skill to determine the truth as suggested in the quote, "Smart is when you believe only half of what you heard. Brilliant is when you know what half to believe."

Observations

In observations, ask people to demonstrate particular tasks. A task analysis, or complete step-by-step breakdown of the duties needed to perform a task, can provide important information about what actually happens. Watch for problems caused by inefficiencies. Determine the difference between actual and optimal performances. Be careful of the "halo effect" where people behave differently because they are being observed. Consider potential problems of people not wanting to be observed. Another observation technique is to analyze work products. Defects can show where problems occur in the process.

Note that there may already be reports, records, and statistics containing relevant information.

Surveys

Surveys can be more effective if the survey is based on earlier observations. This may provide useful information for knowing what questions to ask. In the survey, try to determine feelings. Attitudes can play a major role in job performance. Consider whether the provided information will be accurate. Will everyone honestly fill out the survey? Some incentives may need to be provided to have the surveys completed.

Group Meetings

Group meetings can be an economical method for gathering information. Before the meeting begins, carefully plan on how the meeting will proceed but be flexible enough to allow the meeting to flow in other useful directions. Note that it is important for you to prevent discord between group members and also prevent one or two individuals from influencing the group.

Reviewing Existing Documentation

Existing documentation could provide you with a list of existing goals or even reveal that the problem is already documented. Existing documentation could state that there is a requirement for new instruction (e.g., learning how to use or repair new equipment or technology) or that there is a new mandate that requires an instructional solution.

Documentation can be problematic if the goals and learning outcomes are non-existent or vague, there are contradictions between what is asked for and what is needed, or goals and learning outcomes shift.

5.2-2   Needs Assessment Results *⇒ a def of the exact problem.*

Most importantly, your needs assessment should result in a definition of the exact problem. There should be a clear distinction between "what is" and "what should be". The real problem must be identified. Sometimes symptoms are addressed instead of what is actually causing the problem. For example, a worker's complaint may really be the result of a fear of change.

The defined problem is sometimes linked to:
- environmental or tool problems such as from worn out or outdated equipment
- lack of motivation including low perceived value and low confidence in success
- poor incentives that can be from achievements being ignored or leading to undesired consequences such as extra work, extra responsibilities, or a transfer to an unwanted location
- communication weaknesses
- illiteracy or lack of knowledge
- a combination of these problems

If the problems are ⟶ non-inst. based

Remember that a non-multimedia approach such as a job aid like a checklist, a less expensive print-based package, or a trainer hired for a short time period may be the most reasonable solution. Appendix III contains ideas for solving non-instructional problems.

> **Practical Guideline:**
>
> Remember that many problems can be solved without an instructional multimedia approach.

Avoid letting pre-conceived ideas, one particular idea, or too many ideas overly influence the problem definition or any step in the instructional design process.

A needs assessment can also result in a statement of:
- the difference between wants and needs
- the skills and knowledge that potential users have, optimal users have, and potential users need
- why there is a difference between what optimal and less effective people know and are able to do and whether or not the difference is important
- an individual's opinions and feelings
- factors that can interfere with learning

- potential solutions for problems
- ideas for meaningful examples, cases, problems, and questions for use in the instructional solution

Any resulting clearly defined instructional goal(s) should be:
- cost-effective to solve
  - (Read the Introduction to Instructional Multimedia chapter for details on benefits and costs.)
- accepted by everybody involved
  - This will help ensure that the solution will also be accepted.
- achievable with respect to time and resources

5.3   Conduct a Goal Analysis

A goal analysis results in a general but exact visual statement of what the learner will be able to do. Consider the goal of a learner being able to film with a camcorder. Figure 5.2 illustrates how this general goal can be broken down into specific learner requirements.

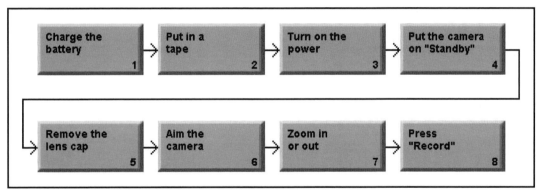

Figure 5.2 – Goal analysis for operating a camcorder

To analyze a goal, simply describe, in detail, the consecutive steps a learner will be doing when performing the goal. The rule of thumb is to have from 5 to 15 steps. If there are more than 15 steps, the goal is too big or the steps are too detailed. Some of these steps can be "mental" steps that cannot be seen, such as estimations. Some steps may require a decision that results in two or more alternate paths. Focus on what learners need to be able to do or perform rather than what learners need to know.

Goal analysis includes classifying the goal into the domain or kind of learning that will occur. The domains can be **verbal information** where students state, list, describe, name..., **intellectual skills** such as learners discriminating, identifying, classifying, demonstrating, generating, originating, creating..., **psychomotor skills** where students make, draw, adjust, assemble..., and **attitudes** such as learners making choices, selecting... These domain classifications are detailed in Appendix IV. Classifying the goal into a domain is important for determining which instructional strategies to use in subsequent steps.

5.4   Conduct a Subordinate Skills Analysis

The sequential steps derived in the goal analysis are often too large to be taught in one step or the learner needs some information prior to learning a step. This can be seen in step 7 in figure 5.2 where the learner needs some information regarding when one should zoom in or out. Subordinate skills are skills that must be learned before performing a step. When identifying subordinate skills, be careful not to make the components too numerous (which can bore students and interfere with learning) or to omit components (which can make the instruction ineffective). For each learning domain classification, you need to conduct a different type of subordinate skills analysis:

Verbal Information

With verbal information, you should derive the subordinate skills through a cluster analysis. In conducting a cluster analysis, identify all of the information that is needed to achieve the goal. After the information is gathered, organize the information into logical groupings. Logical groupings should have up to five pieces of information for weaker or younger students or up to seven pieces of information for brighter or older students. A few students can handle nine pieces of information but it is risky to assume that all students in the target audience can do this. The basic problem is that students can only process a limited amount of information at a time. The human brain has limitations that must be factored into the design. Whenever there is doubt, choose smaller groupings to be safe.

Although verbal information is deemed trivial by some people, treat verbal information seriously since it forms the needed knowledge base for higher-level skills.

> **Practical Guideline:**
>
> Organize the information into small enough chunks for the students to successfully learn.

Given the learning outcome, "learners will be able to state body parts," the verbal knowledge can be organized as seen in Table 5-1.

Table 5-1		
Body area	**Major parts**	**Smaller parts**
Head	Eyes Ears Nose Mouth	 Lips, teeth, tongue
Torso	Shoulder Chest Abdomen	 Belly button
Arm	Upper arm Elbow Forearm Wrist Hand	 Palm, thumb, fingers
Leg	Thigh Knee Shin Ankle Foot	 Heel, toes

Intellectual Skills

With intellectual skills, you need to conduct a hierarchical analysis to determine the subordinate skills. An example of the skills needed to multiply three digit numbers is shown in figure 5.3.

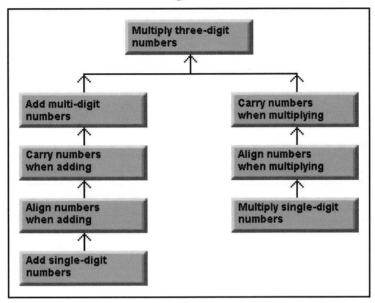

Figure 5.3 – Hierarchical analysis for three-digit multiplication

Do the following steps to conduct a hierarchical analysis:
1) For each step derived in the goal analysis, ask, "What must the student know before this skill can be learned?" This creates the first hierarchical level.
2) For each first level component, ask the same question. This creates a second hierarchical level.
3) Continue this as far as needed.

Assuming a problem-solving goal, the first level may be comprised of rules, the second level may be rules or concepts, the third level may be concepts or verbal information... Each level can have a simpler or equally difficult skill underneath it. (See Appendix IV for more information on rules and concepts.)

Psychomotor Skills

You can derive subordinate psychomotor skills through a procedural analysis. An example of the subordinate skills needed for charging a battery is shown in figure 5.4.

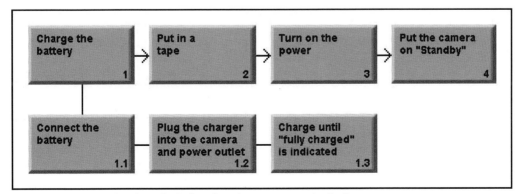

Figure 5.4 – Procedural analysis for charging a camcorder battery

When conducting a procedural analysis:
1) Specify each activity that must be done for each goal analysis step.
2) Ask, "What must the student do or know before this step can be done?"
3) Continue this as far as needed.

The resulting chart can be a few layers deep.

Attitudes

To determine the subordinate attitude skills, you usually need to conduct at least one of the preceding instructional analysis techniques:
- For each goal analysis step, ask, "What must the student do when showing this attitude?" The answer is usually a cognitive, intellectual, or psychomotor skill and then the appropriate analysis is done.
- Ask, "Why should learners show this attitude?" The answer is usually verbal information and then a cluster analysis is done.

The subordinate skill analysis can help determine whether lesson flow or branching should be relatively linear, hierarchical, based on the lesson's difficulty, based on a student's performance, based on a student's choice, or a combination of these. Note that the amount of branching, criteria for branching, and direction of branching (e.g., forward or backward) can vary significantly for different skills.

5.5   Identify Entry Skills and Characteristics

For learning to be effective and to avoid frustrating students, you must create a match or balance between the instruction and the students' capabilities. The instruction must be designed for the target population, defined as the widest practical range of learners. Determine, as discussed below, the students' abilities, language level, motivation, interests, and human factors. You can obtain this information by interviewing teachers and learners, testing students, and reviewing existing documentation such as test scores. Your end result should determine the entry or basic skills that the target population students must have mastered before the instruction begins. In other words, these skills will not be taught. In this step, you may also discover factors that may influence the instructional design.

Practical Guideline:

Create a balance between student capabilities and the instruction.

Based on the completed instructional skills analysis, draw a dashed line just below the skills that most, if not all, of the target population possesses. You will teach the skills above the dashed line and **not** those below the dashed line. In the example shown in figure 5.5, students will not be taught how to add multi-digit numbers, any skill below that, or how to multiply single-digit numbers. It is assumed that target audience students will have these skills.

You should confirm this decision by asking the subject-matter experts whether the entry skills should be tested within the instructional multimedia application. If there is any doubt about whether the target audience students possess the skills, pre-test for those skills. You can do this on paper, computer, or any format providing accurate data. The instructional design process later includes testing the instruction with learners who are truly representative of the target audience population to ensure that the entry-level behaviors are set appropriately.

For computer-managed presentations, clearly define the audience. This includes the number of people as well as their attitude toward the topic, level of expertise, needs, and expectations. Also, ensure that the presentation meets their expectations and needs and is presented at an appropriate level.

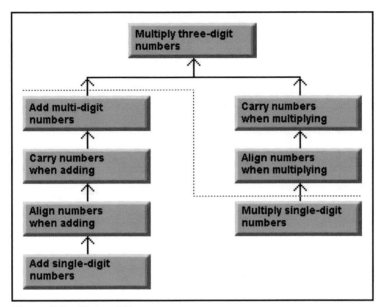

Figure 5.5 – Entry skills

5.5-1 Learner Analysis

You should ask questions about the learners, in order to adapt the instructional design to the correct target audience population. The instructional design must revolve around how students learn rather than a preferred teaching approach. The questions should determine information about the students' abilities, language capabilities, motivation, interests, human factors, and learning styles. Conducting a learner analysis will also let you define a student population that is neither too narrow nor too broad.

If possible, you should observe typical students. For example, this can help in selecting relevant and meaningful examples and appropriate role models and in avoiding stereotyping inappropriately.

Practical Guideline:

To ensure your materials are aimed at the correct student population, consider the students' abilities, language capabilities, motivation, interests, human factors, and learning styles.

Abilities

You should ask the following questions about the learner's abilities:
- What are the students' current skill levels?
  - Sometimes, a student's prior knowledge and experience can interfere with the new learning. For example, the menu items in an old software package may be different than those used in the new version of the software. These differences can be addressed in the instructional materials.
  - Are all of the students computer literate and to what degree? What guidance will they need?
- What are the students' mental capabilities?
  - Are the students fast or slow learners?
  - How well can the students memorize information?
  - Are the learners able to learn on their own?

- Will students be able to choose appropriate learning paths? How will they be guided?
- What are the students' confidence levels?
  - This information can be used to determine the size of the incremental learning steps.
- What are the students' maturity levels?
  - Are the students independent or do they require supervision?
- Are there any learner misconceptions?
  - Misconceptions must be dealt with in the program.

Language Capabilities

You should ask the following questions about the learner's language capabilities:
- What are the students' language levels?
- What specialized vocabulary do the learners already know?
- Is their preferred language style conversational, scholarly, or technical?
- Should the material be taught in one, two, or more languages?
- Will an audio narration be needed for learners who have a weak reading ability but good oral comprehension?

Motivation and Interests

You should ask the following questions about the learner's motivation and interests:
- What would make the material motivating?
  - For example, determine some real-world problems that can be addressed in the materials.
  - Why should the students learn the material?
  - What would make the material particularly relevant and meaningful?
  - Are there any attitudinal or motivational problems? If so, how can these problems be overcome?
- What are the learners' background experiences?
  - Students can bring a vast amount of knowledge and life experiences to a learning situation.
- What will the students find interesting?
- Are students learning the material because they are required to learn it or want to learn it?
- Are there any learner preferences for specific media?
  - Remember that learning effectiveness is a primary concern.
  - Will students be easily de-motivated with certain media? For example, do students presume that materials with a large text component are boring?
  - Are there past failures associated with a particular medium?
- How should testing be done?
  - Are certain test formats preferred over others? For example, would short-answer questions deter students who have a poor keyboarding ability?
  - Should testing be formal or informal?

Human Factors

You should ask the following questions to determine the human factors regarding multimedia instruction for the learners:
- Will students prefer to work alone, in pairs, or in groups?
- For self-paced material, is student-to-student interaction needed?
- For self-paced material, is there a need for teacher intervention or a facilitator?

5.5-2 Learning Style Research

Learning styles, also known as cognitive styles or learning preferences, are characteristic behaviors that indicate how students prefer to learn. Learning styles tend to be relatively stable over time, in other words are predictable, but are not static in that there can be some variation from day-to-day and week-to-week.

To maximize student learning, it is important for you to address learning styles when designing your lessons.

Some of the numerous learning style categorizations and preferences include:
- active experimentation (e.g., trying something out and then thinking about it) versus reflective observation (e.g., watching and thinking about something before trying it out)
- abstract conceptualization (e.g., thinking things through) versus concrete experience (e.g., sensing or feeling the actual experience)
- visually-based activities versus text-based activities
    - Different parts of the brain process different types of information.
    - Note that some references refer to these as right-brained versus left-brained activities. However, the original research was flawed. In reality, both halves of the brain can be involved in processing both visual material and text-based material. The important point is that if you provide both visual and text-based content, more of the brain will be involved in learning and learners will more likely have the content presented in a way that they prefer.
- environmental considerations such as the amount of light and sound in the room or room temperature
- sociological factors that includes working alone or in groups
- physical factors such as the time of day

Within these categorizations and preferences, students generally fall somewhere along the continuum between two opposite extremes. Very few students are found at the extremes.

Research has shown that:
- In general, each learning style is equal in terms of achievement. However, depending on the situation and the material being taught, one specific learning style can be better than another. Also, learning styles can be situation specific. For example, a student can have one preferred method for learning grammar and another for learning how to use a camera. Possibly due to learning styles being situation-specific, research has produced mixed results. For example, some researchers have found a direct correlation between a learning style and achievement while others have found no significant difference. Another factor for the mixed results may be that most students are adaptable and can learn effectively from a variety of methods.
- Matching learning style with the instructional design can lead to increased achievement, better attitudes, and thus cost-effectiveness.
    - One method of matching learning styles with instructional multimedia is to include a variety of media since different students prefer different media. For example, some students prefer visuals while others prefer to read text. If you include both, you are likely to reach more students.
    - Learners who prefer a structured approach to learning and to use their senses, such as sight and sound, tend to match and learn effectively with those types of multimedia instruction. Students who prefer to learn by experimenting or by using intuition, common sense, imagination, or inspiration should be taught with multimedia packages that encourage those preferences. Again, you can include both approaches within one instructional multimedia package.
    - Note that effective learning can still occur when the student's preferred learning style does not match the instructional design. Most students have learned how to effectively handle a variety of instructional approaches.
    - There is some value in occasionally mismatching learning style with instructional design. This can help students learn to adapt to other instructional styles.

Practical Guideline:

In general, no learning style is better than another. However, overall, it is better to match learning styles with the instructional design.

Note that the results are less significant for a single tutorial than for an entire course taught with multimedia. For example, student attitudes can change over continued exposure to multimedia instruction. Attitudes can initially start as negative and change to being positive. Conversely, some students are initially excited about instructional multimedia simply because it is an alternative to traditional instruction. This excitement tends to level out over time. Attitude changes are also affected by the instructional quality and how the program meets the student's learning styles and needs.

5.5-3 Learning Style Conclusions

Students who are more likely to have problems with instructional multimedia packages are those who:
- cannot easily concentrate
- cannot stay with a task until it is completed
- do not pay attention to details
- have poor memories for facts
- have poor reading skills
- work best in groups
- prefer working with people rather than inanimate objects

However, these students are likely to have some problems with any instructional presentation. It can be argued that these students would benefit most from well-designed multimedia lessons. The instructional strategy that you design should ensure that all target audience learners, regardless of their learning style, could effectively learn from the multimedia lesson.

Practical Guideline:

All target audience learners, regardless of their learning style, should be able to learn effectively from the multimedia lesson.

Remember that it is neither important nor necessary to categorize and label a student into a particular learning style. This could have negative consequences if the information is abused or not used properly. The issue is what should be done for students who have some difficulties with multimedia instruction since no one single teaching method or medium is perfect for all learners. This is discussed below in the developing an instructional strategy step.

5.6   Write Learning Outcomes

Learning outcomes or objectives are specific measurable skills. For example, a learning outcome could be to state five differences between teaching via DVD-ROM discs and videotapes. Learning outcomes are more specific than instructional goals. For example, if a goal is to be able to speak conversational English, a learning outcome could be to conjugate the verb "to be".

Learning outcomes communicate to learners, instructors, and other interested people, what the students should be able to do compared to what they can now do. Success occurs when learners achieve the planned outcomes. Learning outcomes help students organize their studying, avoid becoming lost, make appropriate decisions such as whether to study a section or not, and maintain their motivation. If you inform your students of the learning outcomes, they will score slightly but significantly higher results. Even though some students do not read the learning outcomes, state the outcomes for those who want and need them. In multimedia lessons, you can state learning outcomes in an overview or introduction before the learning material is presented. You can present learning outcomes with text, which is quick and easy to do, or video through a person talking. For computer-managed presentations, it is also important for you to clearly define and present the outcome(s) to the audience.

In instructional multimedia software development, it is critical for you to define specific learning outcomes since learning outcomes form the basis of the subsequent instructional development process. Accurate well-written learning outcomes can prevent development time and money from being wasted by helping to keep the process on track. As Robert Mager said, "If you're not sure where you're going you're liable to end up some place else." Without specific learning outcomes, it is easy to start branching off on interesting tangents. Working on tangents could make it impossible to finish a project with the constraints given. Whenever you have doubt about whether some material should be included, refer back to the stated learning outcomes.

Learning outcomes can be the basis for contracts. Many projects have failed because of poorly written or non-existent learning outcomes. For safety, check all learning outcomes for possible flaws. If a learning outcome is not specific and measurable, do **not** proceed with any design and development. Even when you define the learning outcomes, there is no guarantee that you will successfully teach the learning outcomes. In order to ensure that learning takes place, you still need to follow the subsequent instructional design steps.

Practical Guideline:

Well-written learning outcomes help keep the subsequent instructional development process on track.

5.6-1 Steps to Writing Learning Outcomes

There are five steps you need to do to write learning outcomes:

1) Once you have decided on a content area, identify specific behaviors by using action verbs. The verb should be an observable behavior that produces measurable results. The verb should be at the highest skill level that the student would be required to perform. Note that students often need a knowledge base of lower-level skills in order to succeed at higher-level skills. These skills will still need to be taught.

   Examples: Calculate and compute
   Non-examples: Understand and know

2) Specify the content area after the verb.

   Examples: Calculate averages and compute variances.
   Non-examples: Calculate statistical information and compute values needed in economics.

3) Specify applicable conditions.

   Identify any tools to be used, information to be supplied, constraints...

   Examples: Given a calculator, calculate the average of a list of numbers.
                   Given a spreadsheet package, compute variances from a list of numbers.
   Non-example: Given an available tool, calculate the average of a list of numbers.

4) Specify applicable criteria.

   Identify any desired levels of speed, accuracy, quality, quantity...

   Examples: Given a calculator, calculate averages from a list of numbers correctly 100% of the time.

                   Given a spreadsheet package, compute variances from a list of numbers rounded to the second decimal point.
   Non-example: Given a calculator, calculate averages from a list of numbers correctly most of the time.

5) Review each learning outcome to be sure it is complete, clear, and concise.

   Get content experts and students to review them and get signed approval before continuing.

Perhaps the worst example of a learning outcome ever written is:

"The learner will understand and appreciate the objectives of the course."

5.7   Develop Criterion-Referenced Test Questions

Criterion-referenced tests are designed to explicitly measure the determined learning outcomes. Student success is based on the number of learning outcomes passed. Whereas, normative-referenced tests compare students to each other. Student success depends on how well other students perform. For example, assume a student answers eight out of ten questions on a test correctly. If the test is criterion-referenced, a student will pass if the mastery level is less than or equal to 80%. If the test is normative-referenced, a student will only pass if his score is better than a specified percentage of other students. In general, you should use criterion-referenced tests for instructional multimedia applications. Avoid normative-referenced tests for instructional multimedia applications.

The evaluation measures the objectives

You should determine a mastery level for criterion-referenced tests. One hundred percent may be necessary if the skill is critical (e.g., safety) or is needed for subsequent steps (e.g., writing complete learning outcomes before writing test questions). Other skills such as spelling may not require perfect mastery, even though mastery is preferred.

> **Practical Guideline:**
>
> Use criterion-referenced tests for instructional multimedia applications.

Use test and question results to:
- evaluate student progress
- provide recommendations for reviewing material
  - You can base recommendations on a minimum required score for each section.
- provide yourself with information about the instruction's effectiveness
  - For questions that students typically answer incorrectly, ensure that the questions accurately measure the content being taught. Analyze each question to ensure that the question is effective. Appendix VI has details on how to do this.
  - If the questions accurately measure the content being taught, re-evaluate the content areas related to these questions.

To gather accurate information, ensure that testing is as realistic as possible.

You can also use test questions to determine whether the learning outcome was written accurately. If a learning outcome cannot be specifically tested then there is probably an error in the learning outcome. Find the error before continuing. This prevents time and money from being wasted in subsequent development. Note that you may not be able to directly test attitudinal learning outcomes.

> **Practical Guideline:**
>
> If you cannot specifically test a learning outcome, check whether or not it is written properly.

The nature of the test questions can also be used in developing the instructional strategy. For example, if the test question involves a psychomotor skill then your instructional strategy should provide practice in doing that skill.

Test questions may need to be modified when actual materials, such as video clips and photographs, have been produced.

5.7-1 Pre-tests

[handwritten: → previous learners' knowledge]

Pre-tests are tests given before instruction is presented. This is sometimes done before the main menu is presented. Pre-tests can act as a challenge test to determine whether the subsequent lesson or parts of the lesson can be optionally skipped. Pre-tests can also be used to determine whether students should review specific material before continuing.

Pre-test results can provide you with information on the students' entry skills and to determine whether students performed poorly on the material because they did not have the prerequisite entry skills. For reliable results, pre-tests should test all of the learning outcomes.

Practical Guideline:

Pre-tests should test all learning outcomes.

Since pre-tests take time and money to create, consider creating a pre-test only when it is possible that a significant percentage of the students will already know the material or when there is doubt about whether an important number of learners have the necessary prerequisite skills.

Some students find pre-tests boring and a waste of time. Be sure that pre-tests will benefit the students and that you let the students know about the potential benefits. For example, let students know that the computer will highlight material that they understand and give them the option of skipping the material. This customizes the material to the individual's needs.

5.7-2 Post-tests

Post-tests are tests given after the content is presented. In multimedia applications, post-tests are usually selected as a menu item. In general, students should be able to determine when they want to attempt the post-test. If learners are automatically branched into a post-test after the material is presented then they may not review before attempting the test.

Post-tests should:
- be based on the stated learning outcomes
  - Students should know what the test would be based on.
  - This should help keep the test at the appropriate difficulty level for the target audience.
  - Only include validated questions. This becomes particularly important when students are learning on their own.
- test all learning outcomes or at least draw randomly from a pool that contains questions from all of the learning outcomes
  - Each learning outcome should not be tested too much or too little.
- be composed of different question types that test as many of the different thinking levels as possible
  - However, students benefit when post-tests in multimedia applications have similar question types as formal exams.
  - The question types and designs should be familiar to the students. Students should not lose time or marks because they do not understand a question's design.
- have a rationale (e.g., motivation, promotion, diagnosis, placement, certification, evaluation...)
  - Post-tests should specifically inform the student of areas of strength and weakness. For example, the student could be told whether they have mastered each learning outcome and whether review is recommended for each. If review is recommended then the student should be able to immediately or easily branch to that area.
  - There must be a purpose for all tests. If not then the test could be a waste of time.

Practical Guideline:

Post-tests must be based on the stated learning outcomes.

Helpful Hints

Within multimedia applications, tests can be formal where the marks are recorded or be a practice exam to act as an indicator for the student. If marks are recorded, will you spend the needed time to manage and supervise the process?

It is helpful for students to have an opportunity to try sample questions before doing a formal test. You can do this with review questions and self-tests.

Test questions can and often should include media (e.g., photographs and video clips) that are related, similar, or identical to those used in the presentation. Is it fair to teach with visuals and then to test with only text? Can you safely assume that students can make the transition from visuals to text? (See the Question Writing chapter for details on writing questions.)

Practical Guideline:

Consider including test questions that are related, similar, or identical to those used in the presentation.

5.8   Develop an Instructional Strategy

An instructional strategy describes the instructional materials' components and the procedures used with the materials to have the students achieve the learning outcomes. Your instructional strategy should be based on your instructional analysis, the learning outcomes, and other previous steps. You can even base the instructional strategy on previous work or on how others have solved similar problems. Time and money can be saved by not re-inventing the wheel.

At the end of this process, you should have a clear set of specifications describing how the material will be taught. This can include a flowchart representing the instructional pathway. You will use the instructional strategy as a framework for creating a storyboard and further developing the instructional materials or evaluating whether existing materials are suitable or need revision. As a general rule, use the strategy to set up a framework for maximizing effective and efficient learning. This often requires using strategies that go beyond basic teaching methods. For example, discovery-learning techniques can be more powerful than simply presenting the facts. One common pitfall in creating instructional multimedia lessons is teaching in the same way as was done with traditional methods. If this is done then there may only be minimal value in transferring the material to a computer. As Emile Chartier said, "Nothing is more dangerous than an idea, when it is the only one you have."

As you proceed through developing an instructional strategy, start specifying the media that would most effectively teach the material. (Read the Media Selection, Text, Audio, Visuals, Video, and Animation chapters for more information.)

Each learning domain classification (i.e., verbal information, intellectual skills and cognitive strategies, psychomotor skills, and attitudes) is best taught with different instructional strategies.

Practical Guideline:

Different skills require different instructional strategies.

5.8-1 Verbal Information

When teaching verbal information:
- Organize the material into small easily retrievable chunks. This is based on the cluster analysis done earlier, as shown in table 5-1.
- Link new information to knowledge the learner already possesses. For example, use statements such as "Remember how" or "This is like..." Linking information helps the learner to store and recall the material.
- Use memory devices like forming images or using mnemonics for new information. For example, the musical notes of the treble clef staff lines can be remembered with the mnemonic Every Good Boy Deserves Fudge.
- Use meaningful contexts and relevant cues. For example, relating an example to a sports car can be relevant for teenage boys.
- Have the learners generate examples in their minds, "do" something, such as create a song or game, with the information, or apply the knowledge to the real world. If the student only memorizes facts then the learning will only have minimal value.
- Avoid rote repetition as a memorization aid. Rote repetition has minimal effectiveness over time.
- Provide visuals to increase learning and recall.

5.8-2 Intellectual Skills

When teaching intellectual skills:
- Base the instructional strategy and sequencing on the hierarchical analysis done earlier. See figure 5.3. Always teach subordinate skills before higher-level skills.
- Link new knowledge to previously learned knowledge. This can be explicitly done (e.g., the bones in your feet are comparable to the bones you have learned about in your hands) or implicitly done (e.g., compare the bones in your feet to other bone structures you have learned about).
- Use memory devices like forming images or mnemonics for new information. For example, help students remember rules by using rhymes such as "i before e except after c". Remember that rules often have exceptions. Tell your learners about the exceptions.
- Use examples and non-examples that are familiar to the student. For example, when classifying metals, iron and copper are examples while glass and plastic are non-examples.
- Use discovery-learning techniques. For example, let students manipulate variables and see the consequences.
- Use analogies that the learners know. However, be careful that learners do not over-generalize or create misconceptions.
- Provide for practice and immediate feedback.

5.8-3 Psychomotor Skills

When teaching psychomotor skills:
- Base the instructional strategy on the procedural analysis done earlier. See figure 5.4.
- Provide directions for completing all of the steps.
- Provide repeated practice and feedback for individual steps, then groups of steps, and then the entire sequence.
- Remember that, in general, practice should become less dependent on written or verbal directions.
- Consider visuals to enhance learning.
- Consider job aids, such as a list of steps, to reduce memory requirements. This is especially important if there are many procedures or if the procedures are infrequently used.
- After a certain point, allow learners to interact with real objects or do the real thing. How much can you learn about swimming without getting wet?

Note that some skills involve other learning domain classifications. For example, when learning how to operate a camcorder, many of the skills are psychomotor. However, deciding how to light an image is an intellectual skill. Also, note that the required proficiency level can affect the instructional strategy. There is a big difference between being able to imitate a skill and being able to automatically do a skill.

5.8-4   Attitudes

When teaching attitudes:
- Base the instructional strategy on the instructional analysis done earlier.
- If you can, show a human model to which the students can easily relate. For example, it may be better if the model is of the same socio-economic class.
- Show realistic consequences, such as through a simulation, to appropriate and inappropriate choices.
- Consider using video.
- Remember that attitudes taught through computer technology are **not** guaranteed to transfer to the real world. If appropriate and possible, consider arranging for practice opportunities to make the choice in real life. Alternatively, use role-playing to reinforce the attitudes taught.

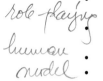

role-playing
human
model

Note that it can be difficult to test whether the attitudes taught have transferred to real situations. For example, learners may not behave as they naturally would if they know that they are being observed. If learners have not voluntarily permitted observations to be made then you must ask whether it is ethical to make the observations.

5.8-5   Sequencing Learning Outcomes

Using the subordinate skills analysis done earlier, determine the sequence of how the learning outcomes will be taught. In general, to best facilitate learning, you should sequence the learning outcomes from:
- lower to higher-level skills
  - For example, teach verbal information and then intellectual skills.
  - For example, cover multiplying decimals with a calculator and then manually.
- easy to hard
  - For example, teach adding fractions with common denominators and then with different denominators.
  - For example, cover writing complete sentences then writing paragraphs.
- simple to complex
  - For example, teach recognizing weather patterns then predicting the weather.
  - For example, cover replacing a washer and later replacing a faucet.
- specific to general
  - For example, teach driving a specific car then transfer the skills to driving any car.
  - For example, cover adjusting the brakes on a specific mountain bike and then generalizing the procedure to other mountain bikes.
- concrete to abstract
  - For example, teach measuring distances with a ruler then estimating distances without a ruler.
  - For example, cover writing learning outcomes to evaluating learning outcomes.
- the known to the unknown

Practical Guideline:

Be sure to teach learning outcomes in the order that best facilitates learning.

Each of these methods of sequencing learning outcomes aim at allowing students to acquire the needed knowledge base for learning higher-level skills. Note that these guidelines are **not** "black and white" rules.

When assigning learning outcomes to lessons, consider the time needed for teaching a learning outcome, the time available per lesson, and the learner's attention spans.

5.8-6 Overcoming Learning Style Problems

If students are not learning in the way they are taught, they should be taught in the way that they best learn. There are a number of strategies that you can use to teach students in the way they learn best:

- Include a variety of instructional activities so that each student is likely to have at least one preferred activity.
  - For example, an instructional multimedia application could include typical theoretical approaches, discovery-learning techniques, drill and practice, simulations...
- Create lively, interesting, and interactive instructional software.
  - For example, include the different media, use a variety of instructional activities, and use a variety of question types (e.g., matching, selecting a part of an image, drag and drop objects).
  - Get ideas by viewing programs created by others. There is no need to constantly re-invent the wheel.
- Create learning materials that help ensure success.
  - Success can make the learner not notice when there is a mismatch in teaching style and learning style.
  - Ensure success through organizing the material into small incremental steps and by providing numerous practice opportunities with immediate and detailed feedback.
  - Another method that helps ensure success is to allow students to have control over the instruction's pace and sequence. Note that some students, especially younger or immature learners, need explicit recommendations on how to proceed.
- Encourage students to work in pairs while learning from the computer.
  - Working in pairs can help increase performance since students who work in pairs or groups tend to discuss and thus think about the material and questions more than when they are working alone.
  - Working in pairs can help those who are uncomfortable with computers and those who do not like to work alone, such as extroverts.
  - Some students do not perform as well when working in groups of three or more. This may be because they allow the other students to do the thinking.
- Include varied non-computerized instructional activities and tools.
  - Use group discussions, research projects, and written assignments. These activities can be done with or without computers.
  - Include a workbook with summaries of the multimedia material so that students do not have to take detailed notes. Taking notes can become tedious and eliminate the "fun" of working with a computer.

This particularly affects students who are inclined to copy everything presented by the computer. Simply copying the computer-based lesson's summary onto paper can be effective. Alternatively, allow students to print out summaries that they need from within the program.

Note that well-designed interactive multimedia lessons overcome learning style problems by inherently including many of these solutions. For example, many of the different learning styles are addressed simply by teaching with a variety of different methods and media.

> **Practical Guideline:**
>
> To address a variety of learning styles, teach with a variety of different methods and media. No one single teaching method or medium is perfect for all learners.

5.8-7 Motivating Students

It is important for your multimedia lessons to motivate learners because without motivation learning is unlikely to occur. Lao Tzu illustrated this well by saying, "You can no more teach without the learner than a merchant can sell without a willing buyer." Follow the ARCS motivation model to ensure that students will be motivated to learn.

> **Practical Guideline:**
>
> Motivate learners because without motivation learning is unlikely to occur.

ARCS Motivational Model

Motivation can be enhanced through addressing the attributes called Attention, Relevance, Confidence, and Satisfaction (ARCS). In multimedia lessons, try to include all of the attributes since each alone may not maintain student motivation. The learner analysis may have provided useful information for motivating students.

You should build motivational strategies into the materials throughout the instructional design process. This is challenging since each learner is an individual with unique interests, experiences, and goals.

> **Practical Guideline:**
>
> Motivational strategies require effort to determine since each learner has unique interests, experiences, and goals.

Attention

Gain attention and then sustain it. You can gain and sustain attention by using human-interest examples, using emotional or personal information, creating mental challenges, showing exciting video or animation sequences, stating conflicting information, using humor, and asking questions. An example is shown in figure 5.6.

Figure 5.6 – Gaining attention with an explosion

You can also sustain attention by making the program highly interactive. (See the Interactivity chapter for more details.)

Relevance

Relevance helps the student to want to learn the material. For example, when teaching adult students how to solve percent problems, a problem that relates to a salesperson's profit on a selling a car is more relevant than a problem that compares two people's ages. You can provide relevance through testimonials, illustrative stories, simulations, practical applications, personal experience, and relating the material to present or future values or needs. Relevance is also useful in helping to sustain attention.

For material to be perceived as being relevant, you must match the learner's expectations to the material you provide.

Confidence

If students are confident that they can master the material, they will be much more willing to attempt the instruction. You will need to convince students with low confidence that they can be successful. You can do this through presenting the material in small incremental steps or even by stating how other similar students have succeeded. You should group learning outcomes into small enough chunks so that the task seems achievable rather than insurmountable.

You should also convince students who are over-confident that there is material that they need to learn. You can do this by giving a challenging pre-test or presenting difficult questions.

Satisfaction

You also need to deal with "satisfaction". Satisfaction provides value for learning the material. Satisfaction can be intrinsic from the pleasure or value of the activity itself, extrinsic from the value of the activity's result, or a combination of the two. Examples of intrinsic satisfaction include the joy of learning, the challenge, increased confidence, positive outcomes, and increased feeling of self-worth. Examples of extrinsic satisfaction include monetary rewards, praise, a certificate, and unexpected rewards. Some evidence suggests that extrinsic motivation, such as a certificate for completing a course, does not last over time. So, try to provide your learners with some intrinsic rewards.

Remember to let the students know that the material to be learned with the computer is important. Consider increasing extrinsic motivation through recording test and quiz results. Alternatively, give traditional tests and surprise quizzes based on the instructional multimedia material.

5.8-8 Instructional Events

As Robert Gagné described, the instructional events (gaining attention, informing the learner of the learning outcome, stimulating recall of prerequisites, presenting the material, providing learning guidance, eliciting the performance, providing feedback, assessing performance, enhancing retention and transfer) represent what should be done to ensure that learning occurs. If you address each instructional event, you will have a solid foundation for creating effective instructional multimedia applications. You will need to determine what will be done for each instructional event for each learning outcome.

Gaining Attention

In this event, get the students involved and motivated to participate. Do this by introducing a stimulus change or something different such as video or audio to stimulate the senses. Gain the learner's attention by something as simple as a beep or as complex as arousing emotions by showing a student being wheeled into an ambulance. Consider using a snappy, animated, or video title page. This is called an attract sequence. Note that video tends to be more effective than still images in gaining attention.

Remember that you also have to keep the students attentive throughout the entire program. You can maintain attention by using different media, asking questions, and providing different learning activities.

Informing the Student of the Learning Outcome

Help students focus their efforts in this event. You can do this with simple statements or thought-provoking questions. If possible, also make the students feel that they need to learn the skills.

You can inform the learner of the learning outcome in an introduction or overview before major learning occurs. This can be a good use of video. Text can be used but text is often boring and is consequently skimmed by some students.

Stimulating Recall of Prerequisites

Prepare students for what is to come in this event. One strategy you can use is simply stating the needed prerequisite skills. Alternatively, pre-tests can remind learners of the prerequisites and also be used to determine a student's current skill level. You should advise students who do not have the prerequisite skills to learn the skills before continuing. Stimulating recall of prerequisites should be done before major learning occurs. This is often done in an introduction or overview.

The learner analysis should have previously determined the relevant knowledge and experiences that typical students will bring into the learning situation.

Presenting the Material

Present material to the students in this event. Generally, you should sequence the material in increasing difficulty and in small incremental steps. This helps ensure success and increases learner confidence. For computer-managed presentations, the main points and sub-points of the presentation must be sequenced logically.

A variety of methods can inspire interest. No single approach can be used to teach all learning outcomes. The activities you provide must match the learning outcomes being taught. As much as possible, the activities learners do on the computer should match what will be done in the "real world". Learning by doing is very powerful. This was stated well by Guatama Buddha who said, "Teach you? I cannot teach you. Go, experience for yourself."

Practical Guideline:

Use a variety of methods to present the material.

Remember to provide examples that are meaningful, relevant, and realistic. Base some of the content on the potential for making mistakes. Ask the subject-matter expert about typical mistakes made after the content is taught in the traditional way. If one only teaches what is correct, the learner may never learn what can go wrong. For example, teaching what can go wrong is important in teaching physicians how to make an accurate diagnosis.

Practical Guideline:

Consider teaching both the correct material and what can go wrong.

Base the total amount of material presented in a lesson on the learners' age, the learner's expected attention span, the material's complexity, the activities needed, and the time needed for all of the instructional events. A rough estimate of the proportional amount of content (e.g., a percentage of the number of screens) needed to cover a learning outcome should be based on the learning outcome's frequency, importance, and difficulty.

Frequency   -   How often is the behavior needed?
Importance   -   How significant is the behavior to job performance?
Difficulty   -   How hard is the behavior to master?

For each learning outcome, give a rating (e.g., a number out of five) for the frequency, importance, and difficulty and then add the total. Base the estimated amount of content (e.g., a percentage of the number of screens) proportionally for each learning outcome. Table 5-2 shows an example.

Table 5-2					
Objective	Frequency	Importance	Difficulty	Total	Percent
Number 1	2	1	1	4	10%
Number 2	4	3	5	12	30%
Number 3	2	3	3	8	20%
Number 4	3	1	2	6	15%
Number 5	1	5	4	10	25%
Total				40	100%

Providing Learning Guidance

In this event, which is usually integrated with "presenting the material," help students learn the material. For example, you can provide ways to categorize materials, provide memory devices, and link new knowledge to previously learned knowledge. You can also emphasize differences between related skills. For example, state that adding two digit numbers is similar to adding single digit numbers except that a value may have to be "carried". Another thing you can do is provide students with strategies for recalling information and encourage them to create their own memory recall techniques. Providing guidance is particularly important because many students have not learned or been taught how to effectively learn.

(Specific ideas for each learning domain classification are also presented in this section on "Developing an instructional strategy.")

Eliciting the Performance

Learners must find out how well they are doing in this event. You can do this by asking questions or providing opportunities to practice the skill and then giving feedback. This event is also integrated with "presenting the material".

You should provide for spaced practice (less, more often) since it is more effective than massed practice (more, less often). Allow for practice as it is logically needed rather than at fixed intervals such as every third screen or only at the end of each lesson. Remember that students will need to practice sub-skills before proceeding to higher-level skills. Make the difficulty level of the practice proportional to the difficulty of the task. Practice should not be so easy that it is trivial nor so difficult that it is frustrating. Remember to check whether the learner can successfully do the correct skill as well as ensure that they do not make expected mistakes.

(Read the Interactivity and Question Writing chapters for more information.)

Providing Feedback

Your feedback should be positive, constructive, and immediate. Your feedback should provide complete information as to why the answer and other answers are right or wrong or guide students in how to attain the stated learning outcome. This event is coordinated with "eliciting the performance". (See the Feedback chapter for more details.)

Assessing Performance

Students are tested in this event. This step is basically more formal than the "elicit the performance" event. As much as possible, the tests you create should approximate or be based on real situations. Test all learning outcomes and only the learning outcomes. Tests should be criterion-referenced (performance based on achieving the specified learning outcomes).

You should provide the students with their test results as soon as possible. The feedback you provide should pinpoint areas in which the student had difficulties.

Enhancing Retention and Transfer

In this event, ensure students retain the information and that the information can be transferred beyond the specific ideas presented in the lesson.

More exposure leads to more retention. You can increase retention through questioning, giving reviews, paraphrasing, and providing summaries. Retention activities should occur at spaced intervals and occur before more complex skills are learned.

Practical Guideline:

Increase retention by exposing the learner to the material in a variety of ways.

You can facilitate transfer by providing links to related situations, related information, or novel problems and solutions. If possible, transfer should focus on real-world situations.

5.8-9   Types of Instructional Strategies

Where appropriate, the instructional strategy you create should include "fun" ways to learn. (However, remember that some learning is simply hard work.) Consider using any or all of the four basic types of instructional multimedia strategies. These are drill and practice, tutorials, simulations, and educational games. Other strategies include intelligent tutoring systems and virtual reality systems. Each type of instructional strategy has strengths and weaknesses depending on the problem being solved. Incorporating a variety of creative instructional approaches can help maintain student interest and motivation. Many effective multimedia solutions include more than one type of instructional strategy.

Practical Guideline:

Consider using more than one type of instructional strategy to create an effective multimedia solution.

You can gain ideas for the instructional strategy through brainstorming activities with all team members and even target audience students. You can also review existing products for ideas. You should not be responsible for generating all of the creative ideas.

Remember that people are social. Collaborative programs are possible with computers. In groups of two, students can discuss, debate, and explore many things. Imagine how much can be learned if students are discussing issues presented by the computer. Also, consider using the Internet as a tool to connect many learners to each other.

With computers, it is possible to tap into real data or tools such as those used by scientists. Wouldn't students enjoy learning about weather if they could use real data and models to predict the weather?

The different types of instructional multimedia strategies are discussed below.

Drill and Practice

Drill and practice is a common instructional multimedia strategy that provides repeated activity (drill) and opportunities (practice) to try skills or concepts learned elsewhere. This is shown in Figure 5.7. The aim is often to achieve mastery.

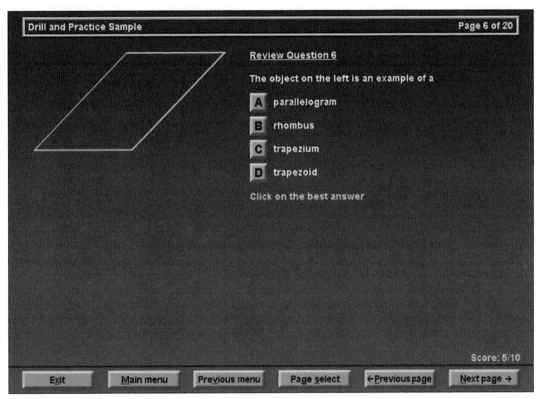

Figure 5.7 – Drill and practice sample

Drill and practice:
- usually takes place after the content has been taught
- does not teach new material
- can and often should include extensive diagnostic feedback
- can be used for many diverse skills such as learning language, learning factual information, and solving problems
- can have a varied difficulty level depending on the learner's ability
  - The difficulty level can be based on the learner's performance.
- can be boring
  - Counter boredom with competition, using visuals, providing variety, stating the progress made...

Tutorials

Tutorials are programs in which the computer imitates a human tutor. This is shown in figure 5.8. In tutorials, information or concepts are presented, questions are asked, responses are judged, and feedback is provided.

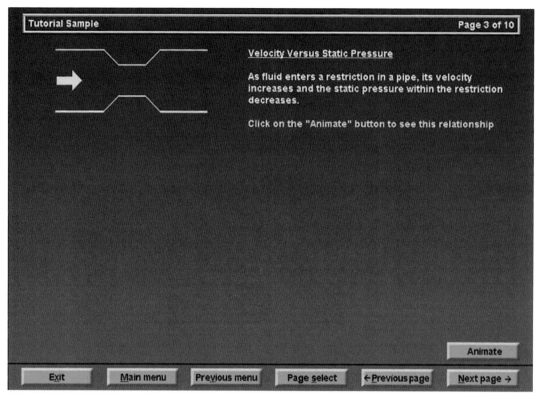

Figure 5.8 – Tutorial sample

Tutorials:
- should include frequent questioning
  - This reinforces learning and increases retention.
- can be used for many low and high-level skills
- can include drill and practice
- can include problem solving and problem analysis
- often include branching to remediation and enrichment
- often include testing

Simulations

Simulations present or model the essential elements of real or imaginary situations. This is shown in Figure 5.9. Instructional multimedia simulations (e.g., flight simulators) allow students to learn by manipulating the model in similar ways to real world situations. Simulations can immediately respond with consequences to learner decisions. However, some consequences may not initially be apparent depending on when the effect is normally seen (e.g., the effects of changes in interest rates may be seen "years" later). Students can learn by observing the results and relationships or receiving specific diagnostic feedback.

Ideally, simulations should approximate real systems as closely as possible. This helps facilitate transferring the knowledge learned to the real world and can make the simulation particularly meaningful to the learners. How closely a simulation must approach reality depends on the complexity of the real situation, how well the skills learned will transfer to the real situation, and the benefits and costs of making the simulation more realistic. Conduct a detailed analysis to determine all of the relevant skills needed and their criticality.

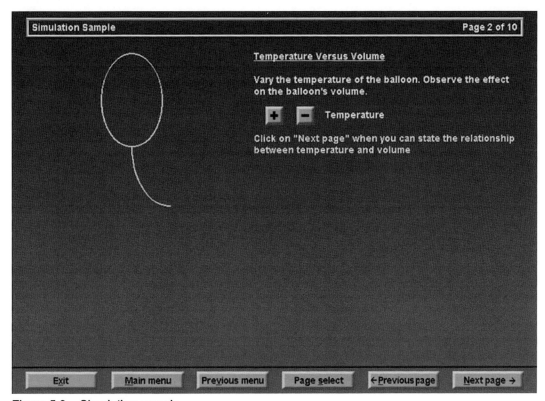

Figure 5.9 – Simulation sample

Simulations can be used for teaching many diverse skills including:
- properties of physical objects such as a comet in its orbit
- rules and strategies such as in war games, making predictions about forest fire behavior or avalanche potential, or building a city
- processes such as laws of supply and demand
- procedures such as diagnosing illnesses
- situations such as teaching instructors about student behaviors and attitudes

Simulations are often used when real situation training is:
- dangerous (e.g., nuclear power plant procedures)
- expensive (e.g., landing a space shuttle)
- not easily repeatable (e.g., avoiding a "run on a bank")
- unavailable (e.g., historical events such as the economics of the Great Depression, how to respond in a robbery, or operating a business)
- not conducive to learning (e.g., when learning is difficult because the learner must consider too many stimuli at once such as in the cockpit of a modern airplane)
- affected by reality (e.g., simulations can provide genetic data about successive generations in seconds where reality could take months or years)
- inconvenient (e.g., experiencing Arctic survival conditions)

Simulations can be very effective:
- The knowledge gained tends to transfer well to real situations especially if students can apply their existing knowledge and experience into their interactions and thoughts.
- Active student participation is critical.
- Effectiveness increases if the simulation is logical or comparable to real situations.
- Effectiveness increases if students are aware of the learning outcomes.
- Effectiveness increases if students can gradually build their skills. For example, when first learning how to control the operation of a nuclear power plant the student should start by learning each system one at a time then combinations of systems and then the entire system.
- Effectiveness can stem from students being very motivated to learn. Imagine your motivation if you are involved in a life and death situation or investing someone's life savings.

Note that students may not necessarily believe the results of a simulation. For example, in a simulation, students may end up in a car accident if they chose to drink and drive. However, there is no guarantee that the student will believe it would happen to them in "real" life.

Attaining excellent results tends to require more explanations of the goals, learning outcomes, and directions than tutorials or drill and practice methods. Some learners, such as young or immature students, will have trouble explaining what has happened in a simulation or transferring the knowledge to real situations.

Simulations can be very efficient.
- Learning can be relatively quick compared to other methods.
- Efficiency increases if the model or simulation closely represents reality.
- Learning efficiency depends on the feedback students are given with respect to the learning outcomes.
- Efficiency depends on whether the model or simulation is aimed at the appropriate learning level. For example, novices may learn best when only some of the variables can be manipulated and experts when presented with the entire model.
- Efficiency depends on how much detail is shown. If too much detail or too many parts of the system are shown, learning may be hindered since the learner may not be able to mentally process all of the information.
- Efficiency can be increased if supplementary material is provided for instructional purposes. For example, text summaries and checklists can be very beneficial.

Gaining this effectiveness and efficiency is usually expensive and time-consuming. Cost-justification is particularly important before creating a simulation.

Educational Games

Educational games are usually decision-making activities that include rules, a goal, conditions or constraints, competition, challenge, strategies, and feedback.

Educational games:
- should encourage the development of specific skills
    - The skills can be in specific subject areas such as science and math or general skills like problem solving, critical thinking, and decision-making.
    - Success should be based on whether or not the learning outcomes have been met rather than good hand-eye coordination.
- can be used for many different skills
    - The example shown in figure 5.10 illustrates how a game can be used to teach keyboarding skills.
    - One difficulty is that games tend to require more explanations of the goals, learning outcomes, and directions than tutorials or drill and practice methods. Without guidance, learning is less effective.

- can be an effective, motivational, and fun way to learn
  - To be effective, the game must be challenging, students must be actively involved, and students must be given feedback and guidance with respect to the learning outcomes.
  - Educational games have been found to be the most preferred way students like to learn.
  - Some educational games are a part of a simulation when the simulation involves competition and/or cooperation.
  - Both males and females can enjoy and learn from games suited to their interests.
- are sometimes a waste of time
  - Some products are fancy but do not teach well.
  - Evaluate a game before purchasing it to ensure that the game teaches an important skill effectively. Some games may lead to violent and aggressive behaviors.
  - Some people erroneously believe that games cannot be effective teaching tools.

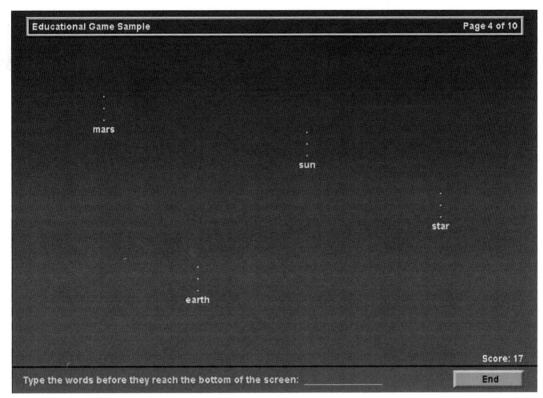

Figure 5.10 – Educational game sample

Intelligent Tutoring Systems

Intelligent tutoring systems attempt to mimic the "perfect instructor". The basic requirements of intelligent tutoring systems include the ability to:

- model the learner
- track misunderstandings
- generate appropriate responses

None of these basic requirements have been perfectly resolved.

Although it is possible to incorporate a model or two of student learning into an instructional multimedia application, a fixed model does not represent "intelligence". How can a student be modeled when students and their learning preferences are so diverse? It is not sufficient to simply categorize students into one of two types and then simply create two ways for students to learn the material. This has been the premise in some "intelligent" tutoring systems. A compounding factor is that learner preferences vary depending on the situation and material being taught. It is impractical to create a different teaching strategy for every individual.

Although intelligent tutoring systems should be able to learn from previous instructional successes and failures, it is a challenging goal to achieve. It is simple to record where students make mistakes but a challenge to know when there is a misunderstanding, what caused it, and what to do about it. In a sense, the computer would have to be able to read each student's mind.

Generating the appropriate response would be difficult even if the first two needs were met. How can a designer determine all of the response possibilities? Every possibility must be based on a known rule. Intelligent tutoring systems can and should have responses for expected misunderstandings but this is at best limited to the finite expressed problems.

There are some excellent "intelligent" tutoring systems available. However, for practical purposes, these tend to be labor-intensive and expensive to develop. Although the potential of intelligent tutoring systems is exciting, the reality is that much research still needs to be done. In other words, if you are an instructor, do not worry about being replaced by an intelligent tutoring system. Given the present state of intelligent tutoring system technology, it can be argued that well-designed instructional multimedia applications are essentially the same from a student's perspective.

Virtual Reality

Virtual reality (VR) allows people to be totally immersed in an artificial or simulated environment yet retain the feeling that the environment is real. This feeling that the environment is real happens because the participant has a "first-hand" or personal experience of the events, "real" distractions are minimized since only virtual images are seen, and because the participant can interact naturally in real time such as by pointing and looking rather than by using a joystick, mouse, or keyboard. Virtual reality systems can include a variety of media such as video, visuals, animation, and audio. In a sense, virtual reality is an extension of simulations that can be created with readily available hardware and software.

A distinctive feature of VR is that learners are an integral part of the synthetic VR world. Users can simultaneously interact with computers in complex ways. Computers can sense body movement and voice commands and respond almost naturally. For example, for teaching students about interior decoration, you could let students walk through a house and allow them to change colors of walls, rearrange furniture, change the lighting, remove a painting and place it elsewhere... To interface with the virtual world, learners must wear specialized equipment such as body suits, goggles, and/or gloves.

Although most applications are found in the entertainment industry, numerous educational products have been and are being developed. Since VR allows participants to feel that they are in another place in which they can move and look around based on a prescribed set of rules, VR offers incredible educational potential. Imagine how much doctors, firefighters, law officers, and soldiers could safely learn in a virtual environment. Abstract ideas, such as the movement of electrons in an atom that cannot be physically presented, can be taught with VR. Since virtual objects can behave as their physical counterparts and be manipulated by the learner, students can experience natural laws such as the law of gravity. Alternatively, learners can experience laws created by developers. For example, energy could be created or destroyed. With the ability in VR to manipulate abstract information, the potential exists to improve a student's understanding and memory of complex ideas.

Learning can be by discovery, experimentation, through guidance using a variety of instructional approaches, or by practice and feedback. The potential for testing in a virtual environment is exceptional. For example, students could virtually perform an operation, put out a fire, or apprehend a thief.

For practical reasons, it can be risky to develop an educational VR system at this time:
- There are few experts in VR design and programming
- The authoring software is mediocre but getting better.

- Extra equipment is needed for developing and using these programs.

A key to effective VR design is to focus on the potential to teach and learn rather than on the hardware and software tools.

Given the potential of multimedia technology, where is the boundary between traditional multimedia applications such as simulations and virtual reality applications?

5.9   Develop and Select Instructional Materials

Based on the instructional strategy for each learning outcome and information from the other steps of the instructional design process, you need to determine whether materials should be gathered or developed. The main reason for using existing materials is to save time and money. It can be cheaper for you to buy materials instead of developing them.

5.9-1   Gather Existing Material

Compare any existing material to the instructional strategy. Determine whether it is suitable and cost-effective. (See Appendix II for a checklist of instructional features.) You may prefer existing materials if the content will be obsolete before or soon after it can be developed. Beware of the "if we didn't make it, it can't be any good" syndrome.

Some but not all of the needed material may exist. Determine whether the existing material can be adapted or supplemented. One alternative is to get permission to repurpose existing media collections, such as those found on DVD-ROMs and the Internet, for your own purposes. Remember, if you include work done by others in your materials, you may not have permission to sell the product with their content. You may be able to work out a revenue sharing agreement.

Note that not all copyrights will be cleared and some promised materials might not be provided. Remember to check all digital materials for viruses.

5.9-2   Develop the Needed Material

When you develop the needed materials, refer to the instructional strategy and all of the information gained through the systematic instructional design process. Use this information to write a storyboard and to finalize the media selection. (Read the Media Selection chapter for more details on selecting media.)

Writing Storyboards

A storyboard is a paper-based scale replica draft of each screen that will appear on the computer. See figure 5.11. Typically, one page represents a single computer screen.

For computer-managed presentations, the content is often directly put onto the computer. The content is frequently based on existing course materials. Decisions still need to be made for media selection, how students will think about the material presented...

Create a storyboard on a word processor. (Hand-written storyboards are hard to edit and can be hard to read.) Since some authoring tools can bring in text created on word processors, use the same fonts and font sizes so the paper version closely matches what will be seen on the computer. Using a word processor can save a lot of time if you can access existing text such as course outlines, the subject-matter expert's notes, training materials, and policy manuals.

The instructional designer collaborates with the subject-matter expert to create the storyboard based on the tentative design. The storyboard must be written and designed for the computer screen. If this is not done well, time must be spent adapting the material. If possible, follow standardized specifications to help with consistency. This can be facilitated by using design templates – as long as the templates do **not** inhibit creativity or compromise learning. As much as possible, each storyboard page should also contain the programming requirements listed in figure 5.12. Storyboards should also contain the interactions, such as questions and feedback, and can contain flowcharts to illustrate branching information.

Video of a teacher being animated and talking energetically while **standing still** and saying:
"Lao Tzu stated, 'You can no more teach without the learner than a merchant can sell without a willing buyer.'"

Video feedback of the same teacher being animated and **moving around** and saying energetically:
"Lao Tzu stated, 'You can no more teach without the learner than a merchant can sell without a willing buyer.'"

Review Question 8

True or false? This example shows how to keep a lesson interesting.

Click on "Play" to watch the video to answer the question.

False

Feedback:
This example does NOT show how to keep a lesson interesting. To keep a lesson interesting, you should create energy by moving around as you speak, being animated, and showing your enthusiasm.

Click on "Play" to see how the content should have been presented.

Figure 5.11 – Storyboard for a sample screen

Lesson: _____   Section: _____   Page number: _____   Page title: _____

Video clip name or description: _____   File type: _____

Audio clip name or description: _____   File type: _____

Visual clip name or description: _____   File type: _____

Branching information: _____

Feedback information: _____

Special instructions: _____

Figure 5.12 – Programming details for each storyboard screen

Leave room for visuals on the screen or pull in digitized images and try to estimate the amount of text that is reasonable for each screen. A problem with trying to exactly match storyboards to computer screens is that the video images, visuals, and text can take more or less space than expected. The storyboard should indicate the expected screen positions for the media. If there is a standardized location then you only need to specify deviations from the standard. It is not necessary to have all of the media at this point. For example, written scripts can substitute for video, audio, and photograph descriptions while stick diagrams can represent visual images.

Initially work with one typical learning outcome and evaluate the storyboard before continuing with other learning outcomes. This helps prevent problems from being perpetuated throughout a lesson.

> **Practical Guideline:**
>
> If you develop one learning outcome at a time, you can prevent problems from being copied throughout the program.

After the storyboard is written, distribute the storyboard or pin it up and ask for feedback from other subject-matter experts, especially others who will use the product, and potential learners. Thoroughly evaluate the material for flow, clarity, accuracy, completeness, pace, interaction, and length. As a general rule, if the storyboard has problems then the material will have problems when it is transferred to the computer. However, there can be inherent improvements in the computer-based materials when actual components (e.g., video and photographs) are added.

Expect revisions to be necessary. Make revisions and evaluate the revised materials before transferring the material to the computer using an authoring tool. It is generally easier to make revisions on paper than on the computer. After the first learning outcome has been transferred to the computer, thoroughly evaluate it. Evaluate the material as well as the user-interface. After revisions have been made, continue developing subsequent learning outcomes and lessons. Repeat the revision and evaluation process as often as is needed for each learning outcome, group of learning outcomes, and lesson.

> **Practical Guideline:**
>
> Thoroughly evaluating a storyboard can help prevent the team from wasting a significant amount of time making revisions.

Based on the storyboard, make final decisions about the media needed to effectively teach the material. These decisions are based on what will most effectively teach the material as well as practical considerations such as cost, hardware capabilities, available expertise... Once you make the decisions, start developing the media. (See the Media Selection, Text, Audio, Visuals, Video, and Animation chapters for more information.)

You must consider the file formats that will be used and where the media will be stored (e.g., DVD-ROM, CD-ROM, hard drive, or network). Read Part 6: Final Steps to determine how to best store the media.

A final storyboard must be created for the programmer. An accurate storyboard will reduce the number of subsequent revisions needed. Programming the materials and utilities can now be completed. After you develop the media, individual pieces can be incorporated into the computer program.

When the programming is completed, you can begin the final formative evaluation.

The components of an existing or a developed instructional multimedia package can also include:
* an easy to use student manual with directions, strategies, learning outcomes, and summaries
* remedial and enrichment materials
* an easy- to-use instructor's manual with a description of the complete package

5.10 Conduct Formative Evaluations

Formative evaluation involves collecting data and information that is analyzed and used to improve the instruction's effectiveness. You should conduct formative evaluation throughout the instructional development process to minimize the loss of time and money due to errors. Imagine the cost of discovering a mistake in identifying an instructional goal after instructional materials have been developed. Consider creating small prototypes or sections for initial evaluation. In formative evaluation, you must collect data and information from target audience learners. See Appendix II for more details on how to evaluate software.

Subject-matter experts should evaluate the first drafts (which are initially done on paper) with respect to accuracy, currency, clarity, the instructional strategy, spelling (especially technical terms), and appropriateness to the target audience.

Practical Guideline:
Conduct on-going formative evaluations to minimize the costs of errors.

During evaluations, it is safer and easier to focus on single tasks. For example, on the first pass consider accuracy, on the second pass focus on currency... This requires a significant amount of time but the thoroughness will show in the final product. Be sure the evaluators are interested in giving a thorough evaluation, have the time to do the task well, and can easily provide feedback (i.e., allow "off-site" evaluators to comment by phone, fax, or electronic mail).

In initial (beta-test) evaluations, consider asking perfectionists to check for grammar and punctuation errors. Request those who tend to see the big picture to consider larger design problems. Also, ask computer novices to check the overall navigation and prompts or directions.

Formative evaluations should include one-to-one evaluations, small group evaluations, and field trials.

5.10-1 One-To-One Evaluations

One-to-one evaluations involve yourself and an individual. This can be done with anyone, including students, team members, and visitors, who is willing to give a few minutes. As a minimum, evaluate with at least three target audience students. Involve weak, average, and strong students. Working with weak students can help verify the determined entry skills requirement.

In this evaluation, encourage everybody to freely give constructive feedback. Simply state that their feedback will help make the product excellent and that if they do not share their concerns then future students could be inflicted with the same problems. A positive rapport helps facilitate this process. The setting should be quiet and private. You can and should interact with the individual and ask specific questions about any area of concern. This is particularly important since some people are reluctant to state problems. You should carefully observe the individual to check for non-verbal cues, such as hesitations, getting questions wrong, frustration, not proceeding as expected, not knowing where to click, and confusion, that indicate problem areas.

During the post-test, you should find out why errors were made. This can help you modify the instruction.

The one-to-one evaluation phase should remove the most obvious errors, provide information on initial reactions, and the time required for completing lessons. An attitude questionnaire should determine:
- the material's strengths and weaknesses
- whether the instruction was interesting, relevant, motivating, and enjoyable
- if the learner understood all of the skills and sub-skills (e.g., was the material clear, sequenced appropriately, and organized logically)
- if the material (e.g., hardware and software) is easy to use
- whether the learning outcomes were covered
- if there were enough relevant practice opportunities
- whether the feedback was instructive
- if the test was a good measure of their skills
- whether the learner was confident in answering the test questions

The questionnaire should also determine if the student has any biases towards multimedia instruction. For example, find out the degree to which the student prefers to learn from people, computers, or a combination of the two. Similarly, determine if the student would like to learn more through computers. This information can be used for assessing the accuracy of the data collected. If possible, pinpoint any areas of concern.

Analyze all of the data and make the necessary revisions.

5.10-2 Small-Group Evaluations

Small-group evaluations involve eight to twenty target audience representatives. Less than eight may not provide enough data while more than twenty may provide more data than needed. With computer applications, individuals and groups of two or three students at a single terminal can be evaluated. Due to limited hardware availability, some situations will require students to work in groups of two or three. Try to have a representative of each type of target population student. This helps avoid any bias or skewed results. Representatives can be from low, average, and high achievers, learners with different language abilities, students with varied attitudes, learners with different degrees of familiarity with the material, males and females, and young and experienced learners.

In the small group evaluation:
- You should only have an observing role to see how students naturally interact with the software.
- Collect data to analyze each question's effectiveness. (See Appendix VI for details.)
- Determine the effectiveness of the changes made after the one-to-one evaluations, identify remaining problems, and gather information on attitudes and initial reactions.
- Analyze all of the data and make the necessary revisions.

5.10-3 Field Trials

In a field trial, evaluate a wide representation of at least thirty target audience students. With computer applications, individuals and groups of two or three students at a single terminal can be evaluated. The learning situation should be as close to the intended real situation as possible. all materials for the instructors (if any) and students should be ready.

In field trials:
- Collect data to analyze each question's effectiveness. (See Appendix VI for details.)
- Determine the effectiveness of the changes made after the small-group evaluations and whether the instruction will be effective in the "real" environment. Instructional effectiveness can be measured by giving students a pre-test and post-test. This can be done on paper or computer.
- Analyze all of the data and make the necessary revisions.

Note that the results of each formative evaluation step may be skewed if learners are forced to participate in the evaluation or if learners rush to complete the evaluation. You should motivate and encourage the students to try to learn the material well.

It may not be possible to change materials developed by others. However, the information and data provided through evaluations can be used for adapting supplementary materials that are being developed.

For computer-managed presentations, practicing the presentation a few times will help everything run smoothly. This includes rehearsing everything aloud. Leave enough time between the rehearsal and the presentation to make adjustments. As the presentation proceeds, note student reactions that may indicate that future changes are needed. You can ask students to provide feedback on the presentation and valuable information can also be gained from noting student test results.

Summary

Instructional design is the systematic process of activities aimed at solving an instructional problem.

After each of the following instructional design steps, evaluate the results, make revisions, and get approval before proceeding:
- Identify the instructional goal. This involves conducting a needs assessment to determine the actual problem and clearly defining and verify the instructional goal.
- Conduct a goal analysis. This entails providing a visual statement of what the learner will be able to do and classifying the goal into a learning domain.
- Conduct a subordinate skills analysis. A subordinate skills analysis is based on the goal's learning domain classification. Perform a cluster analysis for verbal information, a hierarchical analysis for intellectual skills, a procedural analysis for psychomotor skills, and the appropriate instructional analysis for attitudinal skills.
- Identify entry behaviors and characteristics. This is based on the instructional skills analysis and a learner analysis that are used to determine which skills will be taught. Undertaking a learner analysis helps in identifying the target audience population and discovering factors, such as abilities, language capabilities, motivation, interests, human factors, and learning styles that may influence the instructional design. The learner analysis should also lead to defining a student population that is neither too narrow nor too broad. This information can be obtained from personal experience, interviews with students and instructors, questionnaires, tests, and literature.
- Write learning outcomes. Learning outcomes are specific measurable skills that students need to learn. Steps to writing learning outcomes include:
  - Identifying specific behaviors by using action verbs.
  - Specifying the content area after the verb.
  - Specifying applicable conditions.
  - Specifying applicable criteria.
  - Reviewing each learning outcome to be sure it is complete, clear, and concise.
- Develop criterion-referenced test questions. Criterion-referenced tests relate student success to achievement of the learning outcomes. Test questions must measure the stated learning outcomes.
  - Pre-tests are tests given before instruction is presented. Pre-tests can act as a challenge test to determine whether the subsequent lesson or parts of the lesson can be optionally skipped, students should review specific material before continuing, and the entry-level skills are set correctly.
  - Post-tests are tests given after instruction is presented. Post-tests should be based on the learning outcomes, be fair and balanced, be at the appropriate difficulty level, test all or a representative sample of the learning outcomes, be composed of different question types that test as many of the different thinking levels as possible, have a rationale, have familiar question types and designs, and only include validated questions.
- Develop an instructional strategy. An instructional strategy clearly describes the instructional materials' components, the media selection, and the procedures used with the materials to have the students achieve the learning outcomes. The instructional strategy is based on the instructional analysis, the learning outcomes, and other previous steps. The instructional strategy will be used as a framework for developing the instructional materials or evaluating whether existing materials are suitable or need revision.
  - In general, to best facilitate learning, learning outcomes should be sequenced from lower to higher-level skills, easy to hard, simple to complex, the specific to the general, the concrete to the abstract, and the known to the unknown.
  - Although multimedia instruction is best suited for certain individuals, there are many things that can be done to overcome learning style problems. One solution is to teach with a variety of methods and media.
  - Without motivation, learning is unlikely to occur. Motivation can be enhanced through addressing the attributes called attention, relevance, confidence, and satisfaction.
  - To help ensure effective learning in multimedia lessons, include all of the instructional events.

- The proportional amount of content needed to cover a learning outcome should be based on the learning outcome's frequency, importance, and difficulty.
- The general types of instructional multimedia include drill and practice, tutorials, simulations, and educational games. Consider using more than one of these types to teach a skill. Intelligent tutoring systems and virtual reality can be considered but they are not practical solutions for typical developers.

- Develop and select instructional materials. When existing materials are available, evaluate the material to determine if the material is suitable or can be adapted or supplemented. When the needed material must be developed, have the instructional designer work with the subject-matter expert(s) to write storyboards and fill in the instructional strategy details. After finalizing the media selection, develop and/or gather the media and complete the programming.
- Conduct formative evaluations. Formative evaluation involves collecting data and information, which is analyzed and used to improve the instruction's effectiveness. This can be done in one-to-one, small group, and field trial evaluations. Formative evaluation must occur throughout the instructional development process to minimize the loss of time and money due to errors.

Application Exercises

1) Categorize the following scenarios into one of the types of instructional multimedia:
   a) Students play the role of detective in trying to capture a criminal hiding in Europe. By correctly answering geography questions, students get closer to capturing the criminal.
   b) Students are taught how to calculate mortgage payments. This is done through presenting the material and providing numerous questions and extensive feedback.
   c) Students are taught the principles of calculating mortgage payments. This is done through allowing the students to vary the starting principal, interest rate, and time length of the mortgage to see the resulting monthly payment requirement.
2) If an employee says to you that he has **not** been able to follow the procedure because the steps are written poorly, what can you conclude? What can you do to obtain accurate information?
3) If you are planning to create and implement a new computerized system, what are some problems you can expect? List ways you could deal with these problems.
4) Imagine that for an instructional multimedia project a subject-matter expert does **not** want to write formal learning outcomes because he has always been able to teach effectively without specifying learning outcomes. What would you do or say?
5) For the following statements:
   - State whether the statement is a well-written learning outcome or not.
   - If the statement is a poorly written learning outcome, explain why the learning outcome is **not** well written.
   - If the statement is a poorly written learning outcome, rewrite the learning outcome into an acceptable learning outcome.

   a) Students will understand how to design multimedia tutorial screens that effectively use color.
   b) Students will be able to distinguish between squares and rectangles.
   c) Using a caliper, students will be able to measure the thickness of different objects.
   d) Students will choose to use calipers when precise accuracy is needed for measuring the thickness of different objects.
   e) Students will appreciate the accuracy that can be attained when measuring the thickness of different objects with calipers.
6) Assume a multimedia tutorial starts off with a title screen that simply states "Driving Safety". What could you improve to help ensure you gain a student's attention?
7) Describe how you could motivate a student in a lesson on chemical safety.
8) If your learner analysis shows that the target population has diverse learning preferences, what should you design into the material?
9) If your learner analysis shows that the target population has a markedly varied skill level, what should you design into the material?

10) What can you do to help extroverted students feel comfortable with multimedia instruction?

Case Study

Six instructors were on a four-week professional development leave from their regular duties. During this time, the instructors participated in a workshop on creating instructional multimedia applications. In the first three weeks, the mornings were devoted to learning the principles and guidelines of creating instructional multimedia applications. During the afternoons, the instructors focused on the particular skills that they needed to create a multimedia tutorial. The workshop leader provided the expertise needed to guide the subject-matter experts through the instructional design process. In the fourth week, the storyboard was evaluated and revised, and started to be transferred to the computer.

Case Study Questions

1) Given the lack of time, the title page consisted of a text title and a simple visual image. For a tutorial in your field, what would you do with the title page to help gain a student's attention?
2) It was known that some of the students tend to have a hard time keeping on task. What would you do as a part of the instructional design process to determine what would make the material meaningful and relevant?
3) In the traditional classroom, students had a hard time remembering the relationships between the different variables. For example, as one variable increased the other decreased. What instructional activities would you create to help students remember the relationships?

References

Alessi, S., & Trollip, S. (1991). Computer-based instruction: Methods and development (2nd ed.). Englewood Cliffs, NJ: Prentice-Hall, Inc.

Armstrong, D., Denton, J., & Savage, T. (1978). Instructional skills handbook. Englewood Cliffs, NJ: Educational Technology Publications.

Bastiaens, T., & Martens, R. (2000). Conditions for web-based learning with real events. In Abbey, B. (Ed.), Instructional and cognitive impacts of web-based education. (pp. 1-31). Hershey, PA: Idea Group Publishing.

Beach, B. K. (1993, October). Learning with Roger Schank. Training & Development, 47(10), 39-43.

Billings, D., & Cobb, K. (1992). Effects of learning style preferences, attitude and GPA on learner achievement using computer assisted interactive videodisc instruction. Journal of Computer-Based Instruction, 19(1), 12-16.

Brush, T. (1998). Embedding cooperative learning into the design of integrated learning systems: Rationale and guidelines. Educational Technology Research and Development, 46(3), 5-18.

Butler, K. (1988). It's all in your mind: A student's guide to learning style. Columbia, CT: The Learner's Dimension.

Butler, K. (1986). Learning and teaching style: In theory and practice. Columbia, CT: The Learner's Dimension.

Carlson, H. (1991). Learning style and program design in interactive multimedia. Educational Technology Research and Development, 39(3), 41-48.

Cavalier, J., & Klein, J. (1998). Effects of cooperative versus individual learning and orienting activities during computer-based instruction. Educational Technology Research and Development, 46(1), 5-17.

Chun, D., & Plass, J. (1994). Assessing the effectiveness of multimedia in language learning software. Proceedings of the ED-MEDIA 94 World Conference on Educational Multimedia and Hypermedia.

Churach, D., & Fisher, D. (2001). Science students surf the web: Effects on constructivist classroom environments. Journal of Computers in Mathematics and Science Teaching, 20(2), 221-247.

Danielson, J., Lockee, B., & Burton, J. (2000). ID and HCI: A marriage of necessity. In Abbey, B. (Ed.), Instructional and cognitive impacts of web-based education. (pp. 118-128). Hershey, PA: Idea Group Publishing.

Dick, W., & Carey, L. (1990). The systematic design of instruction (3rd ed.). Glenville, IL: Harper Collins Publishers.

Dunn, R., & Bruno, A. (1985, September). What does the research on learning styles have to do with Mario? The Clearing House, 59(1), 9-12.

Enochs, J., Handley, J., & Wollenberg, J. (1986). Relating learning style, reading vocabulary, reading comprehension, and aptitude for learning to achievement in the self-paced and computer-assisted instructional modes. Journal of Experimental Education, 54, 135-139.

Falk, D., & Carlson, H. (1995). Multimedia in higher education: A practical guide to new tools for interactive teaching and learning. Medford, NJ: Learned Information, Inc.

Ference, P., & Vockell, E. (1994, July-August). Adult learning characteristics and effective software instruction. Educational Technology, 34(6), 25-31.

Fenrich, P. (2005). What can you do to virtually teach practical skills? The Journal of Issues in Informing Science and Information Technology, 2, 347-354.

Gagne, R., Briggs, L., & Wager, W. (1988). Principles of instructional design (3rd ed.). New York, NY: Holt, Rinehart and Winston.

Guild, P., & Garger, S. (1985). Marching to different drummers. Alexandria, VA: Association for Supervision and Curriculum Development.

Hoffman, J., & Waters, K. (1982, March). Some effects of student personality on success with computer-assisted instruction. Educational Technology, 22(3), 8-14.

Jonassen, D., & Hannum, W. (1991). Analysis of task analysis procedures. In G. J. Anglin (Ed.), Instructional technology: Past, present, and future (pp. 170-187). Englewood, CO: Libraries Unlimited.

Keller, J. (1987). Strategies for stimulating the motivation to learn. Performance and Instruction, 26(8), 1-7.

Orey, M., & Nelson, W. (1993). Development principles for intelligent tutoring systems: Integrating cognitive theory into the development of computer-based instruction. Educational Technology Research and Development, 41(1), 59-72.

Orr, J. (1994, Spring). Light from shadow: The virtues of virtual reality. The Human Interface Technology Lab Review. 4, 21.

Magel, M. (1998, June). Splat! There's more than one way to debug a project. AV Video Multimedia Producer, 20(6), 39, 41.

Mager, R. (1962). Preparing instructional objectives. Belmont, CA: Fearon Publishers.

Main, R. (1993, December). Integrating motivation into the instructional design process. Educational Technology, 33(12), 37-41.

Mayer, M. (1988). Test item construction: A self-instructional manual. Victoria, British Columbia, Canada: Province of British Columbia, Ministry of Advanced Education and Job Training.

McCarthy, B. (1987). The 4MAT system: Teaching to learning styles with right/left mode techniques. Barrington, IL: Excel, Inc.

McFarlane, A., Sparrowhawk, A., & Heald, Y. (2002). Report on the educational use of games. Teachers Evaluating Educational Multimedia (TEEM), Cambridge, UK. Retrieved November 12, 2004 from http://www.teem.org.uk/publications/teem_gamesined_full.pdf.

Miller, S., & Miller, K. (2000). Theoretical and practical considerations in the design of web-based instruction. In Abbey, B. (Ed.), Instructional and cognitive impacts of web-based education. (pp. 156-177). Hershey, PA: Idea Group Publishing.

Newby, T., Ertmer, P., & Stepich, D. (1995). Instructional analogies and the learning of concepts. Educational Technology Research and Development, 43(1), 5-18.

Rossett, A. (1987). Training needs assessment. Englewood Cliffs, NJ: Educational Technology Publications.

Salisbury, D. (1990). Cognitive psychology and its implications for designing drill and practice programs for computers. Journal of Computer-Based Instruction, 17(1), 23-30.

Schwier, R., & Misanchuk, E. (1993). Interactive multimedia instruction. Englewood Cliffs, NJ: Educational Technology Publications.

Shi, L., Kinshuk, Lin, T., & Patel, A. (2004). High level intelligence through horizontal and vertical networking of tutoring applications. Proceedings of the Third Pan-Commonwealth Forum on Open Learning.

Thurman, R., & Mattoon, J. (1994, October). Virtual reality: Toward fundamental improvements in simulation-based training. Educational Technology, 34(8), 56-64.

Thurman, R. (1993). Instructional simulation from a cognitive psychology viewpoint. Educational Technology Research and Development, 41(4), 75-89.

Wager, W., Polkinghorne, S., & Powley, R. (1992). Simulations: Selection and development. Performance Improvement Quarterly, 5(2), 47-64.

Winn, W. (1994). Designing and using virtual environments: The advantage of immersion. Proceedings of the ED-MEDIA 94 World Conference on Educational Multimedia and Hypermedia.

Wlodkowski, R. (1985). Enhancing adult motivation to learn. San Francisco, CA: Jossey-Bass Publishers.

Wunderlich, K., Bell, A., & Ford, L. (2005, January). Improving Learning Through Understanding of Brain Science Research. Retrieved Mar. 31, 2005 from http://www.league.org/publication/abstracts/learning/lelabs200501.html

Section 2: Media

A major part of the instructional design process you need to do is select the appropriate media mix to effectively solve the defined problem. The media mix can include text, audio, visuals, motion visuals, animations, and/or real objects. The strengths and weaknesses of these media, which are presented in this section, will help you determine your media mix. Practical guidelines for designing and developing these media are also presented.

Chapter 6: Media Selection

Learning Outcomes

After completing this chapter, you should be able to:
- explain the importance of selecting the best media mix
- describe how the selected media can affect learning and motivation
- list strengths and weakness of the different media
- describe considerations for selecting media
- determine which media are appropriate for different needs

Introduction

Selecting the best media mix to use will enable you to increase learning, ensure the media is effective for the learner, and maximize cost-effectiveness. This chapter first introduces you to the different media categories, explains how each medium relates to learning, and describes how media can affect a learner's motivation. The strengths and weaknesses of each medium are then presented with respect to the different learning outcome classifications. Lastly, this chapter provides considerations to help you select media and some notes on transferring material to other formats.

6.1 Media Categories

The media categories that you can incorporate into an instructional multimedia package are:
- text
  - Text is typically presented on computer screens but the complete resources you provide can also include other formats such as paper handouts that contain summaries.
- audio
  - Audio can be heard from DVD-ROM/CD-ROM discs, computer hard drives, an intranet, and the Internet. However, a complete instructional package can also include resources like tapes (audiocassettes), radio, television, and live commentary.
- visuals
  - Visuals can be stored on DVD-ROM/CD-ROM discs, computer hard drives, an intranet, and the Internet. Other resources can include slides, photographs, overhead transparencies, and paper-based material.
- video
  - Video can be retrieved from DVD-ROM/CD-ROM discs, computer hard drives, an intranet, and the Internet. Other sources can include mini-DV tapes, film, VHS tapes …
- animations
  - Animations can be stored on DVD-ROM/CD-ROM discs, computer hard drives, an intranet, and the Internet. Film, VHS tapes and other sources can also contain animation resources.
- real objects
  - Real objects include actual equipment and models.

Video typically includes natural images recorded with video equipment whereas animations are usually created artificially with computers and/or other tools.

comprise — a cuprinde; a include

6.2   Media and Learning

The media you select do **not** determine whether learning will occur. The media simply carry your message to the learner. For learning to occur your message must be received and understood. This is independent of the media. However, the media you use can influence the amount of learning that can occur. If you combine the media's strengths with instructional methods that take advantage of these strengths, you can positively influence learning.

Complete multimedia packages can, but should not necessarily, include all of the different media. Note that:

the mix of media however

- Learning from material made with more than one medium is usually more effective than material comprised of only one medium. This is partly due to the fact that different parts of the brain process different information. For example, some parts of the brain process text while other parts process visuals. When multimedia packages activate more regions of the brain, there are increases in learning and retention compared to materials that require fewer parts of the brain to process information.

> **Practical Guideline:**
>
> Teaching with more than one medium is usually more effective than teaching with only one medium.

- In many situations, you can and should use more than one medium to teach the skill. You will need to determine the media that will complement the intended instructional strategy.
  - Video materials often include an audio component.
- If you use too many media at one time, you can impede learning.
  - Although multi-sensory learning experiences tend to be effective, learners can only process a limited amount of information at one time. Imagine trying to read text while a supporting animation is being shown on the screen.
  - Media should support and enhance each other.
- Base your media mix decision on what is being taught, how it is being taught, how it will be tested, and the previously specified target audience characteristics.
  - Different media may be needed for different groups of learning outcomes. For example, video may be appropriate for the attitude component but video may not provide the corrective feedback necessary for the intellectual skills component.
  - Do **not** select media simply to dazzle or for convenience.

6.3   Media and Motivation

Consider a student's experience with each media. For example, if the students have typically failed in text-based programs then consider using other media. Students must have confidence or expectations of success with the selected media. To be successful, students must also have the skills to extract information and learn from the media. This is **not** always a safe assumption. For example, many learners are used to passively watching video and do not know how to focus their learning or take effective notes while watching video.

Depending on a student's learning preferences or learning style, the media you choose could be liked or disliked. If the selected media are **not** preferred, enhance motivation through:
- stating how learning the material will fulfill the student's needs
- illustrating how the material is important
- stating that the test will be based on the material.

(Check the Instructional Design chapter for more details on how to motivate students.)

6.4   Text

You can effectively use text to teach most skills (most verbal information, intellectual skills, and cognitive strategies and some psychomotor skills and attitudes) unless the target audience has a poor reading ability or low motivation. However, text alone cannot adequately represent the richness the world offers through our senses and our imaginations. Consequently, for instructional effectiveness, you will often need to combine text with other media.

Practical Guideline:

Text is excellent, as a part of the instructional strategy, for teaching most skills.

Text is better than video and audio when the topic is complex (e.g., forecasting economic trends), abstract (e.g., balancing chemical equations), or has structure (e.g., solving word problems).

Text is especially effective for verbal skills such as describing, listing, and naming. With proficient readers, verbal information can usually be learned faster with text than other media.

For higher-level skills, remember that practice and feedback are particularly critical. You can use text in your multimedia application to provide effective practice and feedback.

Multimedia applications are sometimes weak when students need to later refer to notes. You can provide paper-based summaries to help solve this problem.

(See the Text chapter for more details.)

6.5   Audio

You can use audio for obvious things like music, poetry, and sound effects and also when real sounds, such as heart, animal, and normal and defective equipment sounds, are an integral part of the learning outcome. Audio is also excellent for teaching attitudes, especially if you personalize the material, and intellectual skills such as learning languages.

Audio is more effective when the topic is simple, concrete, and has little structure, as is the case with foreign language vocabulary. However, you can effectively teach many skills with audio, such as intellectual, psychomotor, and attitudes, when the audio is supplemented with other media such as text, especially when providing practice and feedback. You should also supplement audio with effective preparatory and follow-up activities. An advantage of audio over text is that listening is much easier than reading.

You can use audio to gain attention, give feedback, give directions, personalize computers, make annotations, provide multilingual support, teach how to pronounce words, provide meaning for images or image collections, and accommodate weak readers.

Practical Guideline:

Audio can be particularly effective when combined with other media.

You can use audio effectively for students with poor reading abilities. Some instructional multimedia programs successfully teach without using text. Another solution is to provide text but let students click on an audio button whenever they want to hear a narration of the text. One strategy some authors use is to display text and simultaneously play a matching narration. Although this strategy is useful for some students, many learners find this annoying. Audio can be problematic when played at a different speed than the student is able to read. For example, if the audio is played at a slower speed than the learner's reading speed, as is true in most cases, the learner can be frustrated as they continually wait for the audio while they read. If the audio is played at a faster rate than the learner can mentally process the information, learning can be compromised. Alternatively, they may try to ignore the audio – which is not easy to do. Note that it is unlikely that all students in a target audience will have similar reading speeds.

To help learning and facilitate reviewing, let students have control over the audio. For example, many students may want to repeat audio clips. This can be easily done with computer applications.

(Read the Audio chapter for more information.)

6.6   Visuals

You can use visuals for identifying objects, classifying objects, showing spatial relationships, performing psychomotor skills that do **not** need to be recognized or copied, and helping make abstract concepts concrete (e.g., with graphs). When you design multimedia applications follow the old adage, "A picture is worth a thousand words." A visual of an animal that is hard to describe well in words is shown in Figure 6.1.

Figure 6.1 – Visual that is hard to describe with words

Compared to only using text, visuals combined with text reduce the learning time and help students acquire and retain information. You should consider combining visuals with text to provide practice and feedback.

(Check the Visuals chapter for more details.)

6.7   Video

You can successfully use video for showing realism, skills requiring learners to recognize or copy movements such as psychomotor skills, procedures, processes, making abstract concepts concrete, classifying information, comparing information, presenting introductions (which may otherwise be boring), and gaining and focusing a learner's attention.

If you combine video with audio, you can effectively teach attitudes and provide elaborations. Note that video combined with audio requires more mental processing than either alone. Consequently, you can overwhelm students with more information than they can mentally process. One solution is to put pauses after complex elements to allow learners to mentally "catch-up" before you present new material.

Video combined with audio can depict events faster than can be done with only text. However, students perceive video as being easier than text and tend to spend less effort in learning from video than text. Consequently, students may learn less from video than comparable text. You can enhance learning with video by cuing the learner, providing interaction, and keeping the video clips short.

In some situations, you should let the learners control the video (e.g., slow forward, step forward, step backward, slow backward...). This is particularly helpful for reviewing, psychomotor skills such as studying procedures, and noting detailed information.

Video tends to be weak at teaching detailed information. You can provide video control and text-based summaries to help with this problem. Consider combining video with text to provide practice and feedback.

Practical Guideline:

Video has many effective uses but is weak at providing detailed information.

(See the Video chapter and the Final Steps section for more information.)

6.8   Animations

You can use animations for a variety of instructional purposes such as
- showing relationships between objects and ideas such as the effects of gravity on objects thrown into the air
- simulating the results of actions which includes activities like showing the resulting movements of gauges in a cockpit
- showing sequential steps in a procedural task such as how to service a photocopier
- helping explain difficult concepts that can include how food is absorbed from the intestines into the blood stream or how electrons move through different parts of electrical circuits
- making abstract concepts concrete like showing dynamic sine waves or a heart's electrocardiogram based on parameters that students input

Consider combining animations with text to provide practice and feedback.

6.9   Real Objects

Imagine learning how to create multimedia instructional materials without ever using a computer or seeing real examples.

Real objects are excellent when teaching psychomotor skills and when the skill must be practiced and mastered. There is no guarantee that the skill learned on a simulator or other format will be transferred to the real job. So, remember the old saying, "practice makes perfect".

For some training needs, such as are done with simulations, you will also need to provide for real experience. A quote illustrates this: "There is only so much you can learn about skydiving while standing on the ground." At certain points within or after the program, simply direct the student to real objects or activities.

> **Practical Guideline:**
>
> Consider including real objects as a part of the entire instructional package.

Although real objects may be preferred, other media are often used if the real object is expensive, rare, dangerous, fragile, large (i.e., cannot be brought to the classroom), or not easily accessible by the learner.

Models can often successfully replace real objects, at least for some phases of the learning such as is done with simulated aircraft cockpits.

6.10 Selecting Media

When you select media, consider whether the media mix can be used to teach all of the learning outcomes, costs and cost-effectiveness, learner characteristics, and the instructional setting.

6.10-1 Teaching the Learning Outcomes

The media mix you choose must be able to meet the requirements of the instructional strategy and address all of the instructional events. In particular, the media mix should allow for practice and feedback. Use the following general guidelines for selecting the appropriate media mix for the learning domains of verbal information, intellectual skills, psychomotor skills, and attitudes. (See Appendix IV for details on the different learning domains.)

For verbal information such as knowledge and comprehension, you should use text and visuals. You can do this in a computer-based multimedia package but paper-based material can be adequate. If you put the material on a computer then use the computer as a tool rather than letting the computer become a glorified page-turner. For example, use the computer to provide interaction as that can be difficult or cumbersome to do with paper-based materials.

For intellectual skills such as applying skills to new examples, you can effectively use each medium depending on the skill being taught. Following the instructional design process will help you determine the best media mix. Computer-based multimedia instruction can be an excellent tool for teaching intellectual skills.

For psychomotor skills such as those requiring muscular actions, you should use real equipment although for practical reasons, such as cost and safety, you may need to create a simulation that incorporates a variety of media. Video with audio or text support can be superb for teaching psychomotor skills. Similarly, a series of images with text can also be very effective.

Although you can use video and audio to effectively teach attitudes, for example choosing to say "no" to drugs, with a computer-based multimedia approach, your complete instructional strategy should consider other methods such as role-playing.

For computer-managed presentations, all of the media can be used to support text or to effectively make points. However, if the presentation is too "flashy" the main points may not be noticed.

6.10-2 Costs and Cost-Effectiveness

You will need to answer a number of questions to determine costs and cost-effectiveness:
- What are the equipment, media resources, and copying costs?
- Will the media run flawlessly on the expected hardware platforms? For computer-managed presentations, media can be easily presented when it is stored in a standardized format. Media can be retrieved from hard drives, devices such as DVD-ROMs and CD-ROMs, networks, and the Internet.
- Are there costs associated with getting copyright clearance to use existing materials? In general, copyright clearance is required **in writing** from the author or copyright holder for all materials, including print, visuals, video, and software, created by others. Copyright also applies to derivatives or transformations of the original work.

(Read the Introduction to Instructional Multimedia chapter for more details on benefits, costs, and copyright issues.)

6.10-3 Learner Characteristics

Learner characteristics you need to consider include:
- media preferences such as from a lack of success with previous media
- the ability to learn from the media
- reading abilities
  - Factors include grade level and whether it is a first or second language.
- memory skills
  - Print materials are one possible solution.
- motivation to learn and how the media affects motivation
- maturity
  - Some students are more easily distracted than others.
- preferences for working alone, in pairs, or in groups
- the need for self-paced materials
- the need for an instructor's help

(See the Instructional Design chapter for more details on learner characteristics.)

6.10-4 The Instructional Setting

Questions you should consider regarding the instructional setting include:
- Will the setting be a school, office, or home?
- Are the students geographically dispersed?
- Will the material and equipment be accessible to everyone? Remember that paper materials can be read virtually anywhere, most students have or have access to audio cassette and VHS tape players, and that access to computers is generally correlated to socioeconomic status.
- Will you teach the lesson to large groups, small groups, or individuals? If you need to present the content to large groups, you may need access to a projector.

6.11 Transferring Material to Other Formats

If you simply transfer material from one storage format to another, the second's advantages may not be exploited and the first's limitations may be kept. For example, some analog videotapes have been transferred to a CD-ROM format. If the videotape is specifically designed to be played linearly, it may only be educationally sound to play the video on the CD-ROM linearly. In this case, the CD-ROM's advantage of instant access capabilities and interaction are not being utilized. There may only be minimum value in having video contained on a CD-ROM instead of a videotape. In general, if material is designed specifically for one format, be careful about transferring it directly to another format. However, with modifications transferring material from one format to another can be justified and effective.

Note that there is often a quality loss in the image and sound clarity when transferring materials between formats. Working with original materials can minimize losses.

Summary

The general media categories you can select are text, audio, visuals, video, animations, and real objects. The media you select do not determine whether learning will occur. The media simply carry your message to the learner. For learning to occur, your message must be received and understood. This is independent of the media. However, the media you use can influence the amount of learning that can occur. If you combine the media's strengths with instructional methods that take advantage of these strengths, you can positively influence learning.

Complete multimedia packages can, but should not necessarily, include every media. Learning from material made with more than one medium is usually more effective than material comprised of only one medium. In many situations, more than one medium can be used to teach the skill. Determine the media that will complement your intended instructional strategy. Your media mix decision should be based on what is being taught, how it is being taught, how it will be tested, and the previously specified target audience characteristics.

You can effectively use text to teach most skills, especially verbal skills. Consider using text to provide practice and feedback, which is critical for teaching higher-level skills. Text is versatile in that it can be read in many locations.

You can use audio for music, poetry, and sound effects and also for when real sounds are an integral part of the learning outcome. Audio is more effective when the topic is simple, concrete, and has little structure. It is particularly useful when you supplement it with other media such as text. Audio is effective for students with poor reading abilities and can be listened to in many locations. A weakness of audio is that it does not, on its own, readily provide practice and feedback.

Consider using visuals for identifying objects, classifying spatial relationships, and performing motor skills that do **not** need to be recognized or copied. Visuals can enhance learning and decrease learning time. However, visuals, on their own, do not readily provide practice and feedback.
You can effectively use video for showing realism, recognizing or copying movements or procedures, and presenting introductions. When combined with audio, video is very effective for teaching attitudes and for providing elaborations. On its own, video tends to be ineffective in teaching detailed content and readily providing practice and feedback.

Consider using animations to show relationships between objects and ideas, simulate the results of actions, show sequential steps in a procedural task, help explain difficult concepts, and make abstract concepts concrete.

You may need to include real objects when teaching motor skills, when three-dimensional presentations are needed for learning, and when the skill must be practiced and mastered. Real objects are critical for skills that require real experience.

There are many factors you need to consider when selecting media. These factors include whether the media mix can be used to teach all of the learning outcomes, costs and cost-effectiveness, learner characteristics, and the instructional setting.

In general, if material is designed specifically for one format, be careful about transferring it directly to another format.

Application Exercises

1) What is more important for learning to occur, the message or the medium? Explain your answer.
2) When should instructional multimedia packages contain all of the different media?
3) Which of the following statements is **false**?
   a) Text is excellent for teaching verbal skills.
   b) Text is less effective for students with low motivation.
   c) To enhance learning, text should often be combined with other media.
   d) Video is better than text when the topic is complex.
4) Which of the following statements is **false**?
   a) Audio is excellent for teaching attitudes.
   b) Audio is more effective when the topic is simple.
   c) Learners tend to like audio narration when they read text.
   d) Listening is easier than reading.
5) Which of the following statements is **false**?
   a) Some learners spend less effort with video than with text.
   b) Video can be used to gain and focus a learner's attention.
   c) Video combined with audio can effectively teach attitudes.
   d) Video is excellent at providing details.

Case Study

Six instructors were on a four-week professional development leave from their regular duties. During this time, the instructors participated in a workshop on creating instructional multimedia applications. One goal of the workshop was to create a small tutorial so that the instructors could apply what they learned. As a part of the instructional design process, the instructors searched for existing materials. The instructors were not able to find any existing multimedia products on the topic but were able to find print-based materials.

Case Study Question

Given that most of the tutorial was to be completed in four weeks, in general, which media would be the easiest to include in the tutorial?

References

Cennamo, K. (1993). Learning from video: Factors influencing learners' preconceptions and invested mental effort. Educational Technology Research and Development, 41(3), 33-45.

Grimes, T. (1990). Audio-video correspondence and its role in attention and memory. Educational Technology Research and Development, 38(3), 15-25.

Kozma, R. (1991, Summer) Learning with media. Review of Educational Research, 61(2), 179-211.

Reiser, R., & Gagne, R. (1983). Selecting media for instruction. Englewood Cliffs, NJ: Educational Technology Publications.

Romiszowski, A. (1988). The selection and use of instructional media: For improved classroom teaching and for interactive, individualized instruction (2nd ed.). New York, NY: Nichols Publishing.

Chapter 7: Text

Learning Outcomes

After completing this chapter, you should be able to:
* describe features of effectively written text
* list considerations for selecting fonts
* state why variable spacing is preferred over fixed spacing
* explain why scrolling should be avoided
* explain why text should be displayed instantly
* describe the best screen locations for critical information
* describe appropriate screen locations for unimportant information
* write effective text designed for computer screens
* explain why hypertext and hypermedia applications can be weak from an instructional perspective

Introduction

It is important for you to consider text as a part of your media mix in a multimedia production since text can be effectively used to teach many skills to many students. It is common for text to be a significant component of instructional multimedia applications. This chapter presents guidelines for creating effective computer-based text material. For example, ideas are presented for making text understandable, minimizing reading, writing style, spacing text, justifying text, choosing fonts, scrolling text, the speed to display text, and where to place text on the screen. (See the Media Selection chapter for more details about using text.)

7.1   Guidelines for Creating Text

Text often forms the foundation of instructional multimedia applications. For your product to be effective, the text has to be written well. Use the following guidelines for creating effective text:
* Make text understandable.
* Minimize reading.
* Develop a good writing style.
* Follow the basic rules of writing.
* Use a word processor.

7.1-1 Make Text Understandable

In multimedia applications, it is particularly critical for you to make text understandable when students will not have a resource to help clarify poorly written material. Make text understandable by ensuring there is message clarity, using simple words, keeping wording to a minimum, and keeping sentences and paragraphs short. Most subject-matter experts need support in writing materials in this way. Consider utilizing a professional writer to do this task efficiently and effectively.

Ensure There is Message Clarity

Keep the text clear and concise. Clear sentences should have a subject (something being talked about) and predicate (something being said about the subject). For example, in the previous sentence, "clear sentences" is the subject and what the sentences should have is the predicate. Message clarity is critical for effective and efficient learning.

Use Simple Words

Simple words help ensure that the message remains clear. Use simple words such as "pay" rather than "compensation" or "begin" instead of "initiate".

Do **not** try to impress with a difficult vocabulary as this can lead to failure. Similarly, unnecessary and complex jargon can also cause comprehension problems.

Keep Wording to a Minimum

For each sentence, try to eliminate words without changing the meaning. For example, "evaluate your animations with target audience students "is shorter than "your animations should be evaluated with some target audience students".

For computer-managed presentations (CMP), use the 6 by 6 rule. This means that each full screen should have a maximum of 6 lines and 6 words per line. Some presenters follow a similar 5 by 5 rule. This rule is a guideline rather than a strict requirement. The key is to only provide enough information to guide the audience through the presentation.

For CMP, only include the words needed to make the point. Extra words crowd the screen. Too many words may make it unnecessary for you to say anything. CMP are interesting if you elaborate on the points and provide valuable insights. If the screen provides all of the details then it is easier for you to simply provide a photocopy of the presentation.

It is generally wiser for you to have the presentation a bit short where the audience wants more rather than too long, which can bore the audience. More tips for creating CMP can be found in Appendix I.

Keep Sentences Short

In general, keep sentences short. This is more important for younger readers since they have trouble remembering lengthy text. As a rule, as a reader's age decreases the comprehension of longer sentences decreases. For younger students, such as those in elementary school, you should keep sentences short and definitely less than 20 words long. This helps increase comprehension.

Remember to vary sentence length. This keeps the text "natural". Note that this page has a variety of sentence lengths.

Practical Guideline:
Text should be short, clear, concise, and simple.

Keep Paragraphs Short

Keep paragraphs short enough to break up large chunks of information into manageable pieces. This is also useful for enabling the material to fit onto computer screens. Short paragraphs also help learners who are choosing to skim the material. Short paragraphs also increase the amount of white space.

7.1-2 Minimize Reading

It is important for you to minimize reading since it is generally more tiring and time-consuming to read from computer screens than printed material. As well, this helps students with weak reading abilities and those with disabilities. Minimizing reading makes writing for computer screens fundamentally different from writing for printed materials. Be sure that you have this skill or that it is available on the team.

There are a number of ways you can minimize reading:
- Use simple and clear wording.
    - Students with better reading abilities usually do not find simple clear writing offending. They simply read it faster.
    - Highlight key words. This makes important information easy to find.
- Ensure smoothness.
    - Read the text aloud to hear if it flows smoothly.
- Be consistent.
    - Keep screens predictable and regular to minimize searching. There should be a clear underlying structure. Facilitate this with organizational landmarks such as the orientation information and headings. (Read the Screen Design section for more information.)
- Use tables to organize information.
    - This makes the information easy to find and understand.
- Use lists instead of paragraphs.
    - This makes the information easy to find and understand.
    - List items should follow the same grammatical structure.
    - Highlight lists with bullets or dashes.
    - Make lists clear by creating logical groupings.

The time saved in reading may help free up computers when computers are a limited resource.

7.1-3 Develop a Good Writing Style

very imp.!

Your writing style should follow these guidelines:
- Use the active voice.
    - For example, use "text color" not "color of the text".
- Be conversational.
    - Vary sentence lengths.
    - Begin sentences in a number of different ways. *Avoid boreness.*
    - Use effective connecting techniques. For example, start succeeding sentences with "However" or "Similarly" or include key words of the preceding sentence.
    - Use many common one or two syllable words.
    - Include colloquial and idiomatic expressions (but be sure the audience will understand them).
    - Use a minimal amount of abbreviations, proper nouns, and numerals.
- Use the second person (i.e., you rather than we).
- Be unbiased.
    - Eliminate sexist, stereotypic, ethnic, and lifestyle comments.

7.1-4 Follow the Basic Rules of Writing

You need to follow the many rules of effective writing. Some of these rules include:
- Use correct writing mechanics (e.g., spelling and grammar).
    - Errors affect credibility, lead students to take the material less seriously, and can teach poor writing habits.
    - Use a spell check program but remember that spell checkers do not consider sentence context and meaning.

hyphenating – ?

- Avoid hyphenating words at the end of lines.
  - Hyphenated text is harder to read.
- Define all acronyms before using them.
  - For the first instance, write the full term then put the abbreviation in brackets. For example, write Computer-based Training (CBT).
- Minimize punctuation. For example, in acronyms use CBT not C.B.T.
- Use upper and lower case letters.
  - Sentences written in upper case letters take longer to read. Reading speed increases when learners can recognize word shapes.
  - Most students find that text written only with capital letters is hard and somewhat uncomfortable to read.
  - THINK ABOUT WHAT IT FEELS LIKE TO READ THIS SENTENCE. Does it bother you? Compare it to other sentences. Imagine a whole page written in capital letters.
- Only use symbols **every reader** understands (e.g., $ for dollar).

7.1-5   Use a Word Processor

When using a word processor, you can easily make the changes needed to make a high-quality product.

To save time, pull in text from existing word-processed documents into the authoring tool rather then retyping all of the material into the program. Note that word-processed text stored in the RTF (Rich Text Format) can be read on both PC and Macintosh® computers. The text-only format is not fully compatible between PC's and Macintosh® computers, as attributes like bold and underlining are lost. Text brought in through scanners and digitized as an image are accurate, although sometimes fuzzy, but require a lot of storage space and cannot be easily edited. Text can be more easily edited if an optical character reader *(OCR)* is first used to convert the image into text.

The accuracy of optical character readers can be up to 99%, or one or two errors per page, depending on the scanner, font, quality of original material (e.g., faxes can be poor), and type of paper stock (e.g., colored paper is poor) used. Computer spelling and grammar checkers can greatly facilitate proofing and editing. With keyboard text entry, proofing and editing is still necessary.

7.2   Spacing

The spacing you use can greatly affect the "look and feel" of your product. As a guideline:
- Use lots of white space.
  - Crowding reduces readability and can make a screen "feel" unpleasant. If in doubt, use more screens and less text per screen but try to keep complete "thoughts" on one screen. Remember that on computers, extra screens are essentially "free".
  - Since screens should only contain a limited amount of text, take special care to make smooth transitions between related screens.
  - It is easy to find and focus on text that is isolated by white space. Note that white space can be overdone. If there is too much white space in the program (i.e., too little text on each screen) then the learner will spend too much time moving from screen to screen. As a guideline, squint at the screen. Determine whether you focus on the message or the space.
  - Larger font sizes should have greater space between lines.
  - Single line spacing can work well but separate paragraphs with a blank line.
- Keep the top and left margins for text locations constant.
  - This reduces searching time.

7.3   Justification

For the best readability, you should left justify paragraphs. Some materials are written with full justification in order to keep the right margin neatly aligned. Full justification is where spaces are added between words so that the text starts on the left margin and ends at the right margin. For instructional multimedia applications, you should avoid full justification. Full justification is harder to read than left justified text. With full justification, a reader's eyes move more because of the large spacing between words.

Hyphenating words can reduce the large spacing between words in fully justified text but hyphenated text tends to take longer to read than non-hyphenated text.

> **Practical Guideline:**
>
> Left justify paragraphs.

Center-justified paragraphs are also hard to read. Right-justified paragraphs are mainly useful for aligning numbers. The various types of justification are shown in figure 7.1.

Use left justify paragraphs!

full justification (to be avoided!)

> **Justification Samples**
>
> This paragraph is written with left justification. Note how the text only lines up with the left margin.
>
> This paragraph has center justification. Note the spaces at the left and right margins.
>
> This paragraph is written with full justification. Note the larger spaces between the words.
>
> This paragraph has right justification. Note how the text only lines up with the right margin.

Figure 7.1 – Variations of justification

7.4   Fonts

Most authoring tools have an adequate selection of fonts. It is safest for you to use standard system fonts like 'Ariel' that are available on every machine running Windows. If you use an uncommon font then the user's computer could substitute a font that may not be appropriate. If you do not use a system font, determine whether there is copyright clearance for distributing the font with the software. A fee or royalty may need to be paid in order to distribute the font. If there is any doubt, use the system fonts. It can be time-consuming but you could create a unique font if the supplied fonts do not meet your needs.

Choose a font that is clear and easily readable such as Arial, the font you are now reading, or Helvetica. Although some people may call these fonts "boring," readability is critical for instructional multimedia applications — especially when students will use the software for longer time periods. Italic, serif, script, decorative, and small fonts (see figure 7.2) can be hard to read depending on their size and the monitor's clarity. Some people prefer serif over non-serif fonts since the "feet" of serif fonts helps the eye move *and connect the words.* horizontally. This can result in an increase in reading speed. It is impossible to please everybody.

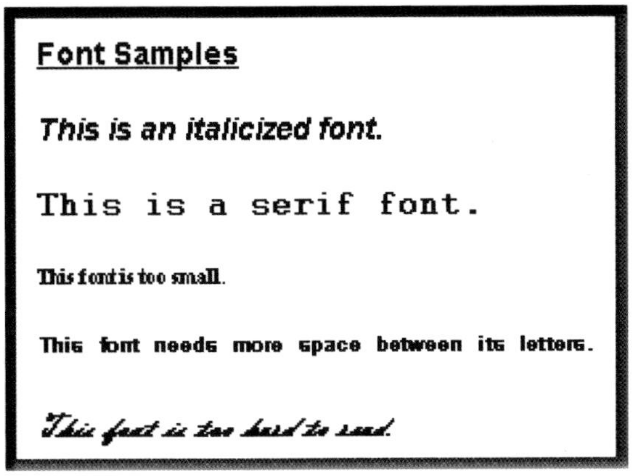

Font Samples

This is an italicized font.

This is a serif font.

This font is too small.

This font needs more space between its letters.

This font is too hard to read.

Figure 7.2 – Variations of fonts

Be sure that you keep the font constant. If a second font must be used, choose one that appears similar to the first. Too many fonts can be distracting, confuse the learner, and reduce the reading speed. This sentence with only three fonts proves the point.

Practical Guideline:

Use an easy to read system font and keep the font constant.

You can use font sizes to organize information, such as in headings, and to indicate importance. Headings should be in upper and lower case letters as uppercase text is less legible. Headings can also help learners quickly find pertinent information, especially when the headings make sense on their own. You can use a slighter smaller font size for labeling.

Use larger font sizes for children and seniors. For other audiences, the font size used should not allow for more than 60 characters on a 6-inch (15 cm) line. This helps increase readability, decrease fatigue, and maintain a student's patience and attention. As a proportional guideline, use a 14-point bold Ariel font for the main text given an 800 by 600 screen size. This is only a starting guideline since readability is affected by the screen size and font used. If there is any doubt, ask typical learners for their opinion.

For computer-managed presentations (CMP), ensure each screen is clearly legible by people in the last row in the room:
- As a guideline, to help ensure legibility, use larger font sizes such as 44 point for headers and 36 point for the main text. The font sizes can be proportionally varied for differently-sized rooms. Find out the size of the audience and room before preparing the presentation. Generally, use an easily readable font, such as Arial or Helvetica. Test the CMP for legibility before giving your presentation.
- If you project the CMP, test out the projection equipment before giving your presentation. The image quality can vary significantly between projectors.
- The projected image height should be about 1/6 of the distance between the first and last seat.
- Remember that future presentations may have people further away from the screen. A CMP designed and tested for a small room may not work in a large room.

There are more tips for creating computer-managed presentations in Appendix I.

7.5   Variable Spacing

Variable spacing (see figure 7.3) reduces the space between letters. This is especially noticed with the letters "i" and "l". Variable spacing allows you more characters per line but is not as "neat" as fixed spacing (see figure 7.3) where all letters use the same amount of horizontal space and consequently line up vertically.

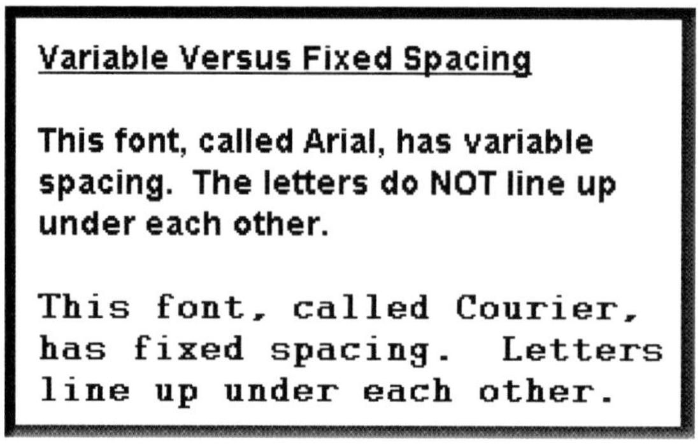

Variable Versus Fixed Spacing

This font, called Arial, has variable spacing. The letters do NOT line up under each other.

```
This font, called Courier,
has fixed spacing.  Letters
line up under each other.
```

Figure 7.3 – Variable versus fixed spacing

For practical reasons, such as screen size limitations and a faster reading speed, you should use fonts that have variable spacing, such as Arial. Note that if the letter spacing is too tight, the letters can be hard to distinguish from each other. Spacing that is too wide can prevent learners from grouping letters into meaningful forms and consequently decrease reading speed. The same holds true for spacing between words.

Practical Guideline:

Use fonts that have variable spacing.

7.6   Scrolling

Scrolling is adding new text lines to the bottom of the display while the top lines disappear. User-controlled scrolling text boxes are time-consuming and cumbersome for students to use. Many readers find scrolling frustrating. Do **not** include scrolling requirements whether the scrolling capabilities are present in the authoring tool or not. Rather than using scrolling, you should use more screens to show the text or allow learners to click on buttons to instantly see previous or subsequent information.

If you are required to use scrolling, allow learners to control the display. Moving text can be a problem for many readers, especially those with disabilities.

7.7   Display Speed

Some authoring tools allow designers to control the text's display speed. For example, the display speed can be slowed down so that individual letters can be seen to appear one at a time. Fast readers find it annoying to be held back by slow display speeds. Learners who read slower than the display speed will be distracted by text appearing below where they are reading. This causes a decrease in comprehension. Some students will wait for all of the text to appear before they begin reading. In the meantime, they can get bored or frustrated waiting for it to appear.

Since the reading rate of most groups will have wide variability, always instantly display text. As a minimum, instantly display at least one paragraph at a time. If reading must be controlled between main points or ideas, allow the student to read a part of the material and then wait for some input (e.g., "Click to continue") before displaying more information.

Practical Guideline:

In general, instantly display text.

7.8   Screen Focus Points

People read English from left to right and top to bottom. Since people tend to focus on a curved path along the screen, you should try to place key points along the curve. The best location for a key point, such as a formula, is the screen's upper left area. Poor areas for key points are the screen's top right and bottom left. Place non-critical or unimportant information in the top right and bottom left. These areas are illustrated in figure 7.4.

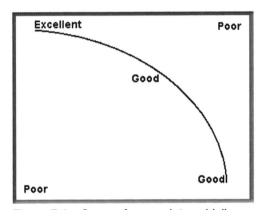

Figure 7.4 – Screen focus points guidelines

There are cases where this curve cannot be used. For example, this can happen if a visual occupies the top half of the screen and supporting text fills the bottom half.

7.9   Hypertext and Hypermedia

Hypertext is text that is indexed and linked in a logical manner to other information. Hypertext allows learners to quickly get more information by activating, such as by clicking a mouse, highlighted parts of the screen. Highlighted active words are sometimes called "Hot words". Hypermedia goes beyond hypertext by providing access to a variety of media. Each object can have one or more links to it. Think of all of the links as being a three-dimensional web.

Hypertext and hypermedia are useful for research projects in that they allow learners to access information in which they are interested, pursue unique ideas, and learn in unplanned ways. Hypertext and hypermedia can also be used for simple information retrieval such as searching an encyclopedia, creative writing projects including a hyper-novel or hyper-report, and specialized reference materials like automobile repair procedures that require a variety of media.

In general, hypertext and hypermedia applications simply provide access to information rather than teaching specified learning outcomes. There are a number of reasons why hypertext and hypermedia can be weak from an instructional perspective. Students may **not**:

- learn effectively if there is no interaction that requires them to think about the material
- be able to differentiate between accurate and inaccurate information (both of which are found on the Internet)
- know how to find needed information if it is not obviously presented
- choose important linked information
- understand the logic or links the author used to organize the material
- have the spatial visualization ability needed to effectively navigate through the content
- be capable of choosing their own paths to acquire specific knowledge
- have the cognitive capacity to deal with the content, especially if there is poor screen design
  - If the learner thinks too much about too many fonts and font sizes, objects, navigation aids, and screen layouts, the learner may not be able to mentally process the content.
- see important information
  - Learners are more likely to miss information if scrolling is needed to find the information or if the information is "deeper" than they searched.
- be able to prevent themselves from getting lost
- be able to prevent themselves from accessing more information than they can mentally process
- spend much time on the content, as learners tend to skim material that they find on the web rather than reflect on the material

---

Practical Guideline:

Do not assume that a hypertext or hypermedia application will result in effective learning.

In other words, for learning to occur in hypertext and hypermedia environments, student learning should be specifically planned and guided. Follow the principles of instructional design. The software's design greatly affects the effectiveness of hypertext and hypermedia systems.

Summary

In a multimedia production, text can be an important part of your media mix since text can be effectively used to teach many skills. For effectiveness, you should keep text short, clear, concise, and simple. There are other guidelines you should follow for minimizing reading, writing style, and writing rules. Use variable spacing and left justify paragraphs.

Other ways you can help the reader include keeping the font constant, using variable spacing, avoiding scrolling, instantly displaying text, and placing key points in the screen's upper left corner.

Hypertext is text that is indexed and linked in a logical manner to other information. Hypermedia provides access to a variety of media. Each object can have one or more links to it. Hypertext and hypermedia are useful for research, information retrieval, creative writing projects, and specialized reference materials. In general, hypertext and hypermedia applications simply provide access to information rather than teaching specified learning outcomes.

Application Exercises

1) The following text appears on a computer screen. List at least seven things you can do to improve it.

   Students should be able to *rite* text that is effective on screens of computers, *describe* features of text that is written good, *list* considerations for the selection of fonts, *say* some reasons why variable spacing may be somewhat preferred over spacing that is fixed, and *state* why text should be fastly rather then slowly displayed.

2) What is the problem with locating important information, such as a formula, in the screen's bottom left corner?

3) State what is wrong with each sentence:
   a) There needs to be a meaning.
   b) Educators should periodically contemplate pedagogical paradigm shifts.
   c) Sometimes but not always you should consider thinking about how you could possibly change some of the ways that you write things.
   d) We should eliminate sexist, stereotypic, ethnic, and lifestyle comments from our writing.

4) Rewrite each sentence in question 3 to meet the guidelines for writing instructional multimedia text.

5) If you create an instructional hypertext application, what are some things you can do to help students learn?

Case Study

Six instructors were on a four-week professional development leave from their regular duties. During this time, the instructors participated in a workshop on creating instructional multimedia applications. One goal of the workshop was to create a small tutorial so that the instructors could apply what they learned. As a part of the instructional design process, the instructors searched for existing materials. The instructors were not able to find any existing multimedia products on the topic but were able to find print-based materials. These materials were used for reference purposes.

Case Study Question

Given that the instructors did **not** have any experience in writing text for instructional multimedia applications, what advice would you give for writing the text component?

References

Alessi, S., & Trollip, S. (1991). Computer-based instruction: Methods and development (2nd ed.). Englewood Cliffs, NJ: Prentice-Hall, Inc.

Ayersman, D. (1993). An overview of the research on learning styles and hypermedia environments. Paper presented at the 1993 Annual Convention of the Eastern Educational Research Association, Clearwater Beach, Florida.

Berry, L. (2000). Cognitive effects of web page design. In Abbey, B. (Ed.), Instructional and cognitive impacts of web-based education. (pp. 41-55). Hershey, PA: Idea Group Publishing.

Ellis, D., Ford, H., & Wood, F. (1993, February). Hypertext and learning styles. The Electronic Library, 11(1), 13-18.

Garner, K. (1991, Summer/Fall). 20 rules for arranging text on a screen. Emerging Technologies Bulletin, 16, 2-4.

Gillingham, M. (1988). Text in computer-based instruction: What the research says. Journal of Computer-Based Instruction, 15(1), 1-6.

Hartley, J. (1985). Designing instructional text. New York, NY: Kogan Page.

Hirai, S. (1994, January). A few words on type. The Computer Paper, 7(1), 94-98.

Jonassen, D., & Wang, S. (1993, Winter). Acquiring structural knowledge from semantically structured hypertext. Journal of Computer-Based Instruction, 20(1), 1-8.

Miller, S., & Miller, K. (2000). Theoretical and practical considerations in the design of web-based instruction. In Abbey, B. (Ed.), Instructional and cognitive impacts of web-based education. (pp. 156-177). Hershey, PA: Idea Group Publishing.

Reiser, R., & Gagne, R. (1983). Selecting media for instruction. Englewood Cliffs, NJ: Educational Technology Publications.

Reizner, D. (1997, October). Tips to clip. AV Video & Multimedia Producer, 19(10), 29.

Romiszowski, A. (1988). The selection and use of instructional media: For improved classroom teaching and for interactive, individualized instruction (2nd ed.). New York, NY: Nichols Publishing.

Rosenborg, V., Green, B., Hester, J., Knowles, W., & Wirsching, M. (1993). A guide to multimedia. Carmel, IN: New Riders Publishing.

Staninger, S. (1994, July-August). Hypertext technology: Educational consequences. Educational Technology, 34(6), 51-53.

Treasury Board of Canada Secretariat (Government of Canada). (2004, March, 5). Common Look and Feel for the Internet. Retrieved January 30, 2005 from http://www.cio-dpi.gc.ca/clf-nsi/guide/guide_e.asp

Vaughan, T. (1993). Multimedia: Making it work. Berkeley, CA: Osborne McGraw-Hill.

Watzman, S. (1995). Information design principles for the interface designer. Session Handout Book of the Performance Support '95 Conference, September 6-8, 1995, Washington, DC.

Xerox Corporation. (1988). Xerox publication standards: A manual of style and design. New York, NY: Watson-Guptill Publications.

Chapter 8: Audio

Learning Outcomes

After completing this chapter, you should be able to:
- list skills effectively taught with audio
- state uses for speech, sounds, and music
- list general principles for writing narration and dialogue scripts
- describe factors affecting audio quality
- explain how a sound designer can help a project
- calculate the storage space required for digital audio
- describe MIDI technology

Introduction

Audio is another medium that you can incorporate into instructional multimedia applications. It is important for you to consider audio as a part of the media mix since some skills are extremely difficult to teach without audio while other skills can be more effectively taught if audio is combined with other media. This chapter describes how audio relates to learning, discusses how speech, sounds, and music can be used in multimedia productions, and provides script-writing guidelines. This chapter also explains how audio quality can affect a product, discusses digital sound, and describes the musical instrument digital interface (MIDI). (See the Media Selection chapter for more details on audio.)

8.1   Audio and Learning

You can use audio to effectively teach many skills such as attitudes and intellectual skills. You can also use audio to gain attention, give feedback, give directions, personalize computers, provide realism such as through presenting actual speeches, make annotations, provide multilingual support, accommodate non-readers, and provide meaning for images or image collections.

> **Practical Guideline:**
>
> Design audio to keep the students attentive.

For audio to be effective for learning, you need to ensure that the students pay attention, as with all media. If a student is not listening, audio becomes a part of the environment. Keep students involved through posing questions that make students think and keeping the audio clips short. This is critical since aural memory is **not** particularly retentive. You can aid a student's aural memory by enabling them to control the audio, such as repeating it as needed. Students must also be able to understand the audio. Consider developing parallel audio versions in other languages.

Audio can be classified into the categories of speech, sounds, and music.

8.2   Speech

You can use speech in the form of a narration or dialogue to teach effectively. To enhance what is directly said, you can also convey meaning through:
- emphasis
    - You can add emphasis through stressing a word.
- inflection
    - Add inflection by altering the pitch or tone, such as raising the pitch at the end of a sentence to indicate a question.
- aural mood
    - Establish aural mood through choosing specific words such as crashed versus hit or fantastic versus good.

To avoid confusion when using narration with text, ensure that the audio exactly matches the text. However, matching the audio to the text can be problematic since changes or edits are common. Since it can be difficult to change the audio, record the audio **only** after your script has been thoroughly evaluated.

Practical Guideline:

Record narration after your script is finalized.

Although using professionals will increase those specific budget items, consider hiring professional actors, narrators, and others like scriptwriters. Their quality will show through and ensure that the audio is effective. After reading the script and context, professionals tend to be able to quickly understand the overall approach and deliver the appropriate style at the right pace. Also, they will complete the recordings in less time than amateurs will need through requiring fewer retakes. They do this by quickly making modifications after you give them feedback.

When you select actors and narrators, ensure that they are credible and appropriate for the audience. For example, be sure that the audience will identify with them. Peers or respected professionals are often good choices. Actors and narrators need to have an appropriate accent, sound the right age, and be of the appropriate sex (if it makes a difference). As a rule, male voices tend to be more authoritative and credible while female voices tend to be friendlier. Note that two or more voices can add variety and thus increase interest and attention.

8.2-1   Script Writing Guidelines

A script is a text copy of a narration or dialogue. When you write scripts:
- Write for listening not reading.
    - Practice the script aloud. The words should flow smoothly.
    - Use a conversational style with the direct "you".
- Use simple sentences with familiar words.
    - The actors/narrators must be able to easily follow the script without faltering.
    - The actors/narrators must be able to easily use the correct pronunciation (e.g., ske-dule versus shed-ule) and provide the appropriate emphasis. The correct pronunciation can be determined as a part of the audience analysis.
- Use short phrases to allow the learner time to understand and synthesize the material.
    - The delivery rate must be appropriate for the audience.
    - Include pauses to let the learners mentally process the information.
- Make the audience think by posing questions.
    - Provide a long enough pause for learners to think and formulate answers.
    - Remember to provide an answer.
- Double space the script so the actor/narrator can make annotations.

- Do **not** have the script split onto two pages.
  - This may lead to an inappropriate pause and/or increase the chance of hearing paper rustle.

Practical Guideline:

Ask the audience questions to ensure they think about the content.

8.3   Sounds

Sounds can be very effective and even necessary to teach certain skills. For example, these include fixing equipment when a sound indicates a specific malfunction as well as diagnosing medical problems such as heart defects. Consider providing sounds that students would not hear in traditional classrooms. Alternatively, sounds can be used to simply "spice up" computer-managed presentations or slide shows. However, if the presentation is inherently weak then sound will not "save" it.

Practical Guideline:

Sound will not save a weak presentation!

You can use sound effects to:
- add realism
- generate emotions
- define space (e.g., distance and direction)
- establish a locale or create an environment (e.g., crashing waves for a beach scene)
- emphasize an action (e.g., screeching tires indicate hurrying)
- intensify an action (e.g., time length or loudness of the emphasis action)
- depict an identity (e.g., slurred speech for a drunk)
- set the pace (e.g., roar of an engine)
- provide a counterpoint (e.g., using unexpected sounds as is done in comedies)
- symbolize meaning (e.g., church bells symbolizing a funeral or wedding)
- unify transitions (e.g., providing continuity between scenes)

Base your sound design on sounds heard in the real world. Sound effects that do not sound right can be distracting.

To decide whether you really need sounds, take the sounds out. If the audience still understands the messages, you probably do not need the sounds. Remember that silence can also send a message.

Note that you should adjust the sound's volume to suit the content. For example, do **not** let sounds overpower a narrator. Also, do **not** use sounds repetitiously. Students sometimes enjoy sounds the first time they hear it but with repetition the sound can become obnoxious.

8.4   Music

Music is a universal language that all learners can appreciate. You can use music to set and change moods, feelings, and atmosphere as well as achieve the same purposes as sound effects. You can add music to slide shows and other applications to provide ambience for the viewer. You may want to add music to an attract sequence or the main menu. Tools exist that enable novices to create customized music based on specified parameters such as music type (e.g., Rock, Pop or Jazz), length, and whether it should be energetic. If you loop the music for continuous play, choose an audio clip designed for that purpose or it will sound like it is skipping when it starts over. Remember that repetitious music can be distracting and become annoying. One solution is to provide a music on/off button.

Note that stock music is less expensive than creating custom or original music. However, be careful in that competitors can also use stock music.

With respect to copyright, you may have to get clearance from both the music composer as well as the music publisher. Remember that even if the copyright to the composer has expired (e.g., older classical music), the publisher will likely retain rights.

8.5 Audio Quality

Audio quality can affect your product's "professional feel" or credibility and even the instructional effectiveness. For example, with respect to effectiveness, higher audio quality can be important for older target audiences since there is a gradual hearing loss with age.

The quality of the equipment and surroundings used for recording and playback affects your product. Professional quality sound requires a quality microphone and cables. The microphone must also be appropriate for the situation. For example, unidirectional microphones are best for recording sounds directly in front of the microphone, multidirectional microphones can be better for recording sounds all around the microphone, and lapel microphones can be effective for recording a speaker even though they are prone to recording clothes rustling. In general, uni-directional microphones are usually preferred over omni-directional microphones. Quality audio can be difficult to record when actors move, microphones need to be hidden, and there are background noises. Tiny wireless microphones, albeit expensive, can eliminate or minimize these difficulties. Wireless microphones are more convenient than wired microphones but have the inconvenience of requiring batteries that sometimes wear out in the middle of a recording. You may need an audio mixer to control the relative volume of different audio sources or to prevent one source from being too loud or dominant.

Your audio output quality can only be as good as the weakest link in the chain. In some multimedia workstations, the weakest link is the speakers. Depending on what you need to be heard, this can be a problem. You can fit workstations with external loudspeakers to help ensure high-quality audio. The weakest link could also be from a low-quality microphone or poor source material, such as recordings from many years ago when high-quality sound recording was not possible.

Practical Guideline:
Audio output quality can only be as good as the weakest link in the chain.

During recording, you should be careful to limit or eliminate unwanted background noises including people talking, air conditioning, fans, wind, echoes, phones ringing, computers, and interference such as between power lines and microphone cables. There are many tricks to solving these problems such as simply turning things off, using a wind screen, using blankets to smother sounds, removing grills from air ducts, and keeping microphones close to the source and away from reflecting surfaces that can cause echoes. However, note that normal background sounds can help create a feeling of realism. For example, including an office's "white noise" can make your recording realistic even if the noise has nothing to do with teaching the skill. This white noise can also be used to replace the extraneous sounds a narrator makes when talking, such as breathing in. White noise is a more natural sound than total silence. You can also shorten the gaps due to breathing in by about one-third to make the narration seem cleaner and more energetic.

As with video technology, using audio technology is an art. To maintain high quality, you should consider hiring a sound designer to help with specifics such as the type of microphone, location of the sound boom, having the microphone or sound boom follow the action, acoustics, and listening for problems as the audio is being recorded. Naturally, a sound designer costs money but "you get what you pay for".

Note that the built-in microphones of camcorders are inadequate for obtaining quality sound. Ideally, use a sound boom, even though it has the associated cost of an operator. Preferably, place a sound boom above the actor's head, out of camera range. Alternatively, placing it beneath the actor's head and pointing it up can work. The closer the microphone is to the actor's mouth, the more of the actor's voice and less extraneous noise is recorded.

8.6   Digital Audio

You can directly record audio into a digital format, transfer audio from other digital sources, or convert an analog audio signal, such as from an audiocassette tape, from a natural waveform to a series of 1's and 0's that computers can interpret. This is shown in figure 8.1.

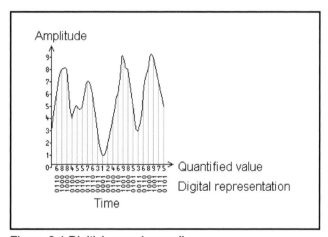

Figure 8.1 Digitizing analog audio

As a general rule, when you record audio with your computer, use at least a 16-bit system to sufficiently minimize the effect of the noise or unwanted sound. As the number of bits increase, more digital data is recorded giving more accurate recordings. A bit represents a "1" or "0," the smallest amount of computer data. There are 8 bits in a byte – the basic storage unit of computer data. 16-bit sound contains twice as much information as 8-bit sound. Do **not** record 8-bit sound. Once you digitize audio at 8-bits, you cannot do better than that minimal quality.

16-bit sound is more accurate than the human ear and is all you typically need especially if your application will only include voice clips. When you need to maintain high quality through the editing process, assume you will need to record with 24-bit or 32-bit sound. You can later reduce the final product to 16-bit or possibly 8-bit sound. Test the final quality of 8-bit sound before you choose to reduce all of the audio to that level, as it may not be adequate. Monophonic (mono) or single-channel sound is adequate for voice and requires one-half of the storage space that stereophonic (stereo) or two-channel sound needs. Most instructional multimedia applications do **not** need stereo sound.

Sampling rates indicate how often data is recorded. Higher sampling rates (e.g., 44 or 48 kHz) provide much better sound than lower sampling rates (e.g., 11 kHz). Higher sampling rates require more storage space. Use higher sampling rates if high-quality audio is needed, such as for listening to bird songs or equipment defect noises, and if the data will be edited. However, for most productions this high quality is overkill. 22 kHz is adequate for voice clips. If you record audio with an uncommon sampling rate that the authoring software does not handle, the software may change the audio to the nearest standard sampling rate and consequently sound differently than the original. Note that you may not be able to simultaneously play audio recorded with different sampling rates or bit sizes.

Digital Audio Tape (DAT) systems can record high-quality sound. However, DAT systems also record unwanted background noises, coughs from other rooms, and noises from the microphone being handled.

Practical Guideline:

In general, record at least 16-bit sound with a 44 kHz sampling rate when high-quality audio is needed or if the data will be edited.

You can create a problem by recording with a higher number of bits, higher sampling rates, or stereo since digital audio inherently requires a large amount of storage space. The number of bytes you need can be approximated with the formula: number of seconds x (number of bits ÷ 8) x sample rate in Hz x number of channels. Approximate storage requirements are shown in Table 8-1. Note that these values are **per second**. CD-Audio recordings are usually recorded with 16-bits at 44 kHz (44,000 Hz). Consequently, CD-Audio applications typically hold a maximum of 74 minutes of music on 700-megabyte discs. Do a calculation to estimate the amount of data your final product will need to ensure that your data will fit on the selected storage medium. Remember that compressing the data increases the amount you can store.

Table 8-1		
Sound quality	**File size/second**	**Recommended uses**
8-bit, 11 kHz, mono	11,000 bytes	Minimal-quality voice playback
8-bit, 22 kHz, mono	22,000 bytes	
8-bit, 44 kHz, mono	44,000 bytes	
8-bit, 11 kHz, stereo	22,000 bytes	
8-bit, 22 kHz, stereo	44,000 bytes	
8-bit, 44 kHz, stereo	88,000 bytes	
12-bit, 32 kHz, 4 channel	192,000 bytes	Mini-DV without compression
16-bit, 11 kHz, mono	22,000 bytes	
16-bit, 22 kHz, mono	44,000 bytes	Record voice, sound effects
16-bit, 44 kHz, mono	88,000 bytes	
16-bit, 11 kHz, stereo	44,000 bytes	
16-bit, 22 kHz, stereo	88,000 bytes	Special sound effects
16-bit, 44 kHz, stereo	176,000 bytes	Music
16-bit, 48 kHz, stereo	192,000 bytes	Mini-DV without compression
24-bit, 11 kHz, mono	33,000 bytes	
24-bit, 22 kHz, mono	66,000 bytes	
24-bit, 44 kHz, mono	132,000 bytes	
24-bit, 11 kHz, stereo	66,000 bytes	
24-bit, 22 kHz, stereo	132,000 bytes	
24-bit, 44 kHz, stereo	264,000 bytes	High-quality music
24-bit, 48 kHz, stereo	288,000 bytes	DVD standard without compression

Practical Guideline:

Estimate the amount of data your final product will need to hold to ensure that your data will fit on the selected storage medium.

With software tools, as shown in figure 8.2, digital audio can easily be edited (e.g., by cutting, pasting, and moving) and manipulated (e.g., amplified or faded).

Compact disc audio is based on the international "red book" standard. This allows you to address audio by minutes, seconds, and frames. For example, the red book address 49:07:63 specifies the audio location at 49 minutes, 7 seconds, and 63 frames. (Compact disc audio plays at 75 frames per second.)

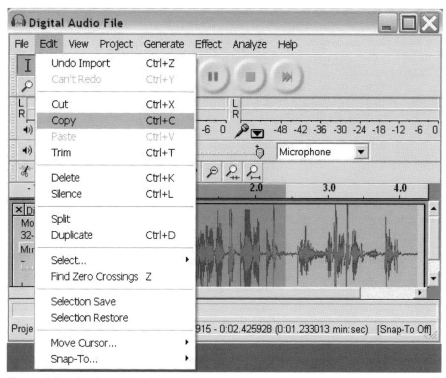

Figure 8.2 – Audio editing tool

There are numerous common file format standards that you can include in your applications. You can recognize them by their extensions (e.g., .au, .aiff, and .wav). Practical factors for choosing a file format include whether your editing tools can edit the file type and whether your authoring tool can play the file.

If you do not have time to record and edit your own audio, you can find clips on the Internet or purchase DVD-ROMs/CD-ROMs containing generic clips such as sound effects and music. Ensure that these audio clips are copyright cleared and can be distributed royalty-free.

Audio quality is partly dependent on the when the recording was made. Since audio technology has improved over the years, newer recordings tend to be of a higher quality than older recordings. However, buying a disc does not guarantee high audio quality. If the material was recorded and edited in analog then the material is more likely to have "noise" than material recorded and edited digitally.

For your computer-managed presentations that require audio from a number of discs, for convenience, consider storing and playing back the audio from a hard drive or a high-bandwidth intranet connection.

8.7   Musical Instrument Digital Interface (MIDI)

MIDI is a standard that allows personal computers, synthesizers, sequencers, keyboards, drum machines... to interface with each other at little cost. You can use MIDI technology to create original music or to play existing music. The "general" MIDI standard specifies instruments that most synthesizers recognize in the same way. Since the general MIDI standard is not perfectly followed, test your MIDI files on a variety hardware systems or consider converting your final MIDI files to wave files. Wave files are always played back accurately.

MIDI files only include instructions for the synthesizer rather than music itself. For example, the instruction may be to play a quarter beat middle C note on the flute as well as a variety of other instruments simultaneously. Consequently, MIDI files require much less storage space than wave files. For example, a typical MIDI file requires 200 bytes/second compared to a range of 11,000 to 264,000 bytes/second.

A limitation of MIDI is that sounds can only be reproduced if they are programmed into the synthesizer. So many sounds, such as the human voice, animal sounds, and sounds of machinery, cannot be reproduced. This is an advantage of "wave" technology over MIDI technology.

Using MIDI in multimedia applications requires both you and the users to have a MIDI chip on the sound card. Many sound cards contain a MIDI chip. MIDI music can be accurately recorded digitally onto your computer for editing or manipulation and playback. If you do not have the necessary hardware and software or know enough about instruments, keys, tempos, pitch, timbre, clefs, and notations, pay professionals to create, record, and edit the music. From a practical perspective, it is easiest and most cost-effective for you to use MIDI files that are readily available on DVD-ROM/CD-ROM discs.

Summary

In a multimedia production, audio can be an important part of your media mix since you can effectively use audio to teach many skills such as attitudes and intellectual skills. Sounds can be very effective and even necessary to teach certain skills. You can also use audio to gain attention, give feedback, give directions, personalize computers, make annotations, provide multilingual support, accommodate non-readers, and provide meaning for images. For audio to be effective for learning, you need to ensure that the students pay attention. Keeping students involved is critical since aural memory is not particularly retentive.

Audio can be classified into the categories of speech, sounds, and music. Speech conveys meaning through emphasis, inflection, and aural mood. Speech can take the form of narration and dialogue. A script is a text copy of a narration or dialogue. There are many guidelines for writing scripts. You should consider hiring a professional scriptwriter.

Audio quality can affect your product's "professional feel" or credibility and even the instructional effectiveness. There are many factors affecting audio quality. A sound designer can help you attain the quality needed. For digital audio, use at least a 16-bit system to maintain high audio quality.
MIDI is a standard that allows personal computers, synthesizers, sequencers, keyboards, drum machines... to interface with each other at little cost. Use MIDI technology to create original music or to play existing music. The "general" MIDI standard specifies instruments that most synthesizers recognize in the same way. It is easiest to use MIDI files that are readily available on DVD-ROM/CD-ROM discs.

Application Exercises

1) Which voice, a doctor's or a rock star's, would be better for teaching teenagers to avoid drugs? Justify your answer.
2) Which of the following statements is **false**?
   a) Audio can be excellent for teaching attitudes.
   b) Aural memory tends to be very retentive.
   c) Speakers should ask the audience questions.
   d) Inflection affects the meaning of speech.
3) Which of the following statements is **false**?
   a) A professional narrator ensures credibility.
   b) Audio quality is determined by the weakest link in the system.
   c) Background noises can be used to provide realism.
   d) Music can be used to set and change moods.
4) If you record a 10-second audio clip in stereo at 24-bits and 22 kHz. How many bytes of storage will you require, assuming no compression?
5) If you record a 15-second audio clip in mono at 16-bits and 11 kHz. How many bytes of storage will you require, assuming no compression?

Case Study

Six instructors were on a four-week professional development leave from their regular duties. During this time, the instructors participated in a workshop on creating instructional multimedia applications. One goal of the workshop was to create a small tutorial so that the instructors could apply what they learned. As a part of the instructional design process, the instructors determined that audio was not required for teaching the concepts. However, audio could be used to provide some realism.

Case Study Question

Given that the project timeline was very short, should audio have been added to provide some realism?

References

Alten, S. (1990). Audio in media (3rd ed.). Belmont, CA: Wadsworth Publishing Company.

Habstritt, G. (2000, February). Sounds important: Spreading the word about new media audio. newmedia.pro, 3(1), 9-13.

Hofstetter, F. (1994). Multimedia presentation technology. Belmont, CA: Wadsworth Publishing Company.

Huntley, J., & Easley, G. (1994). The brown book of multimedia. Dubuque, IA: Wm. C. Brown Communications.

Macromedia. (1994). Multimedia essentials for windows. San Francisco, CA: Macromedia, Inc.

Marchant, B. (2004, March). Music rights and wrongs. AV Video Multimedia Producer, 26(3), 34.

Reiser, R., & Gagne, R. (1983). Selecting media for instruction. Englewood Cliffs, NJ: Educational Technology Publications.

Romiszowski, A. (1988). The selection and use of instructional media: For improved classroom teaching and for interactive, individual instruction (2nd ed.). New York, NY: Nichols Publishing.

Rose, J. (2000, March). Boom Mic Basics. DV, 8(3), 38-44.

Rose, J. (1998, May). Cutting remarks. DV, 6(5), 98, 100.

Rose, J. (1997, May). You can't always fix in the mix. DV, 5(5), 86-87.

Rosenborg, V., Green, B., Hester, J., Knowles, W., & Wirsching, M. (1993). A guide to multimedia. Carmel, IN: New Riders Publishing.

Schwier, R., & Misanchuk, E. (1993). Interactive multimedia instruction. Englewood Cliffs, NJ: Educational Technology Publications.

Stamberg, R. (2004, June). Sound design: Creating big impact with a small budget. AV Video Multimedia Producer, 26(6), 10.

Terwilliger, C. (2004, October). Voiceover 101: How to hire, direct and format scripts to get the most out of your talent in the studio. AV Video Multimedia Producer, 26(10), 20, 22.

Vaughan, T. (1993). Multimedia: Making it work. Berkeley, CA: Osborne McGraw-Hill.

Wood, E. (1993, October). A beginner's guide to multimedia. Computer Graphics World, 16(10), 71-84.

Chapter 9: Visuals

Learning Outcomes

After completing this chapter, you should be able to:
- describe how visuals affect learning
- describe how visuals can be designed to keep the message clear
- list some considerations for displaying visuals
- describe factors that can affect a visual's appearance
- list some considerations for costs of visuals
- design screens that effectively use visuals
- describe methods of digitizing images

Introduction

Visuals are another medium that you can incorporate into instructional multimedia solutions. It is important for you to consider visuals as a part of the media mix in a multimedia production since combining visuals with other media can significantly enhance learning. Some concepts are extremely difficult to teach without visuals.

Visual images can be considered to be "real" as in photographs and slides. Visual images can also be pictorial or diagrammatical representations of "real" objects. Graphic artists often create pictorial or diagrammatical representations.

This chapter describes how visuals relate to learning and presents guidelines on how you can keep the message clear and where to display visuals. As well, the appearance and costs of visuals are discussed. This chapter also provides you with practical considerations for digitizing images. (Check the Media Selection chapter for more details on visuals.)

9.1   Visuals and Learning

For instructional purposes, you can use visuals to illustrate objects and ideas, show relationships about objects and ideas, classify objects, and help teach psychomotor skills and attitudes. You can also use visuals to make abstract concepts concrete. For example, you can do this by graphically showing the relationship between interest rates and the time required to pay off a mortgage. Note that some learners have difficulty learning from abstract sources such as text, numbers, and symbols. Visual images are an alternative that can help these learners. Similarly, you can help these learners by presenting data with graphs, bar charts, and pie charts.

If you provide visuals, you will likely increase learning. Visuals provide an alternate learning path since certain parts of the brain process visuals while different parts process text. The concept that only the right side of the brain processes visuals while only the left side process text is not accurate. The original research was flawed.

> **Practical Guideline:**
>
> In general, adding visuals leads to increased learning.

Visuals become particularly valuable when you direct learners to focus their attention on specific details, which you can do through concise prompts or captions. A combination of text and visual images can result in a 15 to 50% increase in recall over either alone. Recall is increased for both simple skills, such as recalling facts, and complex skills, like performing operations. Lessons with visuals result in higher retention over long time periods (i.e., months). Visuals particularly benefit weak learners. Another reason you should include visuals, is that visuals can be mentally processed much faster than text. As well, students may be better able to transfer the skills learned to other situations.

In general, visuals can be valuable learning tools. Some ideas cannot be adequately expressed in words but can be readily depicted with visuals. How could you adequately describe the surface of Venus or the structure of DNA without a visual? Look at figure 9.1. Think about the words you would use to describe what this rhinoceros looks like. With those words and without seeing a visual, could learners accurately envision the rhinoceros, if the learner has not seen one before? For instructional multimedia applications, visuals can be particularly effective if students can control the length of time the visual remains on the screen, in other words proceed when they are ready.

Figure 9.1 – Hard to describe visual

Note that in some cases, a visual image may be more effective than a real image. Some learners may not be able to focus on all of the details that real images sometimes provide. In a related way, people will usually recognize a cartoonist's sketch of a hand as being a hand faster than a digitized image of a hand, even if a cartoonist's sketch of a hand has three fingers. Look at figures 9.2 and 9.3. Which do you more quickly recognize as a hand?

Complex visuals require more time to mentally process than simple images. Factor this in if the learner does not control the instruction's pace, such as in a computer-managed presentation. Note that learners will sometimes simplify complex visuals into a form they can understand. Given that, it makes sense to simplify images in the first place.

On screens with text and visuals, learners are naturally drawn to the visuals. As a minimum, your visuals will add variety to screens. Although irrelevant visuals do not help students learn relevant content, some images (e.g., humorous) can help "lighten" the material. Screen variety can increase attention and motivation and consequently indirectly affect learning positively.

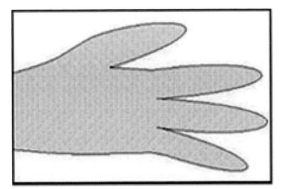

Figure 9.2 – Cartoon hand

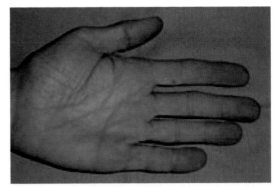

Figure 9.3 – Digitized hand

9.2   Keeping the Message Clear

To keep the message clear, your visuals should be self-explanatory, have labels, and only include relevant information!

Visuals Should Be Self-Explanatory

Self-explanatory visuals illustrate the message. If the image is not self-explanatory then you should determine how it could be done. At times, this goal may not be possible but you should at least aim for it. However, be sure to provide an explanation to link the visual to the idea you are conveying.

> **Practical Guideline:**
>
> As a rule, ensure your graphics are self-explanatory.

You should use the following methods to ensure message clarity:
- Keep the visual simple and only include essential information. For example, crop images to eliminate unnecessary details. Complex visuals can weaken the instruction by confusing or distracting the students.
- Match the visual's complexity to the learner's skill. Overly complex visuals are often ignored.
- Consider using simple diagrams instead of realistic images. Realistic images sometimes contain an overwhelming amount of detail that can distract the learner from understanding the message.
- Use a series of diagrams rather than a single complicated diagram. When explaining a process, use one visual per step. One technique you can use is to gradually build the visual from screen to screen.
- Add labels to diagrams to highlight key points. Horizontal labels are the easiest to read.

Only Include Information Relevant to the Screen

If you include extra information, you could clutter the screen and can cause confusion. On screens that build, some of the previous information may need to be erased or de-highlighted so that new key points are easily found. Build the visuals in logical straightforward sequential steps. Plan to allow the learner the capability to reverse the steps for easy review.

9.3   Displaying Visuals

To facilitate learning and to reduce searching time, you should display visuals consistently on one side of the text, as seen in figure 9.4. Unless you have a reason to do otherwise, place visuals to the left of the text. Since readers tend to start reading a screen from the upper left and examine visuals before reading text, placing visuals in the upper left reduces eye movement. If needed, you can place visuals to the right, above, and below text. However, you should avoid sandwiching images between text.

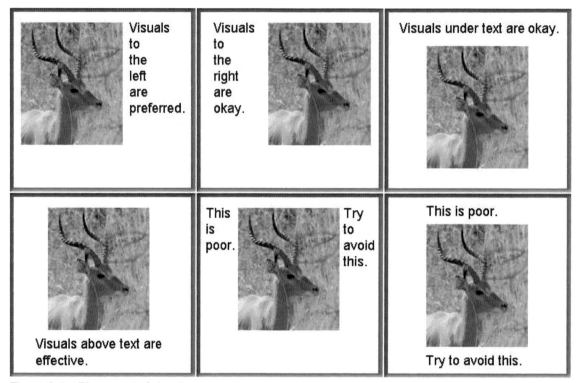

Figure 9.4 – Placement of visuals

Try to standardize the size of images in order to simplify your screen design process. Use what looks best, is appropriate, is necessary, and is logical. If possible, try to balance visuals with the text. Note how figure 9.5 shows an unbalanced screen in that it looks like it may tip to the left. Figures 9.6 and 9.7 show balanced screens, where figure 9.7 is balanced better than figure 9.6.

Keep related text on the same screen as the visual since comprehension is more difficult if students have to flip between visuals and text explanations. In general, display visuals instantly. Reading becomes difficult when other events distract the learner.

Note that the style of your visuals should match the text on the screen. Figure 9.8 shows a mismatch between the visuals and text while figure 9.9 shows a match.

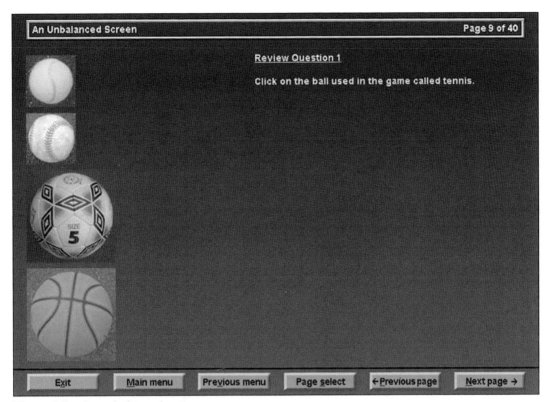

Figure 9.5 – An unbalanced screen

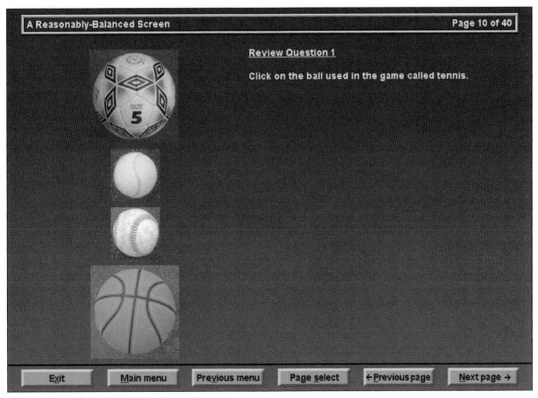

Figure 9.6 – A reasonably-balanced screen

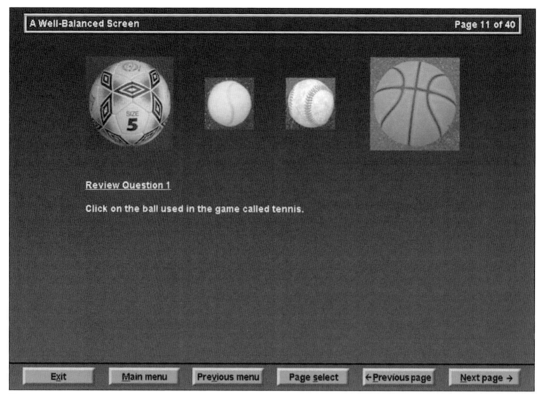

Figure 9.7 – A well-balanced screen

Figure 9.8 – Mismatched visual and text   "Cascades" courtesy of Jane Appleby © 2002

Figure 9.9 – Matched visual and text   "Cascades" courtesy of Jane Appleby © 2002

9.4   Appearance

An image's appearance is affected by many things such as screen size. Screen size refers to the number of pixels or dots on a screen. A minimal screen size of 800 x 600 with 16-bit color is adequate for many applications and can be shown on both new and old computers. When computer images are projected, the images are less clear than can be seen on quality monitors. Consider the quality of your images if you expect that the computer program may be projected. Applications made for larger screen sizes, with more colors, and higher quality source material will look better when projected. Images designed for larger screen sizes require more storage space, which is usually not a factor, and are harder to edit. Note that some people incorrectly use the term "resolution" when referring to "screen size". Resolution refers to the number of pixels per inch.

Graphics may have a staircase appearance in objects such as lines, circles, and arrows. A staircase appearance is affected by the screen resolution and whether the authoring tool has a "rounding" feature to minimize the staircase appearance. A staircase appearance can be acceptable (as in figure 9.10), but for elegance, use vertical, horizontal, and 45 degree lines that appear smooth (as in figure 9.11), assuming learning is not negatively affected.

Where appropriate, visuals should appear similar in color, brightness, and style. This helps provide continuity between screens. Figures 9.2 and 9.3 show visuals that do not match in style while figures 9.12 and 9.13 show visuals that match in style.

Visuals can be more effective when they appear 3-dimensional. Depth can provide extra information or simply provide sight-appeal. 3-dimensional images can be "seen" with special glasses but most applications do not need this level of realism.

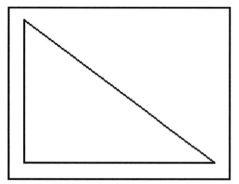

Figure 9.10 – Line with staircase appearance

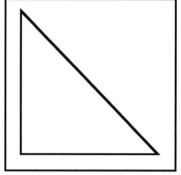

Figure 9.11 – Smooth 45 degree line

Figure 9.12 – Visual that matches in style

Figure 9.13 – Visual that matches in style

9.5   Costs

Since creating visuals can be difficult and costly, be sure your images are educationally sound. Visuals are, in a sense, more worthwhile to include if the students would not be able to view the images in the traditional instructional setting. If you add visuals simply for entertainment purposes, it may not be worth the cost and the visuals may even be viewed negatively.

It can be cost-effective for you to purchase a quality graphics package and hire a graphic artist. Although amateurs can easily create many effective images, only individuals with artistic abilities can fully exploit a graphics package's tools. Some specialized graphics packages can meet specific needs. For example, some packages allow you to quickly create realistic 3-dimensional landscape scenes. If you work with a graphics package other than the one provided in the authoring tool, be sure that the authoring tool can easily incorporate the images and that the graphics package can import images from other needed sources. Check for compatibility before undertaking significant development.

To prevent problems, plan for screen size. In general, you will have the clearest images if you capture your images in the size you need. However, if you capture at a larger size than you need, you can easily shrink the images, at a slight cost of image clarity, but then still have the source material in a larger size for applications that are later redeveloped for larger screen sizes. Remember that data is discarded when images are shrunken. It is also important to remember that you lose a significant amount of clarity whenever you enlarge images. When you enlarge a visual, such as the one shown in figure 9.14, pixels are either duplicated or interpolated. These images may appear "blurry," "blocky," or "jagged," as shown in figure 9.15.

Figure 9.14 – Original visual

Figure 9.15 – Enlarged visual

You should also plan for the color palette you will use. Different tools can have different palettes. Consequently, if different screens in the program have images with different palettes, there may be a "flash" when the user moves from screen to screen. The easiest way to prevent the flashing is to have the authoring tool convert each image to its own color palette when you import the images. Note that the Macintosh® color palette is a little different from the PC standard. Cross-platform applications may not look exactly as intended.

Practical Guideline:

Determine whether the graphics can easily be incorporated into the authoring tool before developing many visuals.

Alternatives to the expensive and time-consuming method of drawing original visuals include using clip art, which is readily available, and digitizing or scanning images. You can quickly and easily re-touch or modify existing images especially if you store the images in an accessible library or database.

9.6   Digitizing Images

You can also reduce costs by digitizing (e.g., with a screen capture utility, with a digital camera, or by scanning images). Alternatively, you can purchase digitized images from stock photo agencies.

Screen capture utilities allow you to digitize any image on the screen. There are many potential uses for captured screens. For example, image how you could use this utility to teach learners how to use a software program. All that you need to do is load the software and press the "hot key" to capture whatever is on the screen. Most tools will let you capture the image in the format you need. You can then use a graphics package to edit the image, as shown in figure 9.16. For example, you will likely need to crop off extraneous information.

Figure 9.16 – *Microsoft®Paint* graphics editing tool

Low-end digital cameras are affordable and can record quality images that can be downloaded to a computer for easy viewing, editing, manipulating, and printing. You can also import high-quality digital images from scanners – an excellent way to tap into the vast non-digital resources of images. Different scanners can capture photographs, positives, negatives, and 35 mm slides. Note that digitizing slides can be beneficial since slides are readily available and are of a high resolution.

Scanned images:
- can be in both color and gray-scale
    - Enhance image appearance by using "dithering" techniques. Dithering is a process that changes the color value of every pixel to the closest matching color value in the target palette. This makes it appear like there are more colors than are actually present. Dithering is particularly helpful when you need to display full-color images with 16 or 256 colors.
    - Note that dithered images may not scale well.
- can be of a very high quality
    - This mainly depends on the quality of the source material.
- tend to be of a poorer quality when the source is black and white materials such as newspapers
- are generally better when reducing large images than enlarging small images

Remember that scanned images may require written copyright clearance. Getting copyright clearance can be costly in terms of both time and money.

Practical Guideline:
Consider the potential time and cost savings from digitizing existing images.

You will find that uncompressed digitized images can require an enormous amount of storage space. For example, an 800 x 600 24-bit image requires 1,440,000 bytes of storage (800 times 600 times 24-bits divided by 8 bits per byte where a byte is the basic unit of computer storage). Most computers and DVD-ROM and CD-ROM drives can easy handle this data. However, as the data size increases, it is harder to smoothly animate the images in that some systems may not be able to process and display the data fast enough. If necessary, animate small-sized (e.g., 320 x 240 or 160 x 120) 16-bit or 8-bit images. If the data is to be delivered over a slow Internet connection, consider 8-bit images that are 160 x 120 in size. As shown in Table 9-1, the number of bits refers to the number of colors that can be simultaneously displayed. 16-bit images are acceptable for many applications. 24-bit images are sometimes necessary when specific details need to be seen. 24-bit images approximate what is called "true" or photorealistic color. Even though 24-bit images show about eight times as many colors as the human eye can distinguish between, 32-bit images more closely represent "true" color than 24-bit images. 32-bit images use 8 bits for buffering requirements such as blends and transparencies. Remember that final images will **not** appear clearer than the monitor can produce. You may need to address this factor.

Table 9-1		
Number of bits	**Number of colors**	**Suggested uses**
1	black and white	Line drawings
2	4	
4	16	Sketches
8	256	Low-quality photographs
16	65,536	High-quality photographs
24	16,777,216	Professional-quality photographs
32	16,777,216	Professional-quality photographs

Practical Guideline:
Estimate the amount of data your final product will need to hold to ensure that your data will fit on the selected storage medium.

You can use compression to reduce the storage requirements needed for visual images. You can use the JPEG (Joint Photographic Experts Group) standard compression technique to reduce image storage requirements of photographs by a 6:1 to 20:1 ratio without significant degradation. Other formats, like GIF – Graphics Interface Format, are excellent for compressing graphic images. The BMP (Bitmap) format has no compression and consequently results in proportionally large file sizes. However, BMP files can be reduced to 8-bit and even 4-bit color and still look reasonable. You should store images in a standard common file format (e.g., JPEG, GIF, BMP, TIFF – Tagged Image File Format...) so that you can easily transfer the image between hardware platforms and software packages. The BMP and TIFF standards are compatible between the Macintosh® and PC platforms. (Given there are so many "standards" it is somewhat ridiculous to call them standards.) If it is not already done, consider setting a visuals "standard" for all internal work. You can use software packages to readily convert images between different file formats. Note that you will lose image quality as you do more conversions.

Vector graphics are an alternative type of image. Vector graphics, sometimes called metafiles, are stored as a set of mathematical instructions. Vector graphics maintain their integrity with differing screen sizes. Vector graphics can be particularly useful when you only have a small amount of storage space. They can be easily resized and manipulated and tend to appear as intended – especially compared to digitized images. One potential problem is that vector graphics tend to look thinner on higher resolution screens. The Encapsulated Post-Script (EPS) format is compatible between the Macintosh® and PC platforms.

Single vector graphics, such as a box, appear relatively instantly on screens. However, a series of vector graphics, for example all of the lines and boxes needed to illustrate a skyscraper, may be seen to gradually display the image on slow computer systems.

Note that many high-quality generic images useful for multimedia presentations and productions are available for a fee. Ensure that these can be distributed royalty-free.

Summary

In a multimedia production, visuals can be an important part of your media mix since combining visuals with other media can significantly enhance learning. Some concepts are extremely difficult to teach without visuals. You can use visuals to illustrate objects and ideas, show relationships about objects and ideas, classify objects, help teach psychomotor skills and attitudes, and help make abstract concepts concrete.

To help ensure your message is understood, your visuals should be self-explanatory, should only include information relevant to the screen, and should not overwrite pertinent information.

Display visuals consistently on one side of the text, with the related text on the same screen.

Visuals are clearer in higher resolution images, may have a staircase appearance, should appear in similar color and brightness, and can be more effective when they appear 3-dimensional.

With respect to costs:
• Visuals can be difficult and costly to create.
• For cost-effectiveness, consider purchasing a quality graphics package and hiring a graphic artist. Determine whether the visuals can be incorporated into the authoring tool before significant development has taken place.
• Consider using clip art and scanning existing images.

Application Exercises

1) Would a videotape or a set of visuals be more effective for showing how to service a photocopier? What else could you do to make your choice even more effective?
2) Which of the following statements is **false**?
   a) Simple visuals can be more effective than detailed visuals.
   b) Students tend to mentally process text faster than visuals.
   c) Using visuals tends to lead to increased learning.
   d) Visuals can be excellent for teaching attitudes.
3) Which of the following statements is **false**?
   a) As a guideline, display visuals to the left of text.
   b) If possible, make visuals self-explanatory.
   c) On screens that build, display all of the previous information.
   d) Display text and visuals consistently with respect to each other.

4) A 320 x 240 screen size 24-bit image requires 230,400 bytes of storage. How much storage would be needed if the image were:
    a) reduced to an 8-bit image
    b) reduced to a 160 x 120 screen size
    c) compressed with a 6:1 compression ratio
5) A CD-ROM has 600,000,000 bytes available for storing visual images.
    a) If the visual images need to be at a screen size of 320 x 240 and 16-bit quality, how many visual images can be stored without compression?
    b) If the images can be compressed with a 10:1 ratio, how many can be stored?

Case Study

Six instructors were on a four-week professional development leave from their regular duties. During this time, the instructors participated in a workshop on creating instructional multimedia applications. One goal of the workshop was to create a small tutorial so that the instructors could apply what they learned. As a part of the instructional design process, the instructors determined that visuals were required for teaching the concepts. There was a problem in that none of the instructors had any experience or expertise in creating visuals. Visuals were found in existing print materials, however, this material was owned by others.

Case Study Questions

1) Given that the project timeline was very short, should visuals have been included in the tutorial?
2) Given the lack of graphics expertise, what are some ways visual images could have been included in the program?
3) If numerous high-quality visual images were added, how might the product's market potential be affected?

References

Alessi, S., & Trollip, S. (1991). Computer-based instruction: Methods and development (2nd ed.). Englewood Cliffs, NJ: Prentice-Hall, Inc.

Aspillaga, M. (1991). Screen design: Location of information and its effects on learning. Journal of Computer-Based Instruction, 18(3), 89-92.

Baek, Y., & Layne, B. (1988). Color, graphics, and animation in a computer-assisted learning tutorial lesson. Journal of Computer-Based Instruction, 15(4), 131-135.

Berry, L. (2000). Cognitive effects of web page design. In Abbey, B. (Ed.), Instructional and cognitive impacts of web-based education. (pp. 41-55). Hershey, PA: Idea Group Publishing.

Leflore, D. (2000). Theory supporting design guidelines for web-based instruction. In Abbey, B. (Ed.), Instructional and cognitive impacts of web-based education. (pp. 102-117). Hershey, PA: Idea Group Publishing.

Hofstetter, F. (1994). Multimedia presentation technology. Belmont, CA: Wadsworth Publishing Company.

Reiser, R., & Gagne, R. (1983). Selecting media for instruction. Englewood Cliffs, NJ: Educational Technology Publications.

Riding, R., & Sadler, S. (1992, October). Type of instructional material, cognitive style, and learning performance. Educational Studies, 18(3), 323-339.

Rieber, L., & Kini, A. (1991). Theoretical foundations of instructional applications of computer-generated animated visuals. Journal of Computer-Based Instruction, 18(3), 83-88.

Sawyer, T. (1985). Human factors considerations in computer-assisted instruction. Journal of Computer-Based Instruction, 12(1), 17-20.

Schwier, R., & Misanchuk, E. (1993). Interactive multimedia instruction. Englewood Cliffs, NJ: Educational Technology Publications.

Villarreal, K., & Oller, B. (1990). A graphic picture is worth... Emerging Technologies Bulletin, 14, 9-10.

Watzman, S. (1995). Information design principles for the interface designer. Session Handout Book of the Performance Support '95 Conference, September 6-8, 1995, Washington, DC.

Wood, E. (1993, October). A beginner's guide to multimedia. Computer Graphics World, 16(10), 71-84.

Chapter 10: Video

Learning Outcomes

After completing this chapter, you should be able to:
- list instructional uses of video
- describe the strengths and weaknesses of video
- describe the pros and cons in gathering existing materials
- describe the pros and cons in filming materials
- determine whether materials should be gathered or filmed
- create video for instructional multimedia applications
- list reasons why hiring a media producer can be advantageous
- describe what you can do to help ensure a professional video production

Introduction

Video is another medium that you can incorporate into your instructional multimedia production. It is important for you to consider video as a part of the media mix in a multimedia production since combining video with other media can significantly enhance learning.

This chapter describes the strengths and weaknesses of video and what you can do to help ensure the production is of high quality. Distinctions are made between high-end and low-end applications. (See the Media Selection and Compression/Decompression chapters for related information on video.)

Note that there are major differences between video and film. However, this book uses the terms film and video synonymously as is done by most lay-people.

10.1 Strengths of Video

With respect to teaching, you can use video, which is usually combined with audio, effectively for:
- demonstrating procedures, changes, and processes
  - Learning can be especially effective when the learner can control the video with features including playing when ready or replaying as needed.
- teaching attitudes and values
  - Emotional material and/or real-life examples can be shown.
  - Text may be needed to help explain the attitudes and values.
- making abstract concepts concrete
- classifying and comparing information
  - For classifying and comparing information, video is particularly valuable when the information can be instantly accessed.

Video can also be useful for:
- gaining and holding attention as well as motivating learners
  - This can be done through special effects, color, motion, audio, historical clips...
  - This can increase retention and recall of information.
  - The use of motion visuals often promotes exploration. Exploration can be powerful in packages that include visual database.

- introducing topics or procedures
    - This can be easy and pleasant for students especially when the alternative is lengthy text.
- presenting visually-rich material that would otherwise be hard to explain (e.g., chemistry and physics experiments, how an amoeba moves, heart valves opening and closing, human interactions...)
    - Information that needs to be visual or have realism can be presented. Examples of these respectively include the courtship rituals of animals and human behaviors for changing attitudes.
    - Audio, such as lung and heart sounds, can also be presented.
- making presentations visual
    - Video can be projected or displayed on televisions or monitors for groups of students.
    - Motion visual databases should be easily and quickly accessible. For example, you can do this through menus.
    - It is helpful if you make the video available to students for studying.
    - Note that video can provide information at a fast rate. However, if you provide information provide at a fast rate then you should likely plan activities to help learners retain the material.
- testing
    - Testing with video can be much more realistic than testing via text.

Practical Guideline:

You can use video to teach skills that are difficult to explain with other media.

The strengths of video are more evident if you tell the students what they are going to learn and what they should focus upon before they view the video. A video's effectiveness also relates to how well the material attracts and directs the learner's attention. Learners tend to have a short attention span for video. If the Grand Canyon, one of the world's most spectacular sights, holds a viewer's interest for an average of 90 seconds then imagine how long your video clip can hold your learner's attention. You can minimize this problem by presenting short clips, as short sequences are helpful in maintaining student attention and interest. This also helps keep the message focused on the learning outcome being taught. Short clips can also be useful in that video is more effective when there is a small amount of presented information. With video, most students remember generalities rather than details.

Practical Guideline:

Prepare students before they watch a video. Let them know where to focus their attention.

10.2 Difficulties with Professional Quality Video

Professional quality video usually requires a large amount of storage space when digitized and significant costs, time, and expertise to develop.

Digitized video (for both professional and non-professional productions) requires a large amount of storage space. Expect to make some compromises. (Read the Final Steps section for more details.)
- Modern video cameras automatically digitize video. However, if you are working with old sources, you may need to convert analog (smooth and continuous) signals into a finite amount (depending on the sampling rate or number of measurements taken) of digital or binary information (1's and 0's) that computers store and process. The large amount of needed storage space needed for digital video can be a significant problem, especially for CD-ROM applications, unless compression techniques are used.
- Minimize digital storage requirements by using short clips and only use the amount of video that is necessary. Some video clips, such as interviews, may not require full-motion, full-screen, or full-color presentations. Although video is typically shown at a frame rate of 30 frames or images per second, as a rule, action sequences should play at a minimum of 20 frames per second while you can reduce non-action clips (e.g., "talking heads") to 10 frames per second if you need to save disc space or

solved by Compressing

reduce bandwidth requirements. Screen sizes for video generally range from 640 x 480 down to very small sizes depending on the computer system and/or speed of the Internet connection. For DVD-ROM and CD-ROM delivery and from a screen design perspective, on a 1024 x 768 screen, video sized at 480 x 360 looks proportional. Similarly, on an 800 x 600 screen, video sized at 320 x 240 works well. For other screen sizes, use proportional sizes for video. Note that these values are for screen sizes that have a 4:3 aspect ratio (4 pixels width for every 3 pixels height). Create proportional screen sizes if you are basing your production on a 16:9 aspect ratio.

- When compressing the video, you can further reduce the storage requirements by minimizing the differences between frames. For example:
  - Keep the scene well lit to maintain high contrast and reduce "noise". When compressing video, noise is interpreted as important changes in the video. Consequently, the information is used rather than omitted. This leads to increased file sizes.
  - Keep the focus constant using manual focus since auto focus may continually make adjustments.
  - Keep the exposure constant.
  - Use simple, preferably single color, backgrounds.
  - Have minimal background activity.
  - Pan or zoom quickly to reduce the amount of time that there is a lot of movement.
  - Use a quality tripod to reduce movement caused by shaking as is commonly seen in home movies when the camera was held in the operator's hand.
  - Minimize the number of file format conversions and dubs as they can introduce noise.
- You can also reduce storage requirements by using cuts or wipes between scenes as compared to high-motion transitions such as dissolves.
  - For wipes, the only pixels changing are those along the boundary of the wipe.
- Depending on the computer's speed, computer's memory size, and the file size, there may be a significant delay while large video files are loaded. Short video clips are often preferable.

Practical Guideline:

Estimate the amount of data your final product will need to hold to ensure that your data will fit on the selected storage medium.

Producing professional quality video particularly needs justification since you will incur significant costs for their production:
- Justification can be from the motion needing to be taught being unfamiliar or difficult to perform.
- Justification can arise from concepts being easily and best understood with video.
- Justification is easier if the material will be useful for a long time. This is particularly important with video since it can be expensive to update the video. Filming, editing, and pressing new discs can have significant costs.
- Typical costs per day for a camera operator, other personnel such as a sound person and actors, a quality camera, and other equipment such as lights tend to be expensive, especially when paying for talented individuals.

Projects requiring professional video can take a large amount of time to produce. For example, a relatively simple project, such as creating a resource that covers each step of disassembling and assembling an aircraft engine, can require 200 hours of development time. Many projects need specific expertise such as media specialists and instructional designers who specialize in multimedia applications.

Professional productions also require relatively expensive filming equipment.
- Although consumer-level digital video equipment tends to be affordable, professional-level equipment can be costly.
- Better filming equipment has high sensitivity (this is a measure of the minimum amount of light to make a usable picture - measured in units of lux), high resolution (this determines the picture's sharpness), and dynamic response (this is the ability to detect rapid changes in a scene's light intensity).

- The good news is that digital video editing systems are relatively affordable. Digital video editing systems allow for quick experimentation with sequencing, special effects, and sounds. It is also easy to assemble individual clips together to make the final video sequence needed for the instructional point. Remember that editing and experimentation can be faster if you film your clips in the sequence needed. Digital video editing systems also allow you to compress the clips in the file format you need.

Practical Guideline:
High quality video takes time and expertise to develop.

10.3 Gathering Existing Materials

Before you go to the effort of recording any video, determine whether any suitable materials exist. Gathering existing materials can save you significant time and money if you do not have to "re-invent the wheel". For any materials you can get, be sure to:
- get copyright clearance **in writing**
  - Copyright clearance is required for all materials owned by others (i.e., authors or copyright holders). Formal copyright clearance is not needed if the copyright has expired or if the clip is "shareware". Copyright clearance is more likely to cost money if you are planning to sell the final product.
- get original materials
  - Each succeeding generation has poorer quality.
- get materials in the format you will use, such as mini DV tapes
  - If you transfer material from one format to another, some image quality will be lost. It also costs time and money to transfer material between formats.
  - Existing materials are often found in a variety of formats (e.g., mini DV, film, one inch, 3/4 inch, Betacam SP, 16 mm, Hi8, 8mm, S-VHS, VHS...).
- determine whether the material's quality is acceptable
  - Sometimes poor quality is better than students never seeing the material.

Practical Guideline:
Get copyright clearance in writing!

Note that many high-quality generic clips that you can use for multimedia presentations and productions are available for a fee in a variety of formats. If it is important to you, ensure that you can distribute the clips royalty-free.

You may have problems in gathering existing materials, in that:
- copyright clearance may cost money
  - Costs can range from being very expensive to being free.
- it may not be possible to locate the copyright owner
- the materials may not arrive or it could take a long time to receive the materials
  - Sending materials can be a low priority of copyright owners.
- copyright clearance may not be granted for some needed materials
- some materials may not be exactly as you need
  - For example, video materials designed to be played linearly, such as in movies, often have audio that overlaps scenes in that the audio may start before or end after the specific video is seen. Also, the video is usually not designed to be shown in a series of short clips, as is often preferred in instructional multimedia applications.

10.4 Producing Video

Professional quality video is needed for many DVD-ROM, CD-ROM, and high-bandwidth intranet or Internet applications. However, from a practical perspective, you may not have the resources or need to produce professional quality video. This section first describes how to produce professional quality video and then what you can do non-professionally. Many of the ideas presented for producing professional video apply to what you can do for "non-professional" applications.

10.4-1 Producing Professional Quality Video

For producing professional quality video, the requirements can vary from requiring a media producer and film crew to having the team members do some tasks. To a degree, "you get what you pay for". Base this decision on the resources available, needed quality, and budget limitations. When producing professional quality video, you should:
- "Sign off" scripts before filming begins.
- Consider hiring a media producer.
- Think about hiring a scriptwriter.
- Consider hiring professional personnel for major acting roles.
- Use professional equipment for best results.
- Have another person view the recording on a separate monitor.

"Sign Off" Scripts Before Filming Begins

Signing off a script provides a contract between the media producer and yourself that specifically outlines the filming requirements. Any changes or additions to the agreement can cost significant amounts of money. Changes and additions are major reasons video productions go over-budget. These extra costs can be hard to justify.

Your completed video scripts should have descriptions for every scene that link to any planned narration. You will need this information to determine the contract specifics.

To help make it possible to film the script, you should have the authority to make decisions. For example, you may need authority to shut down machinery or get employees to cooperate. During the intense activity of filming, you and one or two others may need to be present but you should avoid "getting in the way".

Consider Hiring a Media Producer

Media producers can effectively and efficiently plan and schedule filming, make a detailed shot and script list, make location and studio arrangements, find talent, arrange for props, as well as arrange for editing facilities. They can also offer advice and their skills in making the production professional and effective. For example, media producers may suggest filming the material from the student's point of view so that students will see the object as they would if the object were in front of them. One method for doing this is by filming over a demonstrator's shoulder. Media producers will know how to professionally operate a camera. There will be times when it is beneficial to adjust a camera's shutter speed (e.g., for filming motion images), adjust the iris (e.g., for different light conditions), and use different lenses (e.g., for distant objects).

Media producers often attend to details that amateurs may not know or do. These details can include:
- black-striping the tape before filming to help ensure continuous time codes
- properly setting up and adjusting the lighting
    - For example, you need proper lighting to show the subject clearly and eliminate inappropriate or distracting shadows.

- properly locating a sound boom
- setting sound levels
- setting the white balance at each location or as lighting conditions change to ensure color accuracy
- reminding actors to avoid wearing white, black, very dark, or very bright clothing, and other color combinations that that can cause color problems
- checking that actors are not wearing anything distracting such as jewelry
- filming important details within the centre two-thirds of the frame to guarantee that the important details can be clearly seen on all monitors
- allowing the camera to record for at least five seconds (for cameras that need it) before each action sequence begins
- having participants sign film release sheets
- record-inhibiting tapes after filming to prevent erasure
- labeling tapes
- maintaining a film log

For each clip, the film log should contain:
- the tape number
- a brief description of the clip
  - You can verbally record this on the tape before any action takes place.
- the take number
- the starting time code
  - Time codes are a numbering sequence recorded onto the tape for referencing each frame. Time codes are written in pairs of digits in the format HH:MM:SS:FF where H is hours (typically set to 00), M is minutes, S is seconds, and F is frames. Depending on the equipment used, there are about 30 frames (images) per second of recording. Frames are numbered from 00 to 29.
- the ending time code
- a check mark or "x" signifying whether the clip is okay or not
- a comment on the sound such as "none," "good," "bad," and "background noise"
- any other relevant comments

Remember that the most important reason for whether to film the sequence again is whether the final intended message will be clear.

All of the information recorded on the film log greatly helps the individual who later does the editing.

Practical Guideline:

Before filming the next clip, be sure the clip just filmed will work.

Media producers will plan for a lead-in time of up to one second to allow learners to focus themselves. The starting motion sequence frame should appear "elegant" since this image may be displayed for a length of time before the video clip is played. For example, check for the actor's mouth position and whether the actor's eyes are closed. This is seen in figure 10.1 where editing should start the video clip on frame two. Similarly, carefully select the last frame of a video clip.

Media producers ensure that each tape is clearly labeled to help prevent mistakes when editing. Mistakes are more likely in projects requiring numerous tapes.

Think About Hiring a Scriptwriter

Since, with respect to learning, narration tends to be less effective than visuals, you should minimize the amount of narration and only use it to reinforce the visual content. A scriptwriter can help with this and other tasks.

Especially when filming is complicated, to make filming more efficient, you should consider recording the narration after completing the filming. In other words, it may be unlikely to get both filming and narration perfect at the same time.

| Frame 1 | Frame 2 | Frame 3 |

Figure 10.1 – Choices for starting a video clip

Consider Hiring Professional Personnel for Major Acting Roles

The quality a professional brings into the production is readily seen and can give your production a sense of credibility. Quality acting may be critical when there is a risk that body language and tone of voice can send a different message than actual words. A message's interpretation is influenced more by non-verbal behaviors, such as facial expressions or gestures and tone of voice, than the actual words. As Ralph Waldo Emerson said, "What you do speaks so loud that I cannot hear what you say."

In terms of costs, if you work with amateur actors, you may lose a lot of time if each scene requires numerous takes. The costs due to time lost to the entire video production team can be greater than the cost of doing the recording more quickly with higher-priced professionals. In general, with a professional, if you make a suggestion, such as "sound more sincere," the professional will often make the adjustment on the next take.

Practical Guideline:

In general, it is usually wisest to work with professional actors.

In general, actors should memorize scripts or use a Teleprompter in that productions look amateur if the actors are seen reading. However, in many cases, the words spoken do not have to be exact if the message is still clear. This can allow actors to say things in their normal words. This can make it much easier for the actor to get it right.

It can be a nice reward and reduce costs if you can arrange to have team members filmed in minor roles, especially those not requiring spoken lines. Sometimes, subject-matter experts can effectively play cameo roles. Subject-matter experts are more likely to be successful in this role when they simply say what they would normally say as opposed to trying to repeat memorized lines. However, do **not** assume that they can act well. Many people "freeze" in front of a camera. Remember that special effects cannot compensate for bad acting.

Use Professional Equipment for Best Results

For high-quality final images, you should use mini-DV or higher standards and digital filming and editing equipment. If you use high-quality source materials and equipment, you can maintain image quality during editing. The approximate number of transfers (or generations) within a standard that you can make before significant signal degeneration occurs are listed in Table 10-1. The values listed in Table 10-1 depend on the original material's quality, equipment's quality, and final quality needed. For simplicity, once you are working with digital video, you will maintain high standards. Working with analog will eventually lead to a loss of image quality. Also, consider the equipment's audio recording quality. VHS sound quality is mediocre while the 8mm equipment and better standards can have good to excellent sound quality.

Table 10-1	
Standard	**Number of generations before degradation**
Digital film	64
1 inch	8 to 10
Betacam SP	8 to 10
Betacam	5 to 6
3/4 inch	3 to 4
S-VHS	0 to 1
Hi8	0 to 1
8mm	0
VHS	0

When you work with analog equipment and tape of a lower standard, you can lose a significant amount of quality each time you transfer the footage. For that reason, you should digitize the best source of analog video material that you can get. After that, by working only in a digital environment, you will be better able to maintain the video quality. However, if your initial quality is low, your final product may be unacceptably poor. This can be especially significant if you need clear detailed images, such as in a surgery scene. Lower-quality standards such as 8mm or VHS have a lot of "noise" in that the images appear grainy.

The quality of video possible relates to the standard's lines of resolution, as shown in Table 10-2. As an average, digital video standards have better image quality than analog as they have more lines of resolution, especially high definition (HD) that can have over 1,900 lines of resolution. If you use high quality for recording then you will always have the option of offering equal or lower quality in the final product or to later create higher-quality products when the user's computers or Internet bandwidth improves. If you film in a low-quality format then this low quality is the best your production can ever show! If you stream the resulting product over the Internet, you will also have to consider your learner's Internet connection speed. If your students cannot clearly see the teaching points, you will have to consider other options such as distributing the video on DVD-ROM or CD-ROM. (See the Final Steps section for more information.)

Practical Guideline:

If you film in a low-quality format then this low quality is the best your production can ever show both now and in the future.

Have Another Person View the Recording on a Separate Monitor

At least one person, usually the instructional designer and/or subject-matter expert, should view the images being filmed on a separate monitor to check for errors or problems. This is important since the camera's viewfinder cannot provide the image quality that can be seen on a separate monitor. Lugging the monitor from location to location is inconvenient but is well worth the effort.

Table 10-2	
Standard	**Lines of horizontal resolution**
High Definition	Up to 1,920
Profession DV	≥480
Mini-DV	approximately 500
Betacam SP	550
S-VHS	400
Hi8	400
8mm	250
VHS	240

The individual viewing the monitor must know how the final product will appear. For example:
- Full-screen video should usually be filmed centered.
- In general, video, viewed in a window, should have the acting personnel looking towards the screen's middle.
  - For example, if the window will be on the screen's left side then the acting personnel should look towards the right side (i.e., at the learner).
  - Some tools can be used later to flip or move the images but there may be some degradation in video quality.

The video producer and the individual viewing the monitor should:
- ensure that scripts are followed
- check that the actors' energy levels are appropriate and remain consistent
  - This can be problematic over a long day or if filming takes place over a number of days.
- make sure the actors' clothing is consistent from scene to scene
  - In particular, check this after a break and at the beginning of each day.

You should record each segment two or three times and possibly at different angles in case there is an unnoticed problem. This precaution costs you time and money but can save you the major costs of bringing the team back together to record the material again.

Practical Guideline:

Film each segment more than once in case there is an unnoticed problem.

While editing, adjustments can be made in the luminance (overall brightness), hue (tint or "color"), and saturation (hue intensity). However, adjustments can introduce noise or distortion. Note that adjustments cannot fully compensate for errors made in filming. So, you should film everything right in the first place.

Similarly, for action sequences, you cannot always fix problems. For example, if you edit out a mispronounced word and try to edit in the word pronounced correctly, the person's face or mouth in the new clip would not be in alignment with the old clip. If there is any doubt, film the clip again. One solution is to also film some close-ups of the material. These close-ups can overlay the video portions of clips that have visual errors. Inserting some close-ups also provides variation for the viewer.

10.4-2 Producing Non-Professional Video

Even if you do not have the luxury of professional filming personnel and equipment, you can still produce effective instructional video sequences. As with professional productions, you still need to:
- precisely plan what you need to film
- make any needed arrangements
- attend to all of the details such as ensuring adequate lighting, using a tripod... as described above

If you are buying a consumer-level camera, you will be buying a digital camera that will have excellent quality. If you are adapting old video recorded with low-end cameras (e.g., Hi8 and S-VHS), these can be good enough to play back on typical DVD drives, CD-ROM drives, or hard drives. 8 mm and VHS can be acceptable depending on the quality of video needed.

After recording the video, you will need to download it to your computer. As shown in figure 10.2, this is often done through a FireWire connection from a mini-DV camera. Alternatively, you can digitize analog video. As shown in figure 10.3, with the right cable connections, you can do this with a digital video camera. The video camera automatically translates the analog signal output from a video cassette player or other device into digital computer data. (Check the Final Steps section for more information about digitizing and compressing video.) Due to different playback capabilities on the user's computers or Internet bandwidth, you will need to make "capturing" decisions about the:
- screen size
    - For example, 640 x 480, 320 x 240, or 240 x 180.
- frame rate
    - For example, 30 frames per second for capturing the video are typical. Playback may later be set to a different amount such as 10 frames per second for interview scenes.
- number of colors
    - 24-bit (over 16 million colors) or 32-bit is typical.
- sound quality
    - In general, you should record at least 12-bit audio data.
- compression standard
    - For example, MPEG-1, MPEG-2, MPEG-4, WMV, QuickTime, or AVI (which is minimal).

Figure 10.2 – Downloading video

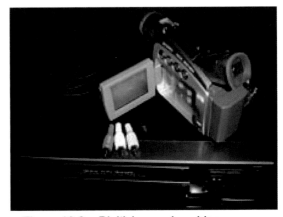
Figure 10.3 – Digitizing analog video

After digitizing the video, you can then edit the clips with digital video editing software. Quality digital video editing systems, as shown in figure 10.4, can have many useful capabilities such as allowing you to:
- select the best clips to use
    - Base your decisions on which clips best convey the intended message, as stated in the learning outcomes and other materials. The amount of work needed to record a clip is irrelevant.
- trim unwanted parts of clips
    - Editing tools allow you to easily mark the start and end point of each clip.

- cut, copy, and paste video clips or parts of clips
- reorder clips
- join clips together
- add audio such as separately recorded narration and sound effects
- create special effect transitions, such as fades and wipes, between clips
  - Although these tools allow you to use a variety of transitions, the basic "cut" (where one clip ends and the next clip immediately begins) is simple to do, unobtrusive, and effective to use.
  - Remember that transitions can become boring if you use them repeatedly.
- add titles
  - Fonts for titles should be plain, sans serif, and bold.
  - A drop shadow can help separate the title from the background.
  - It can be effective to fade the titles in and out.
  - Keep titles uncrowded.
- adjust qualities of the video such as brightness

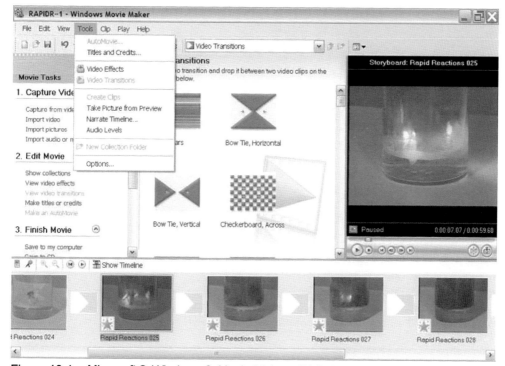

Figure 10.4 – *Microsoft ® Windows ® Movie Maker* – Digital video editing tool

Remember that editing is a distinct skill. Professional video editors can likely work more efficiently than yourself and will be able to "tweak" video and deal with technical issues such as "square" pixels.

After you edit and render (create) the clips, you can use an authoring tool to control where and when to play the digitized video files.

Note that you may need to keep the total time of the video within specified restrictions. For example, you may have limits on storage space or the amount of time students have available for learning.

Note that you may want to display live broadcast signals such as newscasts, web casts, and other special events, especially in computer-managed presentations.

Summary

In a multimedia production, video can be an important part of your media mix since video can significantly enhance learning. With respect to teaching, video is excellent for demonstrating procedures, changes, and processes, teaching attitudes and values, making abstract concepts concrete, classifying information, and comparing information.

You can also use video for gaining and holding attention, motivating learners, introducing topics or procedures, presenting visually-rich material that would otherwise be hard to explain, and testing. However, video is weak in presenting large amounts of information.

Professional quality video can require a large amount of storage space when digitized, significant costs to produce, a large amount of time to develop, and expertise to create.

Gathering existing materials can save you significant time and money if you do not have to "re-invent the wheel". Be sure you get copyright clearance **in writing**, get original materials, and determine whether the material's quality is acceptable.

You may have problems in gathering existing materials, in that:
- Copyright clearance may cost money.
- It may not be possible to locate the copyright owner.
- The materials may never arrive or take a long time to arrive.
- Copyright clearance may not be granted for some needed materials.
- Some materials may not be exactly as needed.

For filming, the requirements can vary from requiring a media producer and film crew to having the team members or yourself do the filming. Base this decision on the resources available, needed quality, and budget limitations.

For professional-quality video, you should:
- "Sign off" scripts before filming begins.
- Consider hiring a media producer.
- Think about hiring a scriptwriter.
- Consider hiring professional personnel for major acting roles.
- Use professional equipment for best results.
- Have another person view the recording on a separate monitor.

You can record adequate non-professional video with consumer-level camcorders.

After recording the video, you will need to make decisions about the screen size, frame rate, number of colors, and compression quality. You can then edit the clips with digital video editing software.

Application Exercises

1) Imagine an instructional multimedia application teaching carpentry students how to use software that helps them estimate the costs of a job. If a video of a businessperson is portrayed explaining the value in using the tool, what could be the consequence?
2) Which of the following statements is **false**?
   a) Learners are usually able to focus on video for a long time.
   b) VHS quality can be acceptable.
   c) Your final video image quality can be worse than your original's quality.
   d) Your final video quality is often comparable to the amount you spent.

3) Which of the following statements is **false**?
   a) Learners should have guidance to learn effectively from video.
   b) Video can be excellent for teaching attitudes.
   c) Video can provide information at a fast rate.
   d) Video is excellent for presenting large amounts of information.
4) List four things you can do to reduce the storage requirements of digitized video.
5) List three things you can do to record high-quality video.

Case Study

Six instructors were on a four-week professional development leave from their regular duties. During this time, the instructors participated in a workshop on creating instructional multimedia applications. One goal of the workshop was to create a small tutorial so that the instructors could apply what they learned. As a part of the instructional design process, the instructors determined that video was not required for teaching the concepts. However, it was tempting to use video to impress people.

Case Study Questions

1) Given that the project timeline was very short, should video have been added to the tutorial?
2) Given the lack of time, what are some ways video could have been quickly produced?

References

Conference Board of Canada. (1991). Employability skills profile: The critical skills required in the Canadian workforce. Ottawa, Ontario: The Conference Board of Canada.

Feeley, J. (2005, February). HDV, film and me: Why HD makes film an undead medium. Studio/monthly, 27(2), 32.

Hedgecoe, J. (1989). John Hedgecoe's complete video course: A step-by-step, self-instruction guide to making great videos. London, Great Britain: Octopus Publishing Group.

Holsinger, E. (2005, February). Sony HVR-Z1U and HDR-FX1 HDV Camcorders. Studio/monthly, 27(2), 12-14.

Huntley, J., & Easley, G. (1994). The brown book of multimedia. Dubuque, IA: Wm. C. Brown Communications.

Johnson, D. (2005, March). Lighting a Video Interview With Arri Fresnels. Studio/monthly, 27(3), 30-31.

Johnson, D. (2005, March). Take Control of Your Lighting. Studio/monthly, 27(3), 44-46.

Kaplow, S. (2002, June). The streamy underbelly: How to avoid pitfalls in producing and delivering web video. AV Video Multimedia Producer, 24(6), 21, 72.

Meyer, T. (1998, February). The pixel formerly known as square. DV, 6(2), 82, 84.

Reiser, R., & Gagne, R. (1983). Selecting media for instruction. Englewood Cliffs, NJ: Educational Technology Publications.

Romiszowski, A. (1988). The selection and use of instructional media: For improved classroom teaching and for interactive, individual instruction (2nd ed.). New York, NY: Nichols Publishing.

Smith, C. (1990). Mastering television technology: A cure for the common video. Richardson, TX: Newman-Smith Publishing Company.

Chapter 11: Animations

Learning Outcomes

After completing this chapter, you should be able to:
- list uses of animations
- discuss reasons why animations enhance learning
- explain how you can design animations to keep the message clear
- describe considerations for displaying animations
- describe costs associated with creating animations
- design programs that effectively use animation

Introduction

Animation is another medium that you can incorporate into instructional multimedia applications. It is important for you to consider using animations as a part of the instructional strategy since animations can significantly enhance learning, motivation, and attitudes as well as reduce the time needed for learning.

Animation means "to give life to" something. Animations, which are a series of visual images that change over time, are like video sequences except that animations are created with a computer, other tools, or manually rather than by filming real objects in motion. For this reason, a video can be easier to make than an animation.

This chapter relates animations to learning, presents practical guidelines for keeping the message clear, provides suggestions on when and where to display animations, and discusses the costs of producing animations. (See the Media Selection chapter for more information on animations.)

11.1 Animations and Learning

You can effectively use animations for:
- showing relationships between objects and ideas
  - For example, animations can illustrate pressure changes in a pressure regulation system or how mechanical systems work.
- simulating the results of actions
  - As an example, animations can show the effects of drug dosage on heart rates.
- showing sequential steps in a procedural task
  - For example, animations can be used to explain how to adjust a camera.
- explaining difficult concepts
  - As an example, you can use animations to illustrate how the body responds to changes in oxygen demand.
- making abstract concepts concrete
  - For example, animations can show how electrons move in orbits around the nucleus of atoms or how information flows in an electronic system.
  - This is important since some learners have difficulty learning from abstract sources such as text, numbers, and symbols.

With respect to learning, you can use animations to:
- enhance performance and retention
  - Note that learning generally requires cues and guidance to specifically direct a student's attention to the pertinent point. This is particularly important for younger and immature students.
  - Ensure that students are not presented with more information than they can handle.
  - In general, animations with text are more effective than visuals with text. This is especially true when the concept involves directional characteristics or changes over time. In these situations, animations can help simplify an abstract idea into a concrete idea.
- reduce the time needed for learning
- gain attention and improve student attitudes
  - This is partly due to animations simply adding variety to pages. You can add some interest to a title page simply by animating text.

11.2 Keeping the Message Clear

To keep the message clear, your animations:
- should be self-explanatory, as a guideline
  - Students do **not** necessarily know how to interpret animations. The ease of interpretation can depend on their age and maturity. Evaluate your animations with target audience students.
  - You can help make the animation clear by providing supporting text and/or labels. Alternatively, focus the student's thoughts on the pertinent information.
  - If it is not self-explanatory, consider redesigning the animation.
- must match the learning outcomes
  - Some animations have been used to impress rather than teach.
- should be set up to allow the learner to control the pace
  - Students should be able to repeat animations since it is easy to miss significant points during minor distractions.

Practical Guideline:

Self-explanatory animations illustrate the message.

11.3 Displaying Animations

You should display animations consistently on one side (preferably the left) of the text.
- If necessary, place animations above or below text.
- Use what looks best, is appropriate, and is logical.

You should only display animations when the reader is ready to view them. Students can do this by clicking an "Animate" button when they are ready. Before showing the animation, it is critical for you to provide guidance to ensure that the students will focus on the important point!

Your animation will appear more realistic if the object's speed, size, and relative motion are accurate. Base the animation's speed on real time (e.g., 0.1 seconds between events) rather than the computer's speed. Otherwise, due to a wide variation in computer speeds, animations may run at different speeds on different hardware configurations.

Practical Guideline:

Animations should only begin when the learner is ready to view them.

You can create and display effective animations by simply plotting and erasing a visual.
- You can do this with many authoring tools.
- The smoothness is affected by each image's size, the number of colors, and the computer's speed. Small visual animations on fast computers can appear very smooth.

You can make animations appear 3-dimensional.
- Use 3D for realistic effects.
- 3D animations can be more powerful than 2D animations, especially if the learner can view the animation from different perspectives such as front, side, and top views. For example, this can be useful for training students to repair equipment.

11.4 Costs

With respect to costs:
- Animations tend to be costly due to the labor needed.
    - It is usually labor intensive to create non-trivial animations. Be sure an animation is justified.
    - Many generic clips useful for multimedia presentations and productions are available for a fee. Ensure that these can be distributed royalty-free.
- You may need to spend money for an animation specialist.
    - Specialists most efficiently and effectively create 3D animations. How can amateurs effectively deal with light sources, perspective, surface textures, and dithering techniques? Even with professionals and the best tools, 3D animations are very time consuming to produce.
- You may need to purchase a specialized animation tool.
    - Purchasing an animation package adds costs to the project but the software can increase production efficiency. Be sure that the authoring tool can easily incorporate animations created with external tools. Common file formats that should be supported by the authoring tool include FLI, FLC, and PIC. The PICS standard is compatible on both Macintosh® and PC platforms. Check for compatibility before completing any significant amount of development. Remember that the authoring tool itself may have built-in tools for creating the animations you need.
    - Some animation tools have a lengthy learning curve. Consider hiring an animation specialist.
    - Creating and rendering (producing the final animation from all of the moving objects) animations usually requires a fast computer. You may need to purchase a high-end computer. After rendering is complete, thoroughly test the animations on the anticipated hardware.
    - Some animation tools can also reduce costs by decreasing the development time needed. For example, morphing packages allow you to quickly change one image into another. You can use morphing for special effects such as stretching, compressing, distorting, and transforming images.
- You may have to purchase high-end playback systems since computer animations can require significant computer processing and/or bandwidth. However, there are things you can do to minimize computer-processing requirements:
    - Avoid animating large objects. If possible, animate small objects.
    - Minimize the number of colors used. Consider using a 16-color palette and dithering techniques to make it appear like there are more colors. You can avoid color conflicts if the colors you use match the color palette of the authoring tool.
    - Make it appear as if the object is moving. For example, instead of animating an entire spaceship across a screen, simply animate small dots (stars).
    - Create small animations that can be combined with others or re-used.
- Note that animations can require much less storage space than digitized video since animations are usually made with fewer colors and have a smaller proportion of the image moving.

Practical Guideline:

Animations of small 16-color objects are better able to run on slow hardware or low-bandwidth systems.

Summary

Animation means "to give life to" something. In a multimedia production, animations can be an important part of your media mix since animations can significantly enhance learning.

You can use animations to show relationships between objects and ideas, simulate the results of actions, show sequential steps in a procedural task, help explain difficult concepts, and make abstract concepts concrete.

With respect to learning, you can use animations to reduce the time needed for learning, effectively teach concepts that involve directional characteristics or changes over time, and gain attention.

Your animations should be self-explanatory, match the learning outcomes, be consistently displayed on one side of the text, and only begin when the reader is prepared and ready to view them.

Your animation will be more realistic if the object's speed, size, and relative motion are accurate. Enhance realism by making the animation appear 3-dimensional. Realism is not cheap. Animations tend to be costly and may need to be created by professionals with a specialized animation tool.

Computer animations that require significant computer processing can run poorly on slower hardware systems. Animations of small 16-color objects are better able to run on slow hardware or low-bandwidth systems.

Application Exercises

1) If an application displays an animation and text at the same time, what could be the consequence?
2) A learner clicks on continue to see the next page. If the page starts with an animation, how might this affect his learning?
3) If an animation is **not** self-explanatory, what can you do to help address the problem?
4) If an animation is created just to add variety to a page, what could be some consequences?
5) What can you do if an animation is displaying too slowly?

Case Study

Six instructors were on a four-week professional development leave from their regular duties. During this time, the instructors participated in a workshop on creating instructional multimedia applications. One goal of the workshop was to create a small tutorial so that the instructors could apply what they learned. As a part of the instructional design process, the instructors determined that animations were not required for teaching the concepts. However, animations could have been used to gain the students' attention and make the learning more enjoyable.

Case Study Questions

1) Given that the project timeline was very short, should animations have been added to the tutorial?
2) If large full-color animations were added, how might the product's market potential be affected?

References

Baek, Y., & Layne, B. (1988). Color, graphics, and animation in a computer-assisted learning tutorial lesson. Journal of Computer-Based Instruction, 15(4), 131-135.

Bennett, G. (1994, June). More, More Morphing! The Computer Paper, 7(6), 24-29.

Park, O. (1998). Visual displays and contextual presentations in computer-based instruction. Educational Technology Research and Development, 46(3), 37-50.

Park, O. (1994, April). Dynamic visual displays in media-based instruction. Educational Technology, 34(4), 21-25.

Park, O., & Gittelman, S. (1992). Selective use of animation and feedback in computer-based instruction. Educational Technology Research and Development, 40(4), 27-38.

Rieber, L., & Kini, A. (1991). Theoretical foundations of instructional applications of computer-generated animated visuals. Journal of Computer-Based Instruction, 18(3), 83-88.

Rieber, L. (1990). Animation in computer-based instruction. Educational Technology Research and Development, 38(1), 77-86.

Wood, E. (1993, October). A beginner's guide to multimedia. Computer Graphics World, 16(10), 71-84.

Section 3: Interaction

For you to ensure that learning is effective and efficient, your instructional multimedia applications must be interactive. This section describes how to make your programs interactive and the various input devices you can select to provide interaction. As well, guidelines are presented for writing effective questions and providing appropriate feedback.

Chapter 12:   Interactivity

Learning Outcomes

After completing this chapter, you should be able to:
- explain why interaction is critical
- describe methods of making programs interactive
- design programs that are interactive

Introduction

Interactivity or active learning is critical for increasing learning and retention in all instructional activities. This chapter defines interaction and presents ways you can make programs interactive. You can create interaction through requiring learners to answer questions that make them think, actively involving learners with a simulation or an educational game, providing feedback, enabling learners to make comments and annotations and/or modify the computer program, and having them discuss the content in pairs or groups of three. This chapter also describes how you can enhance interaction by utilizing the learner's existing knowledge and experience and by learners controlling the instruction's pace and sequence.

12.1 What Makes Interaction?

Interactivity is active learner participation in the learning process. This is essential for effective learning. Learners retain more if they see, hear, and do something than if they just see and hear something than if they just see or just hear something. Your instructional multimedia applications have the potential of enabling learners to "see, hear, and do". Without including interactivity in your program, learning and retention will be reduced. Interaction is one of the fundamental strengths that instructional multimedia applications have over many other delivery methods.

The interactivity you provide can take a variety of forms depending on your instructional strategy. Interactivity includes:
- learners answering questions that require thinking
- students being actively involved with a simulation or an educational game
- providing feedback
- utilizing the learner's existing knowledge and experience
- students making comments and annotations
- learners modifying the computer program
- students discussing the content in pairs or groups of three

For computer-managed presentations, you can provide interactivity by:
- presenting questions on the screen for students to consider
- verbally asking questions

Answering Questions that Require Thinking

Socrates said, "I cannot teach anybody anything. I can only make them think." As he must have thought, it is critical for students to answer questions that require thinking since students are much more likely to learn information that they process mentally. Generally, as the material's complexity increases more questions are needed. Questions should occur after logical blocks of information. Note that mature students can handle larger blocks of material than immature students. Remember that high-level questions, such as, "What would happen if... ?," may be necessary to teach the material. A question may be ineffective if it is trivial. For example, it may be pointless to ask a factual question immediately after presenting the material. Similarly, if a student is wrong on a true-false question, it is relatively worthless to ask the student to try again.

Practical Guideline:

To facilitate learning, ask questions that require students to think.

Ask questions that include visuals and/or video images that have already been seen, are modified, or are unique. Present a variety of question formats such as matching, clicking/touching a part of a video or visual, three correct answers out of five, assemble a series of parts...

Writing good questions does take time. Some instructional multimedia developers have omitted including questions because time was a constraint. If you omit questions due to a lack of time then it is also likely that the program will not be thoroughly evaluated for learning effectiveness. It may never be noticed that learning will likely be compromised.

Active Involvement with a Simulation or an Educational Game

In order to effectively learn with a simulation or game, you need to guide and focus students on to what they are to learn. (See the Instructional Design chapter for more information.)

Providing Feedback

It is more effective for you to provide detailed or elaborative feedback than simply telling the students whether they are right or wrong. (Read the Feedback chapter for more details on providing feedback.)

Utilizing the Learner's Existing Knowledge and Experience

If you utilize the learner's existing knowledge and experience, you can make the instruction much more meaningful and help the learners remember the information by having them relate it to knowledge that they already have. You can gain ideas for this through a learner analysis (as described in the Instructional Design chapter). Alternatively, you can ask learners to relate what was learned in the program to their existing knowledge and experiences, make hypotheses and predictions, make up more examples, or use their imagination to come up with a solution. You could then have the students compare their ideas to a set of parameters.

Making Comments and Annotations

You can choose to enable students to make comments and annotations for a variety of reasons. For example, students could analyze a part of the material and then immediately record their thoughts or questions (e.g., with voice or keyboard input) into the program. Subsequent learners or you could later hear or read this input. In these systems, you should take care to prevent students from becoming overwhelmed with information.

Learners Modifying the Computer Program

Common ways you can do this include enabling students to "paste" a digital image into the program or add to existing lists or databases. This requires the students to have a certain level of maturity. You will need to ensure the integrity of the material.

Students Discussing the Content in Pairs or Groups of Three

Within instructional multimedia applications, you can prompt students to talk about ideas, share their experiences with each other, or discuss answers to questions. All of these lead to discussion. This, in turn, leads to increased learning. With questions in particular, students tend to not let another student answer if they disagree with their answer. Consequently, they discuss the question and answer choices.

12.2 What Isn't Interaction?

Interactivity is **not**:
- choosing menu items to create one's own learning path
  - Note that some people will disagree with this point especially since some multimedia programs only offer interactivity through selecting menu items. The key difference in interpretation is whether significant learning can occur. Interaction that requires thinking is essential for learning. "Menu selection" programs are useful but the real learning comes from doing something significant with the information gained.
  - It may be easier to think of students choosing menu items as being a navigation activity rather than a learning activity.
- clicking a mouse or pressing a key to continue
- answering yes or no to questions such as "Would you like to continue?"

> **Practical Guideline:**
>
> Selecting menu items is not interaction in that interaction requires learners to think about the content.

Summary

Interactivity is active learner participation in the learning process. This is essential for effective learning.

You can achieve interactivity in a number of ways:
- Learners can answer questions that require thinking.
- Students can be actively involved with a simulation or an educational game.
- The application can provide feedback.
- The application can incorporate the learner's existing knowledge and experience.
- Students can make comments and annotations.
- Learners can modify the computer program.
- Students can discuss the content in pairs or groups of three.

Interactivity is **not** selecting menu items. This is really a navigation activity.

Application Exercises

1) What could happen to a student in a one-hour tutorial that does **not** have any interaction?
2) Explain why asking students whether they would like to continue is **not** interactivity.
3) A multimedia program guides students into manipulating variables and seeing the results. If questions are **not** asked, is the program truly interactive? Explain your answer.

Case Study

Six instructors were on a four-week professional development leave from their regular duties. During this time, the instructors participated in a workshop on creating instructional multimedia applications. One goal of the workshop was to create a small tutorial so that the instructors could apply what they learned. As a part of the instructional design process, the instructors determined that students needed to be able to manipulate variables and observe the results.

Case Study Questions

1) What are two ways students could actively learn the material?
2) If the instructors chose to save time and **not** include interactions, what could happen?

References

Alessi, S., & Trollip, S. (1991). Computer-based instruction: Methods and development (2nd ed.). Englewood Cliffs, NJ: Prentice-Hall, Inc.

Begley, S. (1993, May 31). Teaching minds to fly with discs and mice. Newsweek, 121(22), 45.

Dempsey, J., & Sales, G. (Eds). (1993). Interactive instruction and feedback. Englewood Cliffs, NJ: Prentice Hall.

Gagne, R., & Driscoll, M. (1988). Essentials of learning for instruction (2nd ed.). Englewood Cliffs, NJ: Prentice Hall.

Jin, H., & Reeves, T. (1992). Mental models: A research focus for interactive learning systems. Educational Technology Research and Development, 40(3), 39-53.

Li, R. (1993, May). Creating interactive CBT lessons without video. Educational Technology, 33(5), 20-26.

Ormrod, J. (1990). Human learning: Theories, principles, and educational applications. New York, NY: Merrill Publishing Company.

Chapter 13:   Input Devices

After completing this chapter, you should be able to:
* describe the pros and cons of keyboard, mouse, touch, voice, and pen input
* compare and contrast keyboard, mouse, touch, voice, and pen input
* select the appropriate input device for a given audience

Introduction

You can choose from a wide array of input devices that are available for instructional multimedia applications. These range from the standard mouse and keyboard to voice to data gloves and even body suits. Typical input devices are keyboards, mice, and touch screens. You can also purchase specialized input devices for particular needs such as for students who have limited muscular coordination or for when they need tactile feedback. This chapter presents some practical guidelines to follow, describes the pros and cons of the common keyboard, mouse, touch, voice, and pen input devices, and lists devices useful for computer-managed presentations.

13.1 Practical Guidelines

In general, you should keep the input simple and consistent. For example, single mouse clicks or key presses are simple and easy. This helps keep the program user-friendly and helps maintain motivation and interest. To simplify input, only use one input device. Programs can become cumbersome to use when the learner has to flip between using the keyboard and mouse.

> **Practical Guideline:**
>
> Keep the input simple and consistent.

Do **not** force students to go through a routine at the program's beginning that teaches the keyboard or other input device. This is frustrating for students who already know how to use the device. If you need to include these instructions, allow the learners to choose whether the information should be presented.

Each input device has unique strengths, weaknesses, and characteristics. You should match the input device to the learner and the setting. The following pros and cons for each input device will help you make the right decision.

13.2 Keyboard Input

Pros:
* Keyboards are found on every computer.
    - Keyboards do not add extra costs to a basic computer system.
* Many learners are familiar with keyboards.
* Keyboard input allows for short (e.g., one or two word) and long answers (e.g., sentences, paragraphs, and even essays).

Cons:
- Some learners are not familiar or comfortable with keyboards.
- With keyboards, it can be difficult, especially for novices, to edit spelling mistakes or other errors.
- Rules for answer judging, such as spelling, punctuation, capitals, and spacing, can be challenging.
- It takes time for learners, who cannot "touch type," to look back and forth between the keyboard and monitor.

Notes:
- Try to minimize the number of required keystrokes.
- Be careful with how keyboard keys are referenced.
    - The "Enter" key is known by most (but not all) students. This is fairly safe to use.
    - Refer to function keys by their specific names (e.g., "F1") rather than created names (e.g., "Help") as many students will **not** remember the created names. For example, state "Press F1 for help".
    - Remember that keyboards are not fully standardized.

Practical Guideline:

If keyboard input is required, try to minimize the number of needed keystrokes.

13.3 Mouse Input

Pros:
- Mouse input can be effectively used for teaching many skills.
- Mouse input is generally easier than keyboard input.
- Most learners are familiar with using a mouse.
- Mouse input is extremely accurate. This can be important if, for example, the learner has to drag and drop items.
- Most computers have a mouse attached.
- Mice are relatively inexpensive.

Cons:
- Mouse input cannot be efficiently used for teaching some skills such as those requiring keyboarding skills. Keyboarding skills are needed for some instructional activities like writing reports.
- It can take novices some time to learn how to use a mouse. There can be problems if novices have to drag items, "double click," or change between "left clicks" and "right clicks". If possible, learners should only have to use single clicks with the left mouse button.
- Mice are easy to steal.

Notes:
- "Flying" mice can provide 3-dimensional input.
    - The third dimension is based on how high the mouse is lifted up.
- Mouse input can be used to allow students to drag objects. This expands the computer's teaching potential by enabling students to build and assemble or sequence items.
- Mouse input is commonly used in most instructional multimedia applications.
- Trackballs function in the same way as mice.

13.4 Touch Screen Input

Pros:
- Touch screen input can be effectively used for teaching many skills.
- Touch screen input is generally easier to learn and do than mouse and keyboard input.
  - This ease of use makes touch screens excellent for kiosk applications.
- Touch screen overlays are harder to steal than mice.

Cons:
- Touch screen input cannot be efficiently used for teaching some skills such as sentence writing.
- It takes novices some time to learn how to touch accurately.
  - Computers can measure touch screen input locations extremely well but fingers are imprecise and there is a parallax problem. Due to viewing angles, where users think they touch may not be where the touch actually occurs.
  - Accuracy is dependent upon the size of the active touch screen areas.
  - Generally, each active touch screen area should be at least ten percent of the screen's vertical and horizontal size. Alternatively, keep touch screen areas as large as possible while considering elegance and consistency.
- It can become tiring for students to keep lifting their arms to touch the screen.
  - This can be a problem for lengthy programs.
- Touch screens become dirty, typically from fingerprints.
- Touch screens can reduce the clarity as well as the brightness and contrast of the monitor.
- Although touch screens are inexpensive, they are an extra cost over a basic computer system.

13.5 Voice Input

Pros:
- Voice input, with a natural language interface, is perhaps the most practical and natural way to interact with a computer.
  - Further research needs to be done to solve all of the problems inherent in natural language processing.
- Voice input can allow visually impaired, blind, and physically challenged individuals to more easily interact with computers.
  - For students with disabilities, instructional multimedia applications must be adapted to their needs. For example, blind students are usually presented with audio information.
  - There are voice input systems available that will assist the speech-impaired.
- Once set up, voice input for answer responses is fast and easy to do.
- Voice input can also be used for taking dictation and making annotations or comments.
  - Voice input systems can handle homophones (words that sound alike), recognize sentence beginnings, and even provide capitalization.
- Large vocabularies are available.
  - Specific vocabularies are also available for some professions.
- Voice input can "free" an individual's hands.
  - Although most instructional multimedia applications do not need individuals to have their hands "free," voice input can be helpful if students are concurrently working with real objects.

Cons:
- Voice input systems may require learners to train the computer to recognize their speech.
  - This can require a significant amount of time.
  - The words may have to be spoken slowly and with emphasis.
  - Some voice recognition systems are better than others. The amount of training needed is one factor. Thoroughly evaluate a voice input system before purchasing it.

- Computers may make errors interpreting voice input when there is background noise.
  - Speaking directly into the microphone from a short distance can minimize this problem.
- Speech recognition techniques have **not** mastered all of a language's idiosyncrasies.
  - Different words can have the same pronunciation (e.g., for, fore, and four).
  - Intonation (e.g., "What!" and "What?") can affect the meaning.
  - Semantics can be a problem if identical sentences have different meanings.
  - Pragmatic or implicit knowledge can be difficult. For example, if you ask, "Is there time?" then the answer must be "Yes".
  - Idioms (e.g., "Fly-by-night") can be misinterpreted.
  - Slang expressions (e.g., "Cool") may not be understood as intended.
  - Continuous speech can also be a problem, especially when there are no pauses between words.
- Most hardware platforms do not have voice input capabilities.
- Voice input can use up a lot of storage space.
- Voice input can contribute to "noisy" environments.
- There can be difficulties in determining when an answer should be marked.
  - For example, what should the computer do if one student says to another, "The answer is "C" unless..."?

13.6 Pen Input

Pros:
- Pen input can be particularly useful for individuals with poor keyboarding capabilities.
- Once set up, pen input for responses, annotations, and comments is fast and easy to do.

Cons:
- Pen input systems can require learners to train the computer to recognize their writing.
  - This can take a significant amount of time.
- Computers may make errors interpreting pen input when the writing varies.
  - Care must be taken to write consistently.
- Most hardware platforms do not have pen input capabilities.
- With pen input, it can be difficult, especially for novices, to edit spelling mistakes or other errors.
- It can be cumbersome to handle answer judging (e.g., spelling, punctuation, capitals, and spacing).

13.7 Computer-Managed Presentation Input

Computer-managed presentations are often controlled with mouse input. However, it can also be useful to have:
- "digital chalk" that allows presenters or students to draw overtop of what is on the screen
- a wireless pointing device to control the computer from any point in the room
- a tungsten light that is designed to send a beam onto the screen to highlight a part of the projection

Summary

You can choose from a wide array of input devices ranging from the standard keyboard to voice to data gloves and even body suits. Typical input devices are keyboards, mice, and touch screens. You can also purchase specialized input devices for particular needs.

In general, keep the input simple and consistent. To simplify input, only use one input device. Do **not** force students to go through a routine at the program's beginning that teaches the keyboard or other input device.

Each input device has unique strengths, weaknesses, and characteristics. You should match the input device to the learner and the setting.

Computer-managed presentations are often controlled with mouse input. However, it can also be useful to have "digital chalk," a wireless pointing device, and/or a tungsten light.

Application Exercises

1) Which input device would you recommend for students with very weak keyboarding skills? Describe an activity that would require these students to provide keyboard input.
2) Which input device would you recommend for an application that will be used in a public place? Explain your answer.
3) A voice input system has been designed for business applications. A salesperson has suggested that this system can easily be adapted to other applications. If you have English as a Second Language students, what difficulty could you have with the voice input system?

Case Study

Six instructors were on a four-week professional development leave from their regular duties. During this time, the instructors participated in a workshop on creating instructional multimedia applications. One goal of the workshop was to create a small tutorial so that the instructors could apply what they learned. The tutorial was to run in a computer lab where each computer station had a mouse and keyboard. Most of the students had minimal computer experience.

Case Study Questions

1) Which input device(s) do you recommend for the tutorial?
2) If the product were to be marketed, would you use the same input device(s)? Justify your answer.

References

Fenrich, P. (1992). Screen design and user interface needs for successful multimedia applications. Proceedings of the Seventh Canadian Symposium on Instructional Technology.

Sawyer, T. (1985). Human factors considerations in computer-assisted instruction. Journal of Computer-Based Instruction, 12(1), 17-20.

von Wodtke, M. (1993). Mind over media: Creative thinking skills for electronic media. New York, NY: McGraw-Hill.

Wheelwright, G. (1993, December). The talkin' listenin' PC. The Computer Paper, 6(12), 58-61.

Chapter 14:   Question Writing

Learning Outcomes

After completing this chapter, you should be able to:
- describe what you can do to test effectively
- state characteristics of well-written questions
- explain what you can do to reduce frustration during questioning
- list advantages, disadvantages, and characteristics of true-false, multiple-choice, matching, and short-answer questions
- explain why long-answer questions are rarely used in multimedia applications
- write effective true-false, multiple-choice, matching, and short-answer questions
- explain why questions should be analyzed for effectiveness
- determine whether questions and tests are effective

Introduction

You can use questions in both presentations and tests to reinforce learning, test understanding, help your students to apply learning to problems, and keep your students actively involved.

This chapter first presents suggestions for testing effectively, characteristics of well-written questions, and guidelines for reducing student frustration. Advantages, disadvantages, and guidelines for writing each question type are then provided. The types discussed are true-false, multiple-choice, matching, short-answer, and long-answer/essay questions.

Although this chapter focuses on writing questions for instructional multimedia applications, you can use most of the information to create effective questions for other delivery methods.

14.1 Testing Effectively

To test effectively, you should:
- Avoid testing content that is directly based on the material unless it is appropriate to only test recall.
  - If you are only testing recall then your learning outcomes may not be written to a high enough level. (See the Instructional Design chapter for more details.)
- Ensure that earlier questions do **not** provide answers for later questions.
  - Otherwise, this would defeat part of the purpose of testing.
- Randomly select questions from a pool of questions, if the authoring tool allows for it.
  - Each test will be different and more valuable if students repeat it. This is a significant advantage of computer-based instruction over some of the other delivery methods.
  - Note that there can be an advantage in testing each learning outcome separately. This allows students to concentrate on individual instructional areas. Remember that you can randomly select questions from pools of questions categorized under each specific learning outcome.
  - To take this one step further, consider randomly inserting the question's choices each time the question is attempted. If on subsequent tests the student receives the same question, the choices will likely appear in a different order. This forces students to think through the question and helps prevent students from copying each other.

- Consider inserting random numbers in questions that involve numbers.
  - This makes it more worthwhile to answer the question if the question was seen on a previous occasion.
  - For safety, check maximum and minimum value ranges, dividing by zero, and significant digits.
- Consider choosing test questions based on a student's ability.
  - This can be useful in ensuring that each student experiences successes.
  - A student's ability can be determined during the lesson or on a pre-test.
  - Choosing questions in this manner can add significant development time.

> **Practical Guideline:**
> Randomly select questions and insert the question's answer choices to make the test more valuable each time the student attempts it.

You should create programming sub-routines to make these features available for future instructional multimedia projects.

14.2 Characteristics of Well-Written Questions

You should use the following guidelines to create well-written questions:
- Use short statements with crystal-clear wording.
  - Ambiguity causes problems such as confusion and frustration.
  - Long statements can obscure the sentence's meaning.
  - Provide all of the pertinent information.
  - Emphasize important words, by making the words bold, capitalized, or underlined, to ensure they are noticed.
- Use language that is familiar and appropriate to the situation. If not, you may be testing the learner's vocabulary rather than the learning outcome.
- Only use official abbreviations and avoid acronyms that some students will not know.
- Have only one fact or concept determine the answer.
  - Otherwise, it may not be clear which fact or learning outcome is being tested.
- Do **not** ask questions that can be answered by common sense alone.
  - There is minimal value in asking questions that can be answered too easily.
- Do **not** provide clues to the answer.
  - Ensure there is consistent grammar between the question and answer. For example, if the questions states, "Multimedia workstations often include an" then a choice should not be "mouse" since the choice starts with a consonant.
- Randomly insert answer choices into multiple-choice questions to make sure you do **not** give subtle clues to the correct answer, such as through the order you sequence the answer choices. Balance this with minimizing a student's searching time. For example, for numeric answer choices, it is easier for students to find numbers in an ascending or descending order. An easier way to not provide clues to the answer is to put all non-numeric choices for all questions in alphabetic order.
- Avoid broad general statements and specific determiners such as always or never.
  - These tend to make the question too easy to answer.
- Use simple positive statements.
- Avoid negatives and especially double negatives. Negatives are sometimes overlooked and double negatives can cause confusion. Negatives can be a particular problem for learners whose native language is different from the language of your instructional solution.
  - If a negative is required, highlight it to help ensure the word is noticed.

> **Practical Guideline:**
>
> To write good questions, use short statements with crystal-clear wording and have only one fact or concept determine the answer.

14.3 Reducing Student Frustration

In instructional multimedia applications, where learners are usually on their own, your questions should be flawless. Questions with errors or problems frustrate students and detract from the material's credibility. For proofing, use instructors, students, team members, and computers to analyze each question.

There are many things you can do to reduce student frustration:
- Test important ideas that are based on the stated learning outcomes and not trivia.
  - Be sure each question matches a learning outcome.
  - Do **not** try to trick students. Trick questions may test for something other than the specified learning outcome.
- Create fair tests so that student results truly represent their ability. (Check the Instructional Design chapter for more information.)
  - Ensure that each learning outcome is tested.
  - Test each learning outcome to the highest skill level needed.
  - Base the number of questions and score for each learning outcome in proportion to its frequency (i.e., how often the skill is needed), importance, and difficulty.
- Include visuals, video, animation, and audio in questions. This can be similar to what you used to teach the material.

  - If you need media to teach the content then it is likely that testing will also require these media.
  - If you teach students with visuals, video, animation, or audio, it may not be fair or realistic to test only with text. Can you be sure that students can transfer visual and audio materials to an abstract text-based format? Will text-based questions truly represent the skills needed in real situations?
  - Testing with different media can be an excellent use of multimedia technology.
- Arrange questions from easy to hard.
  - This helps build confidence.
  - This arrangement can be difficult to do when randomly selecting questions.
- Group similar question types, such as multiple-choice and short-answer questions, together to keep the instructions simple.
  - The importance of this depends on the program's ease of use. If students intuitively know how to interact with the computer, as they should be able to, then grouping similar question types becomes less important.
  - This grouping is more difficult to do when randomly selecting questions.
- Provide feedback for all possible responses. (See the Feedback chapter for more details.)
  - This can take a lot of time to develop but can be a major strength of your applications.
  - For short-answer questions, first have students answer all of the questions on paper. This provides most of the responses that students will give. Include feedback for each of these responses in the program.
- Allow the slowest student enough time to try each question, if there is a time limit.
  - This can compensate for slow reading and/or keyboarding speeds.
  - Consider giving students more time by minimizing the input or keyboarding needed.
  - You can set up a situation where the students have a set amount of time to answer as many questions as possible. This can be a positive challenge but can be stressful for some students.

Practical Guideline:

Include media in questions. It may not be reasonable to test only with text.

You can also minimize student frustration by ensuring that:
- all questions use realistic situations, numbers...
- there are clear and simple instructions on how to answer each question
- the method for entering a response is appropriate (e.g., mouse or touch input is excellent for identifying parts of diagrams)
- the number of characters that can be entered is appropriate
- you tell students the number of tries allotted per question, how scores are tallied (if it is not obvious), and passing requirements
  - As a maximum, let the student proceed or tell the student the answer after the third try. Do **not** force students into an endless loop if they cannot answer a question. It can also be frustrating for students to have to answer a question after they are told the answer.
- you tell students rules for spelling, grammar, and extra words when keyboard input is required

Practical Guideline:

Proof questions thoroughly so that students are not frustrated because of errors.

14.4 True-False Questions

You can use true/false questions to test a student's ability to:
- determine whether a statement is a fact or opinion
- identify relationships
- identify attitudes, values, and beliefs
- apply known principles to new situations

Advantages, if written properly, include:
- testing the most facts in the shortest time
- being easy to write and score
- only measuring one learning outcome
- questions being non-ambiguous
- taking little screen room
- requiring minimal student input
- giving students a break since there is a 50% chance of answering correctly

Disadvantages include:
- difficulty in measuring complex learning (since true-false questions usually test simple facts)
- not reliably measuring the skill when students answer from recognition not memory
- being subject to guessing

In addition to the guidelines for writing effective questions presented earlier, when you write true-false questions, you should:
- Use statements that are absolutely true or false.
- Check that statements are specific and direct, not implied.
- Ensure that parts of each statement are either all true or all false.
- Name the authority when opinions or values are tested.
- Avoid direct quotes from books.
- Use approximately the same number of true and false questions.

Well-written true-false questions have one fact that determines the answer. Figure 14.1 shows an example of a well-written true-false question. Determine why figure 14.2 shows a poorly-written question.

You can phrase true-false questions to give Yes/No, High/Low, Agree/Disagree, Fact/Opinion answers.

14.5 Multiple-Choice Questions

You should use multiple-choice questions when you need to:
- measure numerous learning outcomes in a short time
- have your students differentiate between a list of similar choices
- reduce the guess factor as compared to true-false questions

Advantages, if written properly, include:
- the ability to test all levels of learning
  - There are some who will argue this point.
- the ability to test subtle differences
- testing many facts in a short time
- being easy to score
- being non-ambiguous
- requiring minimal student input

Disadvantages include:
- difficulty in measuring some skills such as problem-solving or organizational skills
- being difficult to write in that it is challenging to make all of the answer choices believable
- being subject to guessing and to the process of elimination
- not reliably measuring the skill when students answer from recognition not memory
- students being able to learn how to master multiple-choice tests
  - This is not a problem if the questions are well written.
- taking a lot of screen room
  - This depends on the font, font size, and screen size used.

Well-written multiple-choice questions have:
- only one correct or obviously best answer
- the stem, the first part of a multiple-choice question, holding all repeated words
  - The stem is an incomplete statement or a direct question.
- a purpose for each answer choice (i.e., is based on a misconception)
  - When a wrong answer is selected, you can then provide specific corrective feedback to the misconception. Alternatively, provide feedback for all of the misconceptions to be sure that they receive an explanation for each. Do this if you are telling the learners the answer on their first try.
  - Having a purpose helps make each choice believable. Otherwise, the student is unlikely to ever select the alternative.
- rare use of "all of the above" and "none of the above"
- four or five choices
  - When there are fewer choices, students have a better chance of guessing the correct answer.
  - Six choices are the recommended maximum.
  - Three choices are also acceptable, especially if you cannot think of other good incorrect answers. Why create a fourth or fifth choice if a student will never select it?
- short alternatives that are about the same length
- answer choices in a logically-sequenced, when appropriate, vertical list that complete a sentence
- answer choices that are not paraphrases or synonyms of each other
  - Avoid using opposite answer choices. They may be better suited to true-false questions.
- answer choices that have something in common, if possible

Figure 14.1 – Well-written true-false question

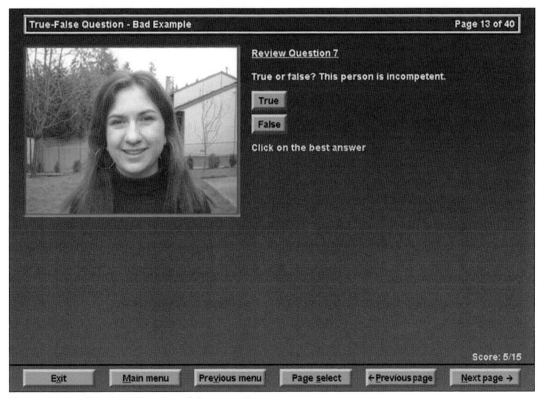

Figure 14.2 – Poorly-written true-false question

Consider writing multiple-choice questions that ask for more than one correct answer. For example, three out of five answers could be correct. These questions can be easier to write because it can be difficult to create four good wrong answers. These questions can also help reinforce learning. For example, there is more than one reason to reduce pollution. If you only ask for one reason, it could imply that there is only one reason.

If you have a penalty for guessing (an assumption for when a student gets a question wrong), say so and state the penalty's size (e.g., minus 0.2 marks for each incorrect answer). Penalizing students is usually unnecessary and is very unpopular.

See figure 14.3 for an example of a well-written multiple-choice question. Determine two reasons why figure 14.4 shows a poorly-written multiple-choice question.

14.6 Matching Questions

You should use matching questions when you need to:
- measure numerous learning outcomes in a short time
- have your students differentiate between a list of similar choices
- reduce the guess factor, as compared to true-false and multiple-choice questions

Advantages, if written properly, include:
- being able to test complex learning
- testing many facts in one question
- being easy to score
- being non-ambiguous
- the ability to test subtle differences

Disadvantages include:
- difficulty in writing good questions
- being subject to guessing and the process of elimination
- not reliably measuring the skill when students answer from recognition not memory

Well-written matching questions have:
- clear directions, on the same page, that include:
  - what is contained in each column
  - the relationship that is the basis for the matching
  - whether choices can be used more than once or not at all
- a maximum of nine matches
  - If you have more than nine matches, create two or more questions.
  - Computer screens may be crowded with over five matches.
  - This is affected by the font size and screen resolution.
- the givens column (left) shorter than the choices column (right) or allow choices to be used more than once
  - This reduces the guessing factor.
- the choices column entries in a logical order to reduce searching time
  - You do this through using an increasing numeric or alphabetic order.
- the choices column entries appearing similar

See figure 14.5 for an example of a well-written matching question. Determine two reasons why figure 14.6 shows a poorly-written matching question.

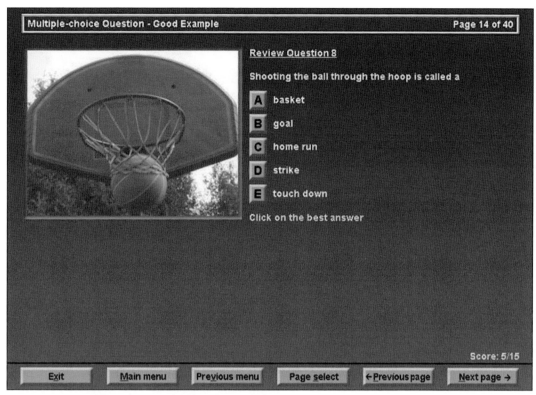

Figure 14.3 – Well-written multiple-choice question

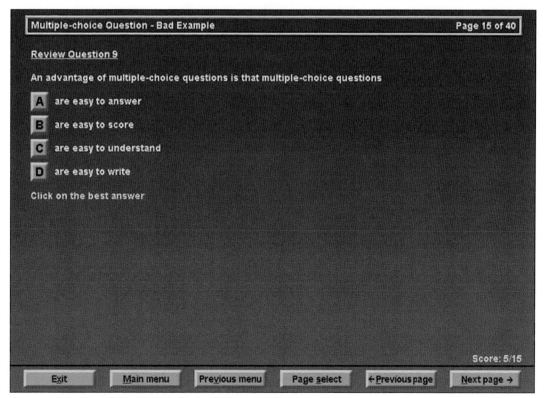

Figure 14.4 – Poorly-written multiple-choice question

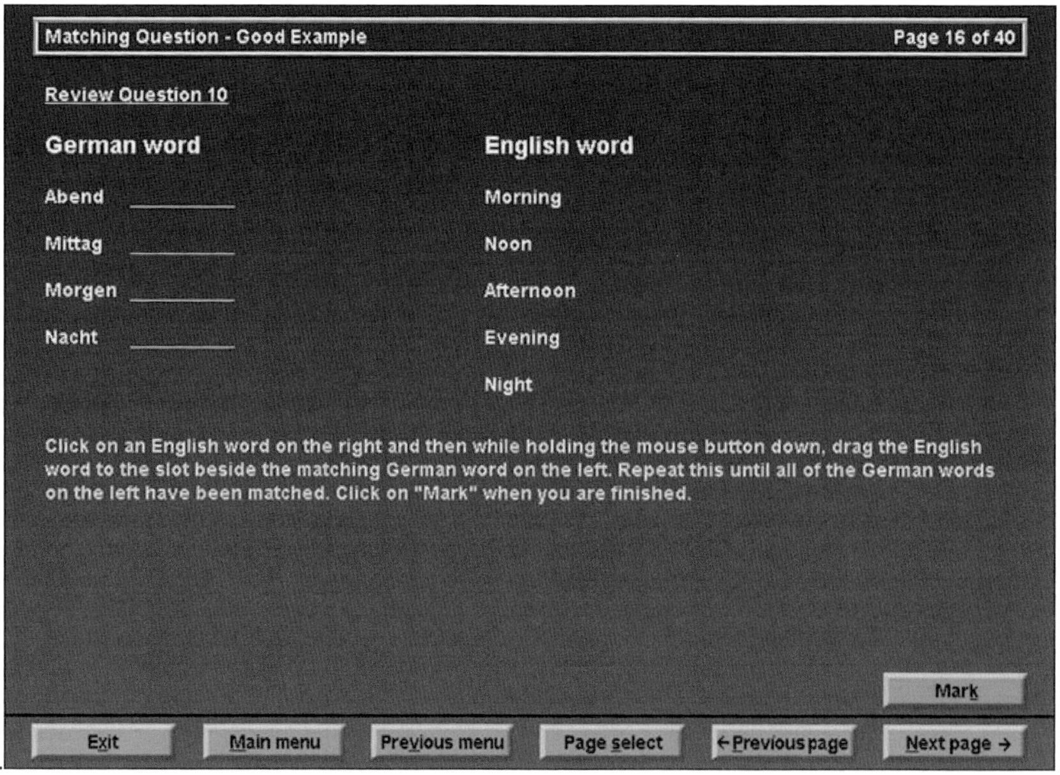

Figure 14.5 – Well-written matching question

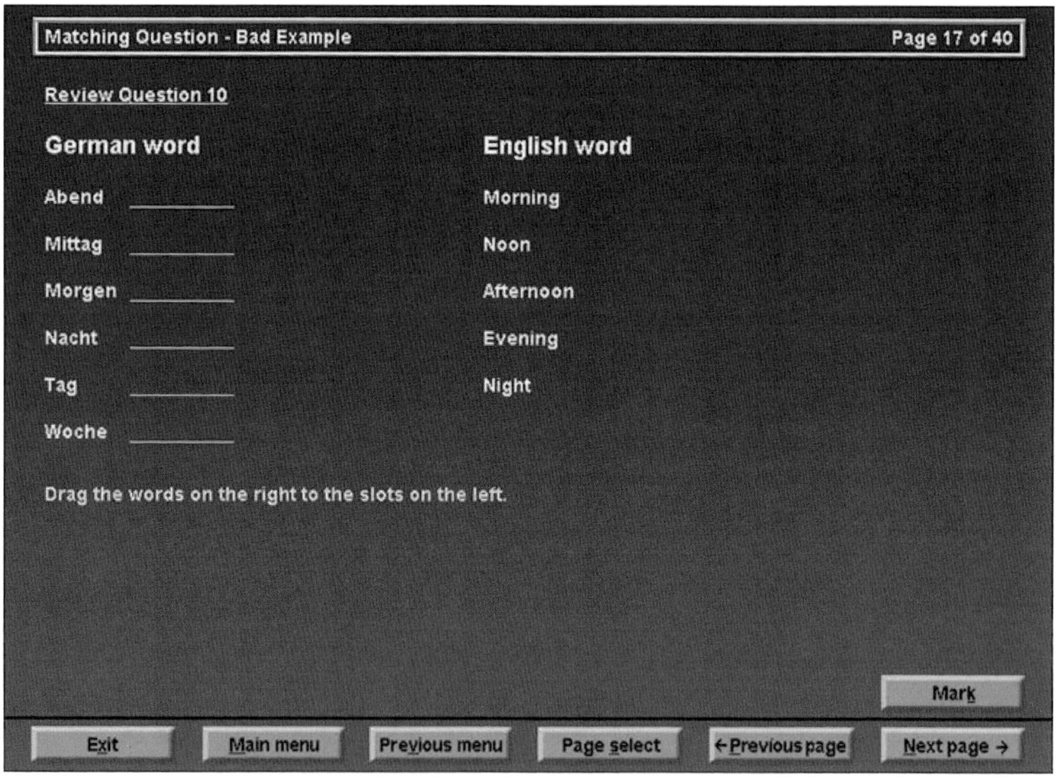

Figure 14.6 – Poorly-written matching question

14.7 Short-Answer Questions

Short-answer questions can have a variety of forms such as completing a sentence, answering a question, and providing a list.

You should use short-answer questions when you need to:
- test recall rather than recognition of information
- check computational and problem-solving skills
- evaluate knowledge of procedural skills
- minimize the guess factor as compared to true-false, multiple-choice, and matching questions

Advantages, if written properly, include:
- testing many facts in a short time
- being easy to score
- having a low guess factor
- taking little screen room
- reliably measuring the skill since students answer from memory not recognition

Disadvantages include:
- being difficult to score objectively
- difficulty in measuring complex learning
- the relatively high likelihood of having ambiguity
- problems in handling spelling, grammar, and extra words
  - Some authoring tools have weak short-answer marking capabilities.
- taking a lot of time to determine and program separate feedback for all of the expected wrong answers, especially you provide different feedback for each try
- sometimes requiring a lot of student input

Well-written short-answer questions:
- have instructions that include rules for spelling, grammar, extra words, units, significant figures...
  - If the detailed instructions are simple, this can be stated in a test's introduction rather than continually providing the detailed instructions for every question.
- have one answer slot per question, unless the learner will provide a list
- only have specific keywords omitted
  - The omitted keywords should preferably be located at the end of the statement. This is less confusing than having the missing keyword at the beginning of the statement and much less confusing than placing the missing keyword in the middle of the statement. For example, a question should be stated as, "Questions that require one to three word answers are called _____." A question should not be written as, "Questions called _____ require one to three word answers."
- only have one word or phrase that can answer the question
- have all answer slots the same size or one size for text and one size for numbers
  - Some programs show or force the number of characters or digits needed. This can provide a clue to the answer.
  - For practical reasons, limit the number of characters a student can enter.

See figure 14.7 for an example of a well-written short-answer question. Determine why figure 14.8 shows a poorly-written short-answer question.

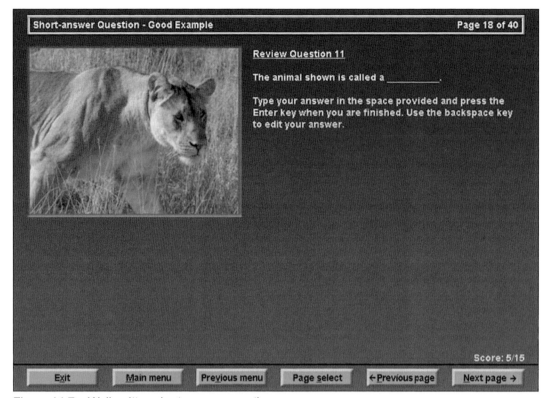

Figure 14.7 – Well-written short-answer question

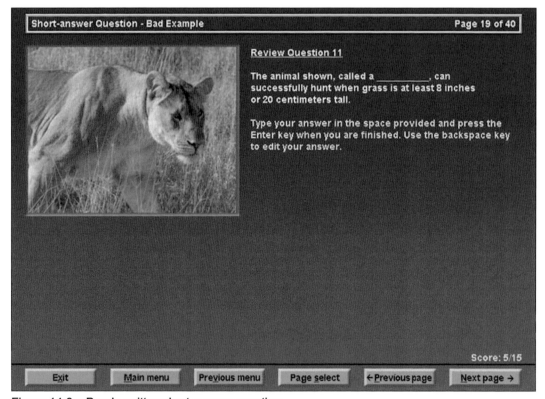

Figure 14.8 – Poorly-written short-answer question

14.8 Long-Answer/Essay Questions

Long-answer questions, sometimes called essay questions, can entail a variety of challenges. These challenges can range from case studies or problem-based learning situations that require the student to apply, analyze, synthesize, or evaluate related products, processes, information, ideas, or procedures. You can decide whether your long-answer questions will refer to resources or have limits on length, time, or scope. Remember that potential problems can stem from students having difficulty with the keyboard and in editing their answers.

Long-answer questions are particularly useful when you need to assess a student's ability to:
• write
• evaluate information
• synthesize ideas
• analyze information
• organize thoughts and ideas
• apply information
• explain, describe, and/or recall content

Long-answer questions can be graded by computers based on provided models. However, there are complexities with marking opinions and ideas. In general, authoring tools do not have built-in capabilities to grade long-answer questions. However, some software tools allow you to record student input to long-answer questions for marking later either manually or by specialized software programs.

In addition to the guidelines for writing effective questions presented earlier, well-written long-answer questions should have:
• clear directions that include:
  - the criteria for scoring (that you should analyze before your students answer the question)
  - guidelines for the length of the response such as the number of words
  - rules, if needed, for marking spelling and grammar
• enough space to fill in the answer

14.9 Question Analysis

By analyzing questions, you can determine whether questions are effective or ineffective and obtain information for improving them. Improving poorly-written questions can help prevent student frustration. However, the reality is that very few people have time to do question analysis and it is rarely a budgeted task. (Details for conducting a question analysis are presented in Appendix VI.)

Summary

You can use questions in both presentations and tests to reinforce learning, test understanding, help the student to apply learning to problems, and keep the student involved.

In situations where learners are usually on their own, write your questions perfectly. Be sure that testing is effective, questions are well written, and students will not become frustrated.

True-false, multiple-choice, matching, and short-answer questions each have many advantages, disadvantages, and unique characteristics. Generally, you should include a variety of these question types. Long-answer questions may not be marked well by computers.

Application Exercises

1) Rewrite the following question to improve it.
   Multiple-choice questions
   a) are excellent for testing many facts in a short time
   b) are very good for measuring more than one learning outcome at a time
   c) are excellent for taking little screen room
   d) are very good for minimizing the guessing factor
2) Rewrite the following question to improve it.
   Common forms of student input include mouse, _____, and keyboard.
3) Rewrite the following question to improve it.
   True or false? The most important component of air is oxygen.
4) As the number of choices in a multiple-choice question increases, the probability of students guessing the correct answer decreases. In a multiple-choice question, is it reasonable to ask students to only choose between three answers? Justify your answer.
5) If a subject-matter expert has a favorite question that fits within a topic but does **not** test a learning outcome, should the question be used? Explain your answer.
6) Should humorous choices be included in multiple-choice questions? Support your answer.

Case Study

Six instructors were on a four-week professional development leave from their regular duties. During this time, the instructors participated in a workshop on creating instructional multimedia applications. One goal of the workshop was to create a small tutorial so that the instructors could apply what they learned. As a part of the instructional design process, the instructors determined that students needed to be able to manipulate variables and observe the results.

Case Study Questions

1) The tutorial included a discovery-learning approach that allowed students to manipulate variables and observe the results. Given this provided a high degree of interactivity, would having students answer questions during the presentation also be useful? Support your answer.
2) The tutorial contained questions during the presentation and self-test questions at the end of each major section. Was there too much interactivity? Justify your answer.

References

Alessi, S., & Trollip, S. (1991). Computer-based instruction: Methods and development (2nd ed.). Englewood Cliffs, NJ: Prentice-Hall, Inc.

Dick, W., & Carey, L. (1990). The systematic design of instruction (3rd ed.). Glenville, IL: Harper Collins Publishers.

Mayer, M. (1988). Test item construction: A self-instructional manual. Victoria, British Columbia, Canada: Province of British Columbia, Ministry of Advanced Education and Job Training.

Williams, R., & Dreher, H. (2004). Automatically grading essays with Markit©. Proceedings of the 2004 Informing Science and IT Education Joint Conference.

Williams, R., & Dreher, H. (2005). Formative Assessment Visual Feedback in Computer-Graded Essays. The Journal of Issues in Informing Science and Information Technology, 2, 23-32.

Chapter 15:   Feedback

Learning Outcomes

After completing this chapter, you should be able to:
* explain why feedback should be included in lessons
* explain why elaborative feedback is more effective than verification feedback
* state characteristics of effective feedback
* state what can be generally included in correct, partly correct, incorrect, invalid, and unanticipated answer feedback
* discuss when audio feedback is appropriate and inappropriate
* discuss considerations in providing learner control over feedback
* create instructional multimedia solutions that include effective feedback

Introduction

Feedback is any information that you give to a learner based on a learner's input. Use feedback to help the learner improve subsequent actions. If you include effective feedback in multimedia lessons, you will help maximize learning. Feedback influences the learning process by motivating the learner and reducing uncertainty. Feedback can also lead to increased attendance.

This chapter distinguishes between elaborative and verification feedback and presents characteristics of effective feedback. This chapter also presents guidelines for providing correct, partly correct, incorrect, invalid, and unanticipated answer feedback. You will also be given recommendations for using sounds and special effects for feedback and the control that you should provide students for the amount of feedback they receive.

Although this chapter focuses on providing feedback for instructional multimedia applications, you can use most of the information to give effective feedback for other delivery methods.

15.1 Feedback Characteristics

The feedback you provide can be for verification or be elaborative. Verification feedback, which is typically used in testing, often only states that an answer is correct or incorrect but can take the form of praise, animations, and sound effects. Verification feedback can include a recommendation for the student to review specific areas of weakness. For example, if testing shows that a student has not mastered a learning outcome then you could give the student the option of going back to review that particular part of the presentation. Note that students can get frustrated if you force them to review material.

Elaborative or informational feedback, which often accompanies an incorrect response, typically takes the form of corrective statements and elaborations (i.e., an explanation of why answers are right or wrong) or guidance in how to attain the stated learning outcome. This additional elaborative instruction is vital for efficient learning and can significantly help students understand concepts and their errors. Although elaborative feedback enhances learning much more than verification feedback, not all students need full elaborations for every answer they provide. However, if you choose to omit elaborative feedback since some students may not need it, you would compromise the learning of students who do need it.

> **Practical Guideline:**
>
> Provide elaborative feedback to enhance learning.

The ability to give specific elaborative feedback is a major strength of instructional multimedia applications as compared to traditional instructional packages. Since you know all of a student's input, you can code the instructional program to provide feedback for any input. You can also use the computer to record which questions the student got wrong and then later ask those questions again.

In general, to be most effective, your feedback:
- should be immediate
  - A delay can decrease its effectiveness.
  - There are a few instances where delayed feedback is preferred. Examples can be found in simulations where learners make choices such as in doctors making a diagnosis, automotive repairs, and life decisions about taking drugs. In these situations, it can be useful to let students see the consequences of their choices at the end of the simulation.
  - Learners seem to expect immediate feedback with computer technology and can become frustrated if you delay the computer's response.
- should be positive and non-threatening
  - Do **not** talk down to students or punish students for making mistakes.

[handwritten in margin: affective feedback]

> **Practical Guideline:**
>
> In general, always provide immediate positive feedback.

- should lead to learning but **not** contain new information
  - If specific information is only contained in the feedback then there is a possibility that the student will not receive the information. If the information is important then the student should receive it as a part of the presentation. Another factor is that students could get frustrated if they did not have a fair chance to correctly answer the question.
  - Remember that feedback can include any effective medium. Text is the most common medium even though it is sometimes ineffective. For example, in an identification task, a visual and label could be more effective than text. For procedural tasks, it can be very effective to show video clips of correct procedures, especially when questions are based on video clips of incorrect procedures.
- can address more than just the content
  - You can also use feedback to provide the learner with information about strategies to try, about how they should proceed in the program, to increase confidence, to provide encouragement, and about how well they are doing.
- can be different for each try
  - If you provide more than one try per questions, consider providing hints with more information on each try. There is no need to tell the student everything right away. Ideally, if the student can think through to the answer, more learning can take place than if you give the most detailed feedback right away. This requires more design and development time.
  - However, the research is inconclusive about whether more learning takes place if learners try questions more than once before seeing the correct answer. You should tell the students the correct answer and give detailed feedback no later than after the third try. Note that forcing students to provide the correct answer after the answer has been given can frustrate them. It is usually best to simply allow the student to proceed in the program after you reveal the correct answer.
  - Avoid repetitious feedback by alternating the wording. For example, cycle between the words "Correct," "Good," and "Right". Repetitious wording can get boring and fail to motivate.

- should be provided for all correct, partly correct, incorrect, invalid, and unanticipated responses
    - For any answer, you should provide enough explanation or guidance to help the student continue working towards achieving the learning outcome. Otherwise, the student may not know what to do.

15.2 Correct Answer Feedback

For correct answers, your feedback can and often should include why the:
- answer is correct
    - This is important in case the student guessed the answer or got the right answer for the wrong reasons. Stating the correct answer also reinforces the correct answer.
- other answers are incorrect
    - This can enhance learning by providing clarification.

An example of elaborative correct answer feedback can be seen in figure 15.1.

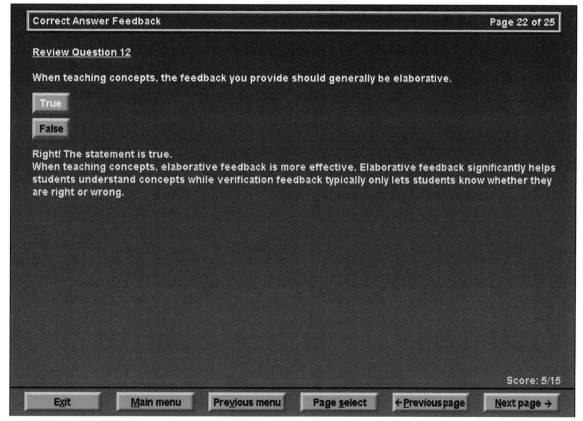

Figure 15.1 – Elaborative correct answer feedback

Practical Guideline:

In general, for correct answers state why the answer is correct and why other answers are incorrect.

15.3 Partly Correct and Incorrect Answer Feedback

For partly correct and incorrect answers, your feedback should usually include:
- a statement of the correct answer
- why the correct answer is correct
- why the student's answer is partly correct or incorrect
- why other answers are incorrect

These details provide students with complete information for analyzing their response. An example of elaborative partly correct answer feedback can be seen in figure 15.2.

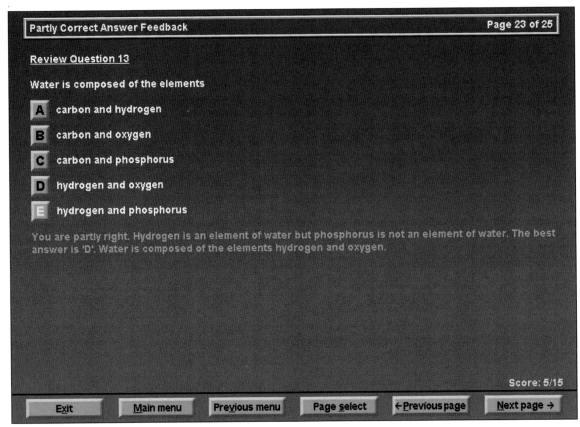

Figure 15.2 – Partly correct answer feedback

15.4 Invalid Answer Feedback

The system must be able to appropriately respond to unexpected input. For invalid answers, your feedback can and often should include:
- what was done incorrectly
- the set of correct responses

This information will help prevent students from making another invalid response.

For example, for mouse input, your feedback could be, "You clicked outside of the diagram. Click on any component in the diagram." For keyboard input, if a student presses "G" on a true-false question, your feedback could be, "Sorry, 'G' is not a valid response. Valid responses are 'T' and 'F'. Please press Enter to try again."

15.5 Unanticipated Answer Feedback

For unanticipated answers, such as in short-answer questions, your feedback can include statements such as:
- the response was not interpreted and the student should phrase the response in another way and try again
- a suggestion to check for spelling
- rules for grammar and extra words if they will impact answer judging
- a hint especially if there has been more than one unanticipated response
- instructions on how to try the question again, if it is not intuitive for all

15.6 Sound/Special Effects

Generally, do **not** use sound/special effects such as beeps, musical tunes, and characters dancing for feedback. Sound effects:
- can distract other students, especially in a lab or library setting
- can be embarrassing if it draws attention to the student's incorrect responses
- may cause students to deliberately provide incorrect responses if the sound/special effect is desired
  - This sometimes happens when the incorrect sound/special effect is humorous or more interesting than the response for correct answers.
- waste development time and money

If you provide sound effects, allow learners to turn the sounds off.

> **Practical Guideline:**
>
> Avoid using sounds and special effects for feedback.

Note that there are some worthwhile uses of audio feedback.
- Audio feedback can be particularly effective when teaching languages.
- Audio feedback, such as sound effects, can be useful in providing realism in simulations and educational games.
- Sound effects can motivate, especially young children.

15.7 Feedback Control

Feedback control refers to the amount of feedback that students can choose to receive. If the amount of feedback can be controlled by students, the amount selected is likely to vary significantly between learners. However, most students typically prefer elaborative feedback to verification feedback.

The amount of feedback selected tends to increase with student maturity and the material's difficulty. Since weaker students are less likely to choose elaborative feedback, it is safer for you to automatically include elaborative feedback – which they need whether they know it or not. Students who do not need or want the elaborations can simply choose to not read the feedback. Another reason to automatically including elaborative feedback is that allowing learners to control the amount of feedback provided adds an unnecessary level of complexity to you, students, and development team members.

Summary

Feedback is any information that you give to a learner based on a learner's input. Feedback helps the learner improve subsequent actions. If you include effective feedback in multimedia lessons, you will help maximize learning. Feedback influences the learning process by motivating the learner and reducing uncertainty.

Your feedback can be for verification or be elaborative. Verification feedback often only states that an answer is correct or incorrect. Elaborative or informational feedback typically takes the form of corrective statements and elaborations. This additional elaborative instruction is vital for efficient learning and significantly helps students understand concepts and their errors.

In general, your feedback should be immediate and positive. Avoid using sounds and special effects for feedback unless you are teaching languages or providing realism in simulations and educational games.

You should provide feedback for correct, partly correct, incorrect, invalid, and unanticipated answers. For any answer, you should give enough explanation or guidance to help the student continue working towards achieving the learning outcome.

Rather than allowing students to control the amount of feedback they receive, you should automatically provide students with elaborative feedback.

Application Exercises

1) A student has just watched a video clip of an explosion. In a question that asks if energy was released or absorbed, the student correctly answers that energy has been released. How could you elaborate to provide better feedback than simply stating that his answer was correct?
2) On a multiple-choice question, a student mistakenly entered a "w". The feedback stated, "That is not a valid answer, please try again." How can you improve the feedback?
3) On a short-answer question, a student enters "beer and whiskey" and the correct answer is "beer and wine". The feedback stated, "Incorrect, please try again." How can you improve the feedback?
4) The feedback for a question provided the student with some new information that was critical for answering the question. What should have been done instead? Explain your answer.
5) One of your team members has read some research that suggests that some learners should be allowed to control the amount of feedback they receive. If he makes this suggestion to you, what could you say to justify why elaborative feedback should automatically be provided?

Case Study

Six instructors were on a four-week professional development leave from their regular duties. During this time, the instructors participated in a workshop on creating instructional multimedia applications. One goal of the workshop was to create a small tutorial so that the instructors could apply what they learned.

As a part of the instructional design process, the instructors determined that questions should be frequently asked and feedback should be provided. Due to the time constraints, there was some question as to whether the feedback should be informative or elaborative. The instructors decided to provide elaborative feedback and **not** put any time into making the presentation "glitzy".

Case Study Question

Did the instructors make a good decision in deciding to provide elaborative feedback? Justify your answer.

References

Clariana, R. (1993, Summer). A review of multiple-try feedback in traditional and computer-based instruction. Journal of Computer-Based Instruction, 20(3), 67-74.

Clariana, R. (1993, Spring). The motivational effect of advisement on attendance and achievement in computer-based instruction. Journal of Computer-Based Instruction, 20(2), 47-51.

Dempsey, J., & Sales, G. (Eds). (1993). Interactive instruction and feedback. Englewood Cliffs, NJ: Prentice Hall.

Romiszowski, A. (1988). The selection and use of instructional media: For improved classroom teaching and for interactive, individual instruction (2nd ed.). New York, NY: Nichols Publishing.

Sales, G., & Williams, M. (1988, Fall). The effect of adaptive control of feedback in computer-based instruction. Journal of Research on Computing in Education, 21(1), 97-111.

Vockell, E. (1990, August/September). Instructional principles behind computer use. The Computing Teacher, 18(1), 10-15.

Section 4: Screen Design

Screen design is an essential and integral part of all instructional multimedia applications. Your screen design can influence your product's success or failure. This section describes the various screen components, how to make programs user-friendly, and how to effectively use color and highlighting.

Chapter 16: Screen Design

Learning Outcomes

After completing this chapter, you should be able to:
*   describe the different screen components
*   explain why screens should **not** be blocked off into components
*   describe the purpose of each screen component
*   explain why icons should contain a meaningful text label
*   list potential problems associated with graphical user-interfaces
*   describe what can be done to make menus easy to use
*   design effective instructional multimedia screens
*   design screens that are sight appealing and easy to read
*   design effective menus

Introduction

Your screen design determines how each screen will appear to learners and how the learners will interact with the computer. Effective screen design is a critical component of successful multimedia applications. This chapter describes the different screen components and provides guidelines for their design. The different screen components are orientation information, presented material, directions and input, feedback and error messages, and control options. This chapter discusses the use of icons and graphical user-interfaces and their potential problems. Different menu types are described and suggestions are given for making menus easy to use.

In general, the presented principles apply to applications delivered on DVD-ROM/CD-ROM and through web browsers. A major difference, however, is that you need to be sure that learners have the bandwidth to handle your web-browser design.

16.1 Screen Components

Screens for instructional multimedia applications should have different components. Common components include orientation information, presented material, direction and input, feedback and error messages, and control options. Figure 16.1 illustrates these components. In computer-managed presentations that do not provide questions and feedback, the important screen components include orientation information and the presented material.

> **Practical Guideline:**
>
> Make screen components consistent, simple, distinct, and easy to find.

You should make screen components distinct and easy to find. You can achieve this through screen location (e.g., top line for the orientation information), foreground color (e.g., bright cyan or white for the main text color), and background color (e.g., dark gray or dark blue for teaching screens). Consistency is important for reducing search time and can help prevent student frustration.

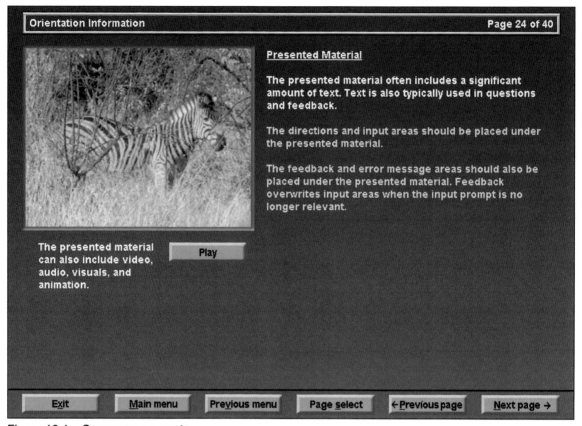

Figure 16.1 – Screen components

Generally, your screen designs should be as simple as possible. (This is not to imply that you should not teach complex information.) As a guideline, if you have to explain how to use the program then there is a weakness in the design. With effective screen design, you can increase user-friendliness, enhance motivation, and reduce learning time.

Practical Guideline:

Develop with the guideline: If you have to explain how to use it, you have done something wrong.

For specific situations, you may have to create a unique design. Thoroughly test the design in the early stages of development. You may want to first test your design using a paper prototype.

Do **not** block the screen into distinct areas. An example is shown in figure 16.2. Blocking off areas can lead to problems such as not having enough room for all of the text that may be needed to teach the concept or situations where two visuals are needed on a screen. Blocking off areas is also restrictive for unique situations such as simulations.

The different screen components are discussed below.

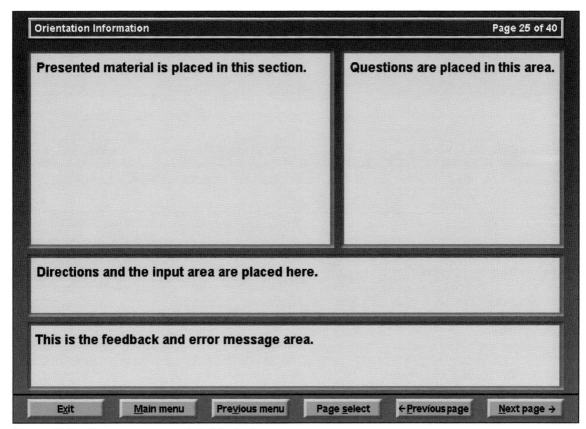

| Orientation Information | Page 25 of 40 |

Presented material is placed in this section.

Questions are placed in this area.

Directions and the input area are placed here.

This is the feedback and error message area.

| Exit | Main menu | Previous menu | Page select | ←Previous page | Next page → |

Figure 16.2 – Screen components in blocked areas

16.1-1 Orientation Information

Orientation information can include the lesson name (usually based on the name of the menu and, if applicable, submenu button), page number, and the total number of pages in the lesson. For example, if this chapter of the textbook was presented in an instructional multimedia application, the orientation information line could read, "16. Screen Design, page 3 of 15".

You can use orientation information to:
- help prevent students from getting lost, especially if you have levels of menus or branch the student out of the main flow
- help students easily return to the same location in the lesson
- provide a reference point for students to later ask questions
- give a reference point for debugging and editing

Page totals provide an estimate of the time required to complete the lesson. This can be useful for helping students decide whether to attempt the lesson. Note that you should **not** state an estimated amount of time that it should take to complete the lesson. It may negatively affect the self-esteem of students who take more than the stated time. Students who finish early may view the lesson as trivial.

You should place orientation information on the screen's top line, starting on the left. With orientation information in this location, students are more likely to "orient" themselves before they proceed with the presented material. It is relatively pointless to orient the student later in the screen.

Practical Guideline:

Place orientation information on the screen's top line, starting on the left.

16.1-2 Presented Material

Your presented material can include text, audio, visuals, video, and animation. Ensure that your presented material appears well organized, uncrowded, balanced, as well as visually interesting. This can make the screen appealing, reduce the total reading time, decrease the chance of reading errors, reduce search time, and be less stressful. Students perceive unbalanced, plain, simple, and bare screens as being undesirable. Key information should be put in pertinent or easily found locations. Critical information should be highlighted.

16.1-3 Directions and Input

You should locate directions so that the students clearly see what they should do next. You should usually place the directions for continuing in the screen's bottom right-hand corner. This is a logical place to look after a learner has read the screen contents. Directions for questions should usually appear directly underneath the question as seen in figure 16.3. Learners should be able to intuitively navigate through the program. It is **not** safe to assume that students will read the directions except, perhaps, as a last resort. **Never** slot directions or a keyboard input area into small open areas between parts of the presented material. Students may not find the directions or easily see where their keyboard input is being displayed. This is shown in figure 16.4. First, display the directions and then cue for input since students sometimes stop reading at prompts.

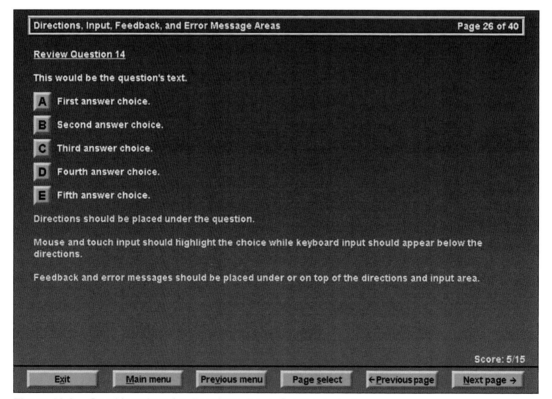

Figure 16.3 – Good locations for directions, input, feedback, and error messages

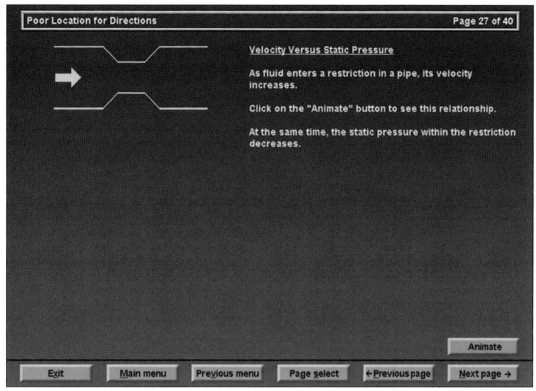

Figure 16.4 – Poor location for directions

Do **not** assume that learners are fluent with computer interfaces. You need to state exactly what the reader must do. Examples include stating:
- click on a button or within a box
- touch the screen at a specific location such as a part of a diagram
- click on each menu item and then on "Continue"
- press a specific key
- press a specific key and then the Enter key

Practical Guideline:
Learners should be able to intuitively navigate through the program.

Standardize terminology and use the conventions consistently. Avoid statements like, "Could you please" or "Would you prefer" as they reduce clarity.

16.1-4 Feedback and Error Messages

You should locate feedback and error messages so that students can clearly see the consequences of their input. Feedback for questions should usually appear directly underneath the question. This can be seen in figure 16.3. Exceptions to this can include feedback that includes video, visuals, or animations. When you show feedback or error messages, erase the question's directions if the prompts are no longer appropriate. **Never** slot feedback and error messages into small open areas between parts of the presented material. Students may miss the information.

Provide simple and meaningful error messages. For example, stating, "The answer should be a number, please try again" is much more effective than a "bad" beep. Standardize the messages and use the conventions consistently. Students should **not** have to spend a lot of time interpreting messages.

Practical Guideline:

Error messages should be simple, meaningful, standardized, and obvious.

16.1-5 Control Options

Control options allow learners to control their own learning paths. You can place control options on the bottom of the screen, in a window, or in a pull-down menu. In general, place control options on the bottom of the screen as this is very convenient for the user. If there is not enough room at the bottom of the screen for all of the needed control options, make the remaining control options available in a pull-down menu or window.

The basic control options, usually in the following order from left to right on the bottom of the screen as shown in figure 16.5, can and often should include:
- Exit (to completely leave the program)
  - If some data needs to be saved, automatically do it for the user.
  - If you record the learner's identification, you can give an option to start where the learner last left off. This does take programming time and has some risk of the learner not being oriented when they return.
  - There is no need to ask a question about whether they really want to exit.
- Main menu (to quickly back out of a section)
- Previous menu (if applicable, such as when the learner selects a submenu of the main menu)
- Page select (to immediately go to any page in the section)
- Previous page (to review)
- Next page (to continue in the normal flow)

Figure 16.5 – Control options shown at the bottom of typical screens

Note that the underlined letter of each control option represents the keyboard key that can used to activate the button instead of using the mouse.

Other control options that can be helpful include:
- Program map (to go to any section in the entire program)
- Glossary (to clarify terminology)
  - This feature is nice to have but is debatably worth the effort given that many learners do not use the feature, especially when the content has been taught well.
- Frequently asked questions
  - This button can be appropriate on the main menu.
- Close, Cancel, or Return (to leave the options menu or return from the glossary ...)
- Restart (to reset variables for the next student)
  - You can place this button on the main menu.
- Technical notes (for describing hardware and software requirements)
  - This information is often placed on the original packaging and/or on a DVD-ROM/CD-ROM jewel case insert. However, it is nice to include it in the program because you cannot be sure that the learner will otherwise have access to the details.
  - You can place this button on the main menu.
- Repeat animation (for seeing an animation again)
- Try again (for games)
- Video control (e.g., fast forward, slow forward, step forward, pause, step backward, slow backward, and fast backward)
  - For many video clips, especially short ones, play, stop, and restart are all that are needed.

As a guideline, you should **not** need a "Help" button. If the user-interface needs explanations then it probably needs to be redesigned. Remember that the user-interface should ideally be intuitive to use. If the learner needs an alternative explanation of the content then consider whether the first version of the content should be rewritten. Another possibility is for you to provide, when needed, a button that leads to detailed descriptions, more sample problems or examples, other diagrams, or references.

If you choose to not have all of the control options available on the screen, have one easy click, touch, or key press for "more options". The "more options" button must be clearly available on each page. Do **not** assume that all students will remember hidden active screen areas or special function keys such as "F3" being "More options". Options must be intuitive to understand, simple to use, and be easily accessible on every page.

Practical Guideline:
Ensure options are intuitive to understand, simple to use, and easily accessible on every page.

In computer-managed presentations, branching options can allow you to quickly move throughout the information.

(Check the User-friendliness chapter for related information.)

16.1-6 Option Availability

You should make most options available on each screen. Some options should not be available in all of the program locations. For example, in many cases a glossary should not be available in test sections. The available options should be consistent in similar sections and be presented in the same sequence to reduce student searching/reading time. This is easily done using computer programming sub-routines.

If you make the options available in a window, include a "Return," "Close," or "Cancel" prompt to allow students to return to where they started without selecting a "branching" option. If a prompt is not provided, as may be done in a pull-down menu, then returning without selecting an option must be easy and obvious. This may be done by simply clicking anywhere outside of the menu.

16.2 Icon Prompts

Icons are graphic or symbolic representations of objects or processes. In general, icons should be relatively small and simple. You can use icons, such as an arrow to represent the next page prompt, for prompts or options if they **also** contain a clear and unambiguous text label. Labels are needed to ensure that students know the icon's function. Without a text label, there is room for error because:

* Icons are not standardized with all past and present software packages and will unlikely be in the future.
* Some learners will expect certain icons to have specific functions.
  - These expectations may not match the program being developed. For example, a "Return" icon of one program could be like the "Previous page" icon of the program being developed.
* Some learners will forget an icon's meaning, especially icons that are rarely used.
* There will always be learners who have not previously experienced a multimedia learning package.

Practical Guideline:
If icons are used, include a clear and unambiguous text label with each one.

Look at the two icons in figure 16.6. Which icon is more clearly understood?

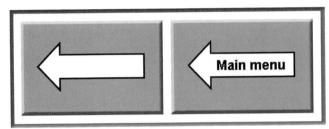

Figure 16.6 – Icons with text labels are clearly understood

You can also use icons or small images to provide learners with a visual clue as to where they are in the program. This allows learners to simply recognize where they are rather than having to specifically think about it. This does not imply that the text orientation information should be omitted.

16.3 Graphical User-Interfaces

From a practical perspective, all of the screen design issues discussed form the foundation for creating a functional and intuitive graphical user-interface. However, you can extend a graphical user-interface further like those found in the *Windows*® operating system. This is seen in figure 16.7. Some learners prefer the "look and feel" of these graphical user-interfaces. However, these graphical user-interfaces can have the same problems as icons, as stated above. In some graphical user-interface environments, learners may be able to accidentally close the window, pick up the window and move it (even partially off the screen), and change the window's size so that not all of the presented material can be seen. You must consider how to handle these potential problems. If the authoring tool cannot solve these problems, consider providing training, having a facilitator present, or even selecting a different authoring tool.

Note that single-window presentations tend to be easier to use and can lead to higher achievement than multiple-window presentations.

If you use a graphical user-interface, as much as is possible or reasonable, follow existing standards to help minimize any possible confusion.

16.4 Menus

Menus allow users to choose their own paths and break large amounts of material into manageable sections containing related information.

As guidelines, your menus should:
- be logical
  - Menus should offer a logical route to the desired information.
  - Meaningful names can help make the menu logical and increase comprehension, retention, and attitude.
- have single clicks, key presses, or touches
  - This makes the menu easy and fast to use.
- be easily accessible at all times
  - Students should be able to quickly move around the program.
- be uncrowded
  - Consider nine choices to be a maximum. However, it is common to have a main menu button for each section of a program.
  - If in doubt, create a submenu.

- be a maximum of three levels deep
  - Too many menu levels can affect student comprehension.
  - A maximum of three levels deep makes it fast for students to reach all of the material.

Practical Guideline:

Keep menus simple, uncrowded, and a maximum of three levels deep.

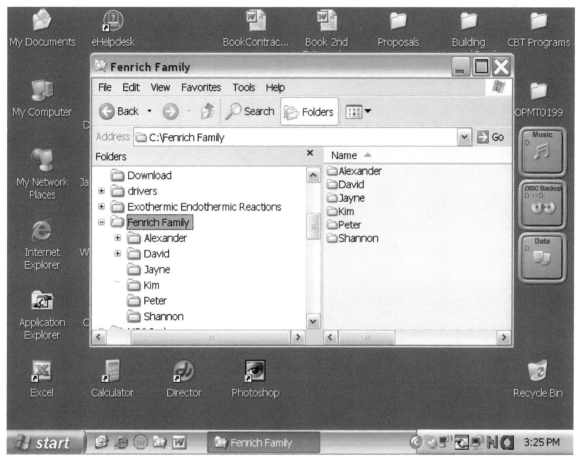

Figure 16.7 – Screen design of the *Windows®* operating system

16.4-1 Menu Types

The three most common types of menus you can use are:
- full-screen (see figure 16.8)
  - These menus often consist of visuals and text labels in boxes that are active selection areas.
  - Full-screen menus are often used for main menus.
- windows (see figure 16.9 - note how the rest of the screen is still seen)
  - In instructional multimedia applications, these menus are often used for control options.
- pull-down (see figure 16.10 - note how the rest of the screen is still seen)
  - In instructional multimedia applications, these menus are often used for control options.
  - Accessing pull-down menus requires skills such as holding a mouse button down and being able to close the menu. Will **every** student know and remember how to work with pull-down menus?

Vertical menus (figure 16.11) are the easiest to read and use. Clear and uncrowded horizontal menus (figure 16.12) can also be effective. If your menu contains boxes then order the boxes sequentially from left to right then down (as shown in figure 16.8). This is logical to most learners since this is the way they read English. However, if menu items are independent of each other, order the menu items sequentially from high to low priority.

Given the ease at which visual images are brought into programs, some multimedia designers have chosen to use menu metaphors in order to make the program more sight appealing. Menu metaphors are visual representations of menu items. For example, an image of a coffee shop could represent where learners can electronically communicate with each other about non-instructional issues while a picture of a bookshelf or the school library could be used to show where reference materials can be found. Menu metaphors can be esthetically pleasing and even lead to exploration but can be problematic. Menu metaphors are indirect in that learners are forced to infer the representation's meaning. You can never be sure if the learner will interpret the metaphor correctly or even if the learner will find the "invisible" input area. For example, a bookshelf metaphor could be interpreted as an area to find reference materials or to find reading assignments, assuming the learner realizes that the bookshelf is a menu item. Over time, this problem is minimized in that menu metaphors are usually memorized. A pleasant compromise between menu metaphors and text buttons is to use buttons that contain a visual and text. Remember that buttons are common in everyday life, such as on elevators and telephones, and are consequently natural to "push" (i.e., click) if you want something done.

16.5 Planning

To ensure that the screens will appear as you intend and to prevent wasted effort, you must plan the screen design. Specifications or guidelines must be set for:
- the screen size to be used
  - Consider possible computer monitor and computer projector limitations.
- the screen locations and sizes of images and video displays
- the color palette to be used
- the locations, colors, appearance, font, and font sizes of each screen component
- how menus will be designed
- which control options will be available at different points in the program
- utilities such as a glossary and program map
- how learners will access control options and control media
- how learners will enter input

Note that these screen design specifications and guidelines need to have some flexibility. It is reasonable to expect that you may need to make exceptions within a program and certainly between programs. If you make a deviation from a specification then it should be an informed and approved decision.

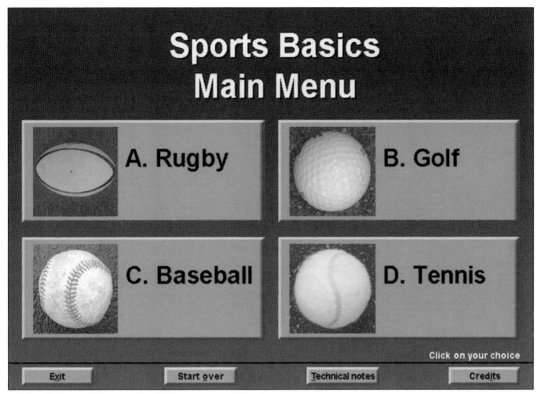

Figure 16.8 – Full-screen menu

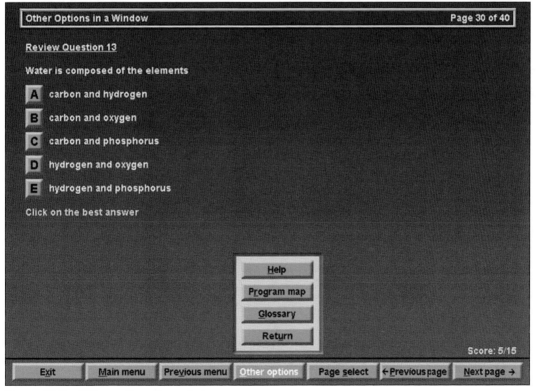

Figure 16.9 – Other options in a window

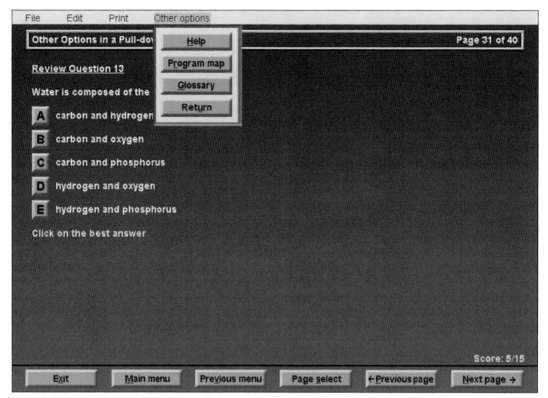

Figure 16.10 – Other options in a pull-down menu

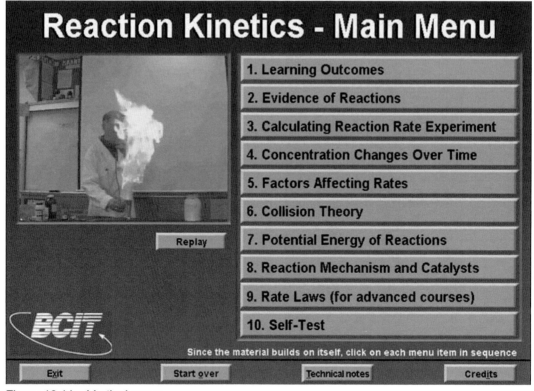

Figure 16.11 – Vertical menu

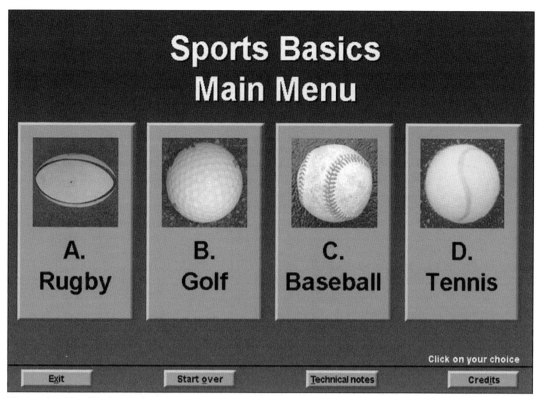

Figure 16.12 – Horizontal menu

Summary

Your screens should have different components or areas including orientation information, presented material, direction and input, feedback and error messages, and control options. Make screen components distinct and easy to find but do **not** block off separate areas. As a rule, screens should be consistent and as simple as possible. Test all screen designs in the early stages of development. Develop with the guideline; if you have to explain how to use it, you have done something wrong.

Orientation information can include the lesson/topic name, page number, and lesson page total. You should locate orientation information on the screen's top line.

The presented material can include text, audio, visuals, video, and animation. Put key information in easily found locations. Highlight critical information. Ensure your presented material appears well organized, uncrowded, and balanced.

Place directions so that the student clearly sees what should be done next. You should usually place the directions for continuing in the screen's bottom line or right hand corner. Directions for questions should usually appear directly underneath the question. First display directions then cue for input since students sometimes stop reading at prompts. State exactly what the reader must do. Learners should be able to intuitively navigate through the program.

Feedback and error messages should be located so that students clearly see the consequences of their input. Feedback for questions should usually appear directly underneath the question. Error messages should be simple, meaningful, and standardized.

Control options allow learners to control their own learning paths. Control options are often found on the screen's bottom line, in a window, or in a pull-down menu. Generally, your control options should be available on every screen, consistently located, and easy to access.

You can use icons for prompts or options but ensure that the icons have a meaningful text label.

Some learners prefer the "look and feel" of graphical user-interfaces. Graphical user-interfaces can be used but there can be problems you must address.

Menus allow users to choose their own paths and break large amounts of material into manageable sections that contain related information. Menus should be logical, have meaningful names, have single clicks, key presses, or touches, be easily accessible at all times, be uncrowded, and be a maximum of three levels deep.

The three most common types of menus are full-screen, windows, and pull-down. Vertical menus are the easiest to read and use. Horizontal menus can be effective if they are clear and uncrowded. Menu metaphors can be problematic if students misinterpret symbolic meanings or do not realize the metaphor's meaning.

To ensure that the screens will appear as you intend and to prevent wasted effort, set the screen design specifications and guidelines in advance.

Application Exercises

1) Imagine working through a tutorial that does **not** present any orientation information. How would this affect you?
2) If an inexperienced designer decided to place the orientation information on the screen's bottom line, how would this affect the students?
3) If an inexperienced designer decided to place the control options down the screen's left side, how would this affect the students?
4) On a multiple-choice question, an error message for **not** clicking on a letter states, "That is not a valid input. Please try again." Provide a more meaningful error message.
5) A main menu contains 20 selections. What could you do to improve this?

Case Study

Six instructors were on a four-week professional development leave from their regular duties. During this time, the instructors participated in a workshop on creating instructional multimedia applications. One goal of the workshop was to create a small tutorial so that the instructors could apply what they learned.

It was decided that the "Next page" button would be available in the bottom right corner and all of the other branching options would be available through clicking a button in the top right corner.

Case Study Question

What are the pros and cons of this decision? Support your answer.

References

Benshoof, L., & Hooper, S. (1993, Autumn). The effects of single- and multiple-window presentation on achievement during computer-based instruction. Journal of Computer-Based Instruction, 20(4), 113-117.

Bonime, A. (1995, April). Menu metaphors and why I hate them. CD-ROM Professional, 8(4), 60-61.

Danielson, J., Lockee, B., & Burton, J. (2000). ID and HCI: A marriage of necessity. In Abbey, B. (Ed.), Instructional and cognitive impacts of web-based education. (pp. 118-128). Hershey, PA: Idea Group Publishing.

Fenrich, P. (1992). Screen design and user interface needs for successful multimedia applications. Proceedings of the Seventh Canadian Symposium on Instructional Technology.

Grabinger, R. (1993). Computer screen designs: Viewer judgments. Educational Technology Research and Development, 41(3), 35-73.

Gray, S. (1988). Sequence control menus and CAI: A follow-up study. Journal of Computer-Based Instruction, 15(2), 57-60.

Milheim, W., & Martin, B. (1991). Theoretical bases for the use of learner control: Three different perspectives. Journal of Computer-Based Instruction, 18(3), 99-105.

Rambally, G., & Rambally, R. (1987). Human factors in CAI design. Computers & Education, 11(2), 149-153.

Sawyer, T. (1985). Human factors considerations in computer-assisted instruction. Journal of Computer-Based Instruction, 12(1), 17-20.

Schwier, R., & Misanchuk, E. (1993). Interactive multimedia instruction. Englewood Cliffs, NJ: Educational Technology Publications.

Chapter 17: User-Friendliness

Learning Outcomes

After completing this chapter, you should be able to:
- list features of user-friendly programs
- describe the different types of instructional control
- explain why guidance should accompany learner control
- list reasons for including learner control
- discuss problems associated with **not** providing learner control
- explain why learners should be able to control video sequences
- design instructional software with appropriate learner control

Introduction

If you create a user-friendly program, you can increase motivation, improve attitudes, reduce fears, and minimize frustrations. This chapter presents guidelines on how to create user-friendliness through ease of use, learner control, clarity, and pleasantness. Specific details are provided on the different types of learner control, the research results on learner control, students controlling media, and the use of humor.

17.1 Creating User-Friendliness

A significant part of your project's success is determined by how easy the product is to use. You can be successful through specific design efforts that consider the user, the user's environment, and the context of use.

Since it is unacceptable to create programs that are "machine-oriented" rather than "people-oriented," you should create user-friendliness through:
- ease of use
- clarity
- learner control
- pleasantness

17.1-1 Ease of Use

You can make a program easy to use if you:
- Create consistent screens.
- Make the program intuitive to use.
- Create single click/touch/key press menus.
- Show attempted menu selections.
- Make the program easy to install and crash proof.

Create Consistent Screens

You should develop a consistent "look and feel". Screen consistency is critical in helping students navigate through the program and finding information since students often rely on recognition rather than recall. Screen consistency can also help learners feel comfortable. Within a program, an unfamiliar "look and feel" can confuse learners.

Make the Program Intuitive to Use

Intuitive programs have a natural interface between the computer and the users or what is known as the user-interface. The user-interface is how the user communicates and interacts with the computer. An intuitive interface is important since learners will have a wide range of computer literacy. Another reason for making an intuitive program is the potential to save money if less support has to be provided. Non-intuitive programs can interfere with learning if students have to think about how to interact with the computer rather than thinking about the content.

Practical Guideline:
Programs must be easy and intuitive to use.

Navigation through the program should be transparent. Students who are not familiar with the program should not have to waste time learning how to navigate through it. If navigation is not obvious then there is a problem with your user-interface. Design the interface with the guideline: If you have to explain how to use it, you have done something wrong. This should hold true whether you are creating a simple program or something complex like a simulation or game.

Practical Guideline:
If you have to explain how to use the program, assume you have done something wrong!

The program should be forgiving for invalid clicks, key presses, or touches. One solution is to have the computer only respond when a button or obvious input area is clicked. Students will intuitively learn where they can click, touch, or provide keyboard input. If you provide a message, be concise to let the student know exactly what was done wrong and what should be done. A statement like, "That is an illegal action" is too vague to be useful. (See the Feedback chapter for more details.)

Create Single Click/Touch/Key Press Menus

Single click/touch/key press menus are the easiest and fastest to use.

Show Attempted Menu Selections

Attempted menu selections let the students know where they have been and help show students what to do next. Attempted sections can be indicated with check marks. Check marks do not have to imply that students have completed every page. Some will argue that check marks should only be provided if every page has been seen. Even if a page has been seen, you would not have any indication that the student learned the content. That information comes independently through informal and formal testing.

Make the Program Easy to Install and Crash Proof

Easy to install, crash-proof programs are particularly important when others may purchase the program. Installation problems can create a negative view that might not be overcome. Program "crashes" are very frustrating. A crash-proof program is generally an achievable goal with thorough testing. However, "it is impossible to make anything foolproof because fools are so ingenious."

17.1-2 Learner Control

Learner control relates to how students are able to navigate through a program. For example, students may be able to branch to anywhere in the program anytime that they want, be totally guided by the computer program, or have partial freedom. Building the appropriate learner control into your instructional multimedia software can help enhance student motivation and thus learning.

In general, the learner control you provide should:
- allow learners to control pacing, sequencing, reviewing, branching, video...
- be available on every screen
  - It can be frustrating to want to branch to another part of the program and not be able to do so.
- be consistently placed in the same location on every screen
  - This allows learners to quickly find the control options.
- allow students to easily recover from mistakes
  - For example, let students back up to the previous page if they accidentally continue to the next page before they are ready. Consider, allowing students to change their selected answer until they choose to have their answer marked. A disadvantage of this is that each question requires the student to provide extra input such as also clicking on a "Mark" button.

You can also use learner control to let students choose how they will be taught such as receiving a generalization and then receiving examples or vice versa, whether to receive supplementary information or a different version of the content, how much practice to receive, and even the material's level of difficulty. Assuming that students can make good decisions about these choices, there is still the practical problem of whether you would be able to spend the time and resources to design and develop these alternatives. This is not practical or justifiable for most applications.

You can determine whether learner control should be by the student, by the program, or shared between the student and the program:

Student Control

Student control allows learners to choose their own learning paths. This control can include students choosing what material is accessed, how much material is viewed, and when the material is seen. (This is discussed in detail below.)

Program Control

When the program controls the instruction, you make decisions about the presentation sequence, practice items like setting question difficulty levels based on performance, and feedback. Program control is recommended when learners, such as immature and young students, cannot accurately assess their learning successes or failures. In other words, learners are not able to make appropriate control decisions.

Program control is **not** suitable for most students.

Shared Control

Shared control occurs when control is shared between learners and the program. In these programs, the design allows for program control when the learner is not achieving desired outcomes. Shared control can be advantageous when the learners vary widely in skill and maturity levels.

Research Results

Generally, the results of learner control research are conflicting. Some studies have favored learner control, other studies have shown increased learning with program control, yet different studies have shown effective results with shared control. However, many studies have shown student control with guidance or recommendations to be very effective.

Practical Guideline:

In general, design programs with learner control but offer students guidance for their selections.

In a learner-controlled program, students who are not be able to assess their learning success or failure might need extra guidance. Even students with high aptitudes and students with previous content knowledge who are well suited for full-learner control should have some guidance. The effectiveness of learner control varies with maturity, learning-style preferences, prior knowledge and experiences, how often an individual uses the program, lesson content, and the control options allowed. You can successfully provide guidance with simple statements such as "Proceed through the menu sequentially since the material builds upon itself."

Even with extensive learner-controlled branching options, many students proceed sequentially. Alternatively, some learners choose to skip material. Generally, these learners realize they are skipping material and realize the consequences of their actions. Students who skip ahead and discover they do not understand the material, typically from not being able to answer questions, often go back to the beginning and then proceed sequentially. However, a few students may wander throughout the program and learn virtually nothing. These students need "live" guidance or need to learn how to learn before they can successfully achieve the learning outcomes of the program.

Why Have Learner Control?

Generally, students prefer having the freedom to proceed at their own pace and move around the program, and can become frustrated when forced to do things. However, some students, such as those who have come from educational backgrounds where teachers control virtually everything, may not initially be comfortable in controlling their own learning. These students can become comfortable with full-learner control through gradual exposure to controlling their own learning.

Practical Guideline:

In general, students prefer to control their own learning.

Since students can choose what they want to learn, learner control may increase motivation, increase time on-task, increase achievement, and improve attitudes since the material is more relevant to their interests. Motivation may also be increased if students choose material at which they expect to be successful. Students can increase their learning if they have the freedom to review when they want.

Requiring students to proceed in a specific order can:
* lead to frustration
    - This can occur if the student already knows the material.
    - Students may not want to start where they left off in that they may want to review material before proceeding.
* prevent students from reviewing
    - Shouldn't students be able to choose when and what to review?

- cause difficulties in restarting students
  - Student identifications and locations must be recorded so students can start where they left off. The feature of restarting students where they left off is called "book marking".
  - Consider what needs to be done if the computer is accidentally turned off or if there is a power outage.
  - Determine whether students will be working at the same computer. If not, and the data is not on a network, then the data must be recorded onto a portable medium.

Media Control

Generally, you should let learners have complete control over media (e.g., video, animations, and audio) sequences. Media control can include fast forward, slow forward, forward one image, freeze, reverse one image, slow reverse, fast reverse, skip, repeat, and stop. However, depending on your development software and the operating system, you may only be able to provide Play, Stop, and Repeat buttons.

Media control enables students to spend the time they need to understand the material. For example, moving forward one frame at a time can allow students to carefully study the changes taking place. This can be important for learning how to do procedural skills.

17.1-3 Clarity

To avoid causing problems such as confusion, ensure clarity with:
- clear orientation information
- clear control options (i.e., the word meanings are obvious to everybody)
- clear messaging and prompting
- language that is simple and is defined when new terms are introduced.

(You can find more details in the Screen design and Text chapters.)

17.1-4 Pleasantness

Create pleasantness through:
- using a program tone that is friendly and relaxed
- teaching in a way students naturally learn
- using real-life examples
- providing feedback that is positive, constructive, and not repetitious
- providing varied activities
- using humor

Humor

Humor can be used to help relax students, gain attention, sustain interest, aid comprehension and retention, and humanize the learning situation. With respect to humor, note that:
- "Humor is one laughing matter that is worth taking seriously."
- Humor should be used to reinforce the material rather than distract the student from learning.
- Humor can be dangerous in that what some people find funny others will find offensive, insulting, childish, or boring while yet others may not even understand the humor. Be sure of an audience's reaction before using humor. Consider cultural differences before using humor.
- Humor should be based on familiar things not subject to being outdated.
- Since sarcasm is not humorous, do **not** use sarcasm.
- Do **not** direct humor at students, the material, the author, or any real third parties.
- Humor does not have to be hilariously funny.
- Humor should not be overused, especially one particular idea. Remember that learning is serious.

Practical Guideline:

Use humor but use it carefully.

(Many other chapters of this book cover these ideas on user-friendliness in more detail.)

Summary

If you create a user-friendly program, you can increase motivation, improve attitudes, reduce fears, and minimize frustrations. Create user-friendliness through ease of use, learner control, clarity, and pleasantness.

You can achieve ease of use through screen consistency and making the program intuitive to use.

Learner control relates to how students are able to navigate through a program. Many studies have shown learner control with guidance to be very effective. Learner control may increase motivation, increase time on-task, increase achievement, and improve attitudes. Without learner control, students are required to proceed in a specific order. This can create problems such as frustration and can prevent students from reviewing.

Media control enables students to spend the time they need to understand the video, animation, or audio.

To avoid causing problems such as confusion, ensure clarity with complete orientation information, clear control options, intuitive messaging and prompting, and language that is simple and is defined when new terms are introduced.

Humor is one of the ways to create pleasantness. Since people are so varied, use humor carefully.

Application Exercises

1) How would you design the learner control for seven-year old children?
2) If a program had inconsistent screen designs, what could be the consequences?
3) If you provide learner control but do **not** provide guidance, what could result?
4) What could the consequences be of requiring students to proceed in a specific order?
5) You have something humorous that you want to include in your program. If you know that most of the audience will find it funny but it might upset a few students, should you use the humor?

Case Study

Six instructors were on a four-week professional development leave from their regular duties. During this time, the instructors participated in a workshop on creating instructional multimedia applications. One goal of the workshop was to create a small tutorial so that the instructors could apply what they learned.

Due to the authoring tool limitations, the initial version of the tutorial allowed students to change their answer but they had to "double-click" on the correct answer. The formative evaluation showed that some students had trouble "double-clicking". The final version did **not** allow students to change their answer but they only had to click on the correct answer.

Case Study Question

Which version would have been better? Explain your answer.

References

Alessi, S., & Trollip, S. (1991). Computer-based instruction: Methods and development (2nd ed.). Englewood Cliffs, NJ: Prentice-Hall, Inc.

Colijn, B., & Petrick, J. (1987, June). Keep your wits about you: Humor in CBT. Data Training, 6(6), 38-41.

Fenrich, P. (1991). The heart of multimedia design: An award-winning approach. Tenfold, 4(1), 10-11.

Friend, C., & Cole, C. (1990). Learner control in computer-based instruction: A current literature review. Educational Technology, 30(11), 47-49.

Gagnon, D. (1986). Interactive television: The influence of user control and interactive structure. Paper presented at the International Television Studies Conference.

Hannafin, R., & Sullivan, H. (1995). Learner control in full and lean CAI programs. Educational Technology Research and Development, 43(1), 19-30.

Jamieson, J., & Chapelle, C. (1988). Using CALL effectively: What do we need to know about students? System, 16(2), 151-162.

Jin, H., & Reeves, T. (1992). Mental models: A research focus for interactive learning systems. Educational Technology Research and Development, 40(3), 39-53.

Milheim, W., & Martin, B. (1991). Theoretical bases for the use of learner control: Three different perspectives. Journal of Computer-Based Instruction, 18(3), 99-105.

Murphy, M., & Davidson, G. (1991, Spring). Computer-based adaptive instruction: Effects of learner control on concept learning. Journal of Computer-Based Instruction, 18(2), 51-56.

Sawyer, T. (1985). Human factors considerations in computer-assisted instruction. Journal of Computer-Based Instruction, 12(1), 17-20.

Schwier, R. (1994). Multimedia design principles for constructing prescriptive, democratic and cybernetic learning environments. Proceedings of the ED-MEDIA 94 World Conference on Educational Multimedia and Hypermedia.

Yung-Bin, B. (1992). Effects of learning style in a hypermedia instructional system. Proceedings of Selected Research and Development Presentations at the Convention of the Association for Educational Communications and Technology, pp. 506-508.

Chapter 18:   Color and Highlighting

After completing this chapter, you should be able to:
* describe reasons for using color
* state meanings associated with colors
* describe guidelines for using color
* state color combinations to avoid
* describe some problems with displaying colors on monitors
* design screens that effectively use color
* explain why highlighting should be used
* describe why too much highlighting can be a problem
* explain when and why blinking should be avoided
* explain why switching foreground and background colors is **not** an effective highlighting technique
* describe the pros and cons of using screen transitions
* design screens that highlight information in effective and sight appealing ways

Introduction

If you effectively use colors and highlighting techniques, you can gain attention, motivate learners, and help programs be user-friendly. This chapter presents uses of color, associations learners can have with colors, and guidelines for using colors. Recommendations are made for using colors for specific screen components. Issues are discussed with respect to colors seen on different monitors. Highlighting techniques are discussed with a focus on highlighting with color, blinking, switching foreground and background colors, and screen transitions.

18.1 Uses of Color

You can use color to:
* gain attention
* motivate learners
* separate screen components including separating orientation information from the presented material
* organize material such as grouping like elements
* guide learners through consistently colored prompts
* show relationships and link logically related information
* distinguish information such as in graphs
* highlight key points, responses, and errors
* help learners find and recall information through highlighting information
* add appeal or an impression of pleasantness to the product
* create user-friendliness

With respect to learning, if you effectively use color, you can increase communication speed, accuracy, and retention. Correct color usage is liked, attractive, and motivating. Remember that highly motivated students tend to perform better than poorly motivated students. However, color presentations do not automatically lead to increased learning over black and white presentations unless color is directly relevant to what is being learned. As an exaggerated example, color would be minimally helpful for students learning keyboarding skills but would be immensely helpful for students learning a rainbow's colors or identifying flowers. Non-realistic colors can inhibit learning.

18.2 Color Associations

You must take care in choosing colors since some colors have associated meanings:
- Blue can be interpreted as cold and far.
- Green can be associated with going and being safe like a green traffic light.
- Yellow can be associated with caution and being near.
- Red can be symbolic for stop, danger, hot, and negative numeric values.

Colors should be appropriate for the target audience's cultural meanings and, if possible, reinforce a company's image.

Note that blue and green tend to be relaxing colors. Consequently, blue is an excellent background color.

18.3 Guidelines for Using Colors

Multimedia applications have the potential to use virtually any color. However, this potential can be used inappropriately. You must take care when using color. When working with colors you should:
- Keep colors consistent.
    - For example, consistently use the same color for text and another for orientation information.
    - Consistency allows learners to quickly find specific information.
    - Without consistency problems can arise since some students try to associate meanings with colors whether there is an implicit meaning or not.

Practical Guideline:
Keep colors consistent!

- Three or four text colors per screen is comfortable and often is all that is needed.
    - For example, use one color for orientation information and highlighting, a second color for text, and a third one for prompts.
    - If you are using more than three or four colors on a screen, justify the need for it.
    - Seven colors is the maximum per screen. This excludes visual images and especially photographs.
    - Too many colors become distracting and irritating. Colors should not be used simply because the system has the capability.
- Use foreground and background colors with high contrast.
    - Use bright-foreground colors and dark-background colors, as opposed to dark-foreground colors on a bright background since bright-background colors cause eyestrain over time. For example, use a bright-white foreground color on a dark-blue background. Note that learners may tell you that they would prefer a bright background. However, they are typically not considering the fact that their choice may cause eyestrain.
    - Drop shadows can be used to increase the contrast between the foreground and background colors. Drop shadows can also be sight appealing.
- Avoid backgrounds that highly vary in colors when the text used for teaching will be placed directly over it. For example, a background with high variation in color would have the top of the screen black and the screen gradually darkens until the bottom of the screen is light blue.
    - These backgrounds can be attractive but can make text harder to read. Text becomes harder to read when the contrast between the foreground and background colors decreases.

- If you use a background that varies in color, only allow the colors to change a small amount. For example, let the background colors range from black to medium blue.

Practical Guideline:

Use bright foreground colors and dark background colors.

- Avoid "picture" backgrounds, even pictures that are muted to be less dominant, when the text used for teaching will be placed directly over it. This is illustrated in figure 18.1.
  - Again, text can be hard to read where there is not enough contrast.

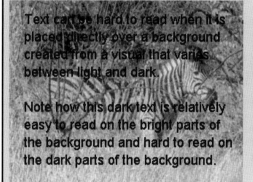

Text can be hard to read when it is placed directly over a background created from a visual that varies between light and dark.

Note how this dark text is relatively easy to read on the bright parts of the background and hard to read on the dark parts of the background.

Figure 18.1 – Text on a varied background

- Avoid using fully-saturated or pure colors.
  - Fully-saturated colors tend to be less clear on computer monitors.
- Avoid using particularly bright colors, such as magenta or neon colors.
  - **Never** use them as the main text color.
  - Bright colors can be hard on the reader's eyes. However, the brightest colors are effective for highlighting.
- Be careful with using red and green.
  - Since about 8% of males and 0.5% of females have a deficiency with seeing color, most often with red and green, it is **not** safe to specifically refer to colors. For example, do not say, "look at the green box". Color-deficient people see red and green as other colors, such as blue, orange, gray, or white, that may not show up clearly or as intended on the screen. For example, if you put green text on a blue background and the learner sees green as blue then the learner may not be able to read the text. See figure 18.2 to test yourself. (This is a simplified test as compared to one that an optometrist would give.)
  - Due to some people having deficiencies in seeing red, do **not** use red as a highlighting color. Red is a psychologically good color for highlighting (i.e., stop and look) but there is another problem in that red can de-emphasize material in that it seems to recede into the screen.
- Use system palette colors whenever possible to help ensure portability from one computer to another.
  - Note that the PC and Macintosh® color palettes are not identical. There can be some color changes when transferring programs between platforms. Thoroughly test the transferred programs to ensure that there are no color problems. Figure 18.3 shows a color palette.
- Consider whether you should use 4-bit (16 colors), 8-bit (256 colors), 16-bit (65,536 colors), or 24-bit (16 million colors) visuals.
  - As the number of bits increases, the storage space and bandwidth needed for the visual increases.
  - 4-bit color may be acceptable for low-bandwidth applications, especially when dithering techniques are used to make it appear like there are more colors. 8-bit dithered color is often acceptable. 16-bit dithered color is excellent. 24-bit color is photo-quality. Note the quality of the

4-bit and 8-bit dithered visuals, shown in figures 18.4 and 18.5 respectively, created from the 24-bit visual shown in figure 18.6. Look closely to see the difference between each.
- Some software tools can more effectively dither than other tools. Evaluate tools beforehand.
- For computer-managed presentations, choose colors with high contrast. For well-lit rooms, use a bright foreground on a dark background. For darker rooms, use a dark foreground on a bright background.

Remember that the above points are guidelines **not** rules. There are always exceptions to rules.

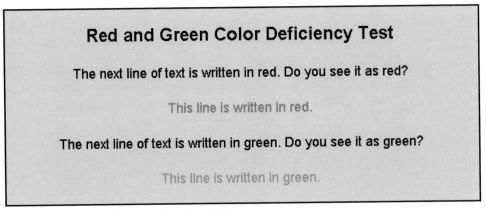

Figure 18.2 – Simplified test for color deficiency

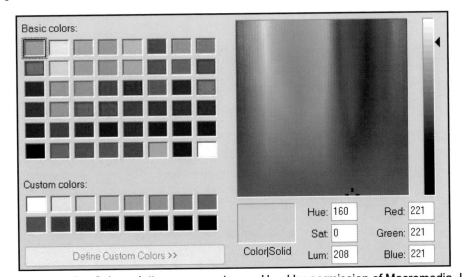

Figure 18.3 – Color palette screen capture   Used by permission of Macromedia, Inc.

18.4 Recommended Colors

There are many effective color combinations. If you use unproven colors, test them thoroughly. Once tested, use the color specifications as a standard to ensure consistency and efficiency.

Practical Guideline:

Use the recommended foreground and background colors or thoroughly test the ones you choose.

Figure 18.4 – 4-bit dithered   Figure 18.5 – 8-bit dithered   Figure 18.6 – 24-bit

Consider the following color combinations, shown in figure 18.7 through to figure 18.10, as experience has shown them to be effective:

- Use dark-gray and/or dark-blue background colors.
  - Dark-gray and dark-blue backgrounds are excellent in that they provide the necessary contrast for easy viewing as well as a professional appearance.
  - A dark-gray background works well but does not have as much sight appeal as a blue background that ranges from very dark at the top to medium blue at the bottom. However, this blue background offers less contrast with bright-foreground text that is written near the bottom of the screen. Consequently, the text near the bottom of the screen may be a little harder to read but not to the point where it is problematic.
  - Black backgrounds allow most foreground colors to show up well but there is a problem in that the highest contrast occurs with black backgrounds. A high degree of contrast can cause eyestrain over longer viewing sessions.
  - Dark backgrounds limit the choices of effective foreground-text colors. Use bright-foreground text colors on dark backgrounds.
- On a dark-gray background, use a bright cyan (baby blue) for the main foreground text.
  - Humans see cyan (and orange) particularly well.
- On dark-blue backgrounds, use a bright white for the main foreground text.
  - White is seen very well at a distance. Consider this for computer-managed presentations.
- Use bright yellow for orientation information and highlighting.
- On dark-gray backgrounds, use white for prompt information.
- On dark-blue backgrounds, use cyan for prompt information.
- Use bright yellow for highlighting correct answers and feedback.
- On dark-gray backgrounds, use a medium-bright magenta for highlighting incorrect answers.
- On dark-blue backgrounds, use a rose or medium-bright magenta color for highlighting incorrect answers.
- Use light gray with black text for buttons. This is relatively standard.

Some applications allow users to change the colors. Most instructional multimedia applications do not need this feature. If you use proven color combinations, you do not need to add this level of complexity to the user-interface or the programmer. There can also be significant consequences if the learner makes some bad choices. For example, if a user changed the dark background to a bright color then bright-foreground text may be hard to read or even be unnoticed.

220   Creating Instructional Multimedia Solutions

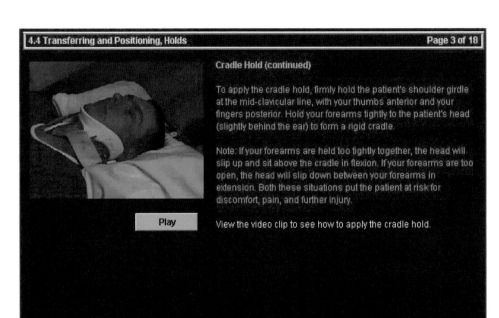

Figure 18.7 – Basic screen colors for a dark-gray background

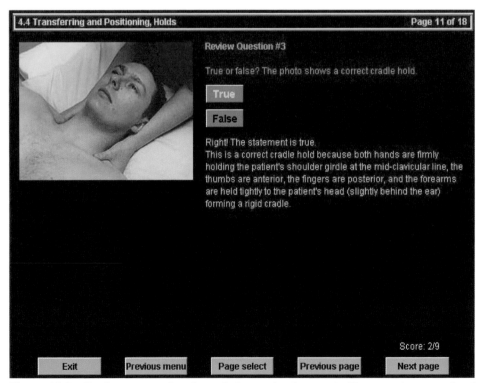

Figure 18.8 – Basic screen colors for a dark-gray background with correct answer feedback

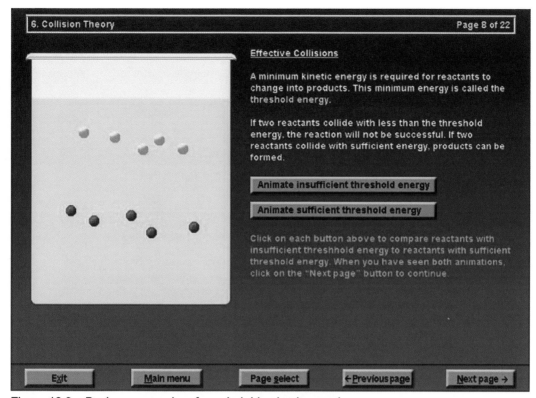

Figure 18.9 – Basic screen colors for a dark-blue background

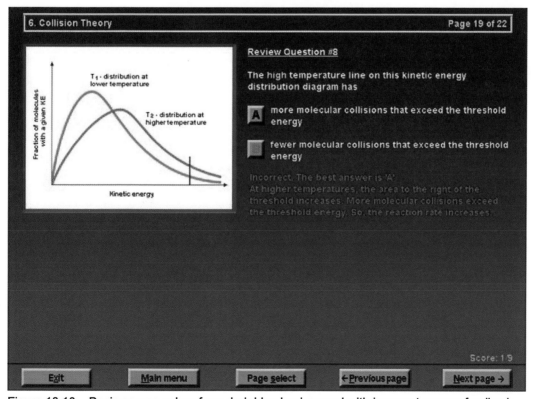

Figure 18.10 – Basic screen colors for a dark-blue background with incorrect answer feedback

18.5 Color Combinations to Avoid

You should avoid the following foreground and background color combinations that tend to be hard to view:
• red with green
• blue with red
• blue with green
• blue with yellow

Colors that have similar brightness values tend to vibrate and become tiring to read.

18.6 Colors and Monitors

The colors displayed on the learner's workstations may not appear entirely as you expect since:
• Colors do not appear consistently among monitors and computer platforms.
   - Cheaper monitors can have problems with some colors, especially fully-saturated colors. Minimize this problem by not using fully-saturated colors and following the guidelines in this chapter. Color saturation can be controlled in some software packages (e.g., through lightening the pure color by adding a white tint to it) but be sure the non-saturated colors transfer to the final hardware and software configurations.
   - Test different monitors thoroughly before significant development has taken place. Finding problems early will save time later on in the development process.
   - Monitor phosphors wear over time.
   - The PC and Macintosh® platforms have different color palettes. Some color modifications may be necessary for cross-platform applications.
• Some students adjust the monitor's intensity or brightness up while others adjust the intensity down.

18.7 Highlighting

You can use highlighting to emphasize information, show relationships, and reduce the time needed to review. You can help learning if you highlight effectively.

18.7-1 Highlighting Techniques

In multimedia applications, you have the potential to use virtually any highlighting technique. Highlighting techniques include bold, color, underlines, boxes, asterisks, bullets, arrows, isolation, larger fonts, different fonts (e.g., italics), switching foreground and background colors, time pauses, and blinking. Some of these highlighting techniques are shown in figure 18.11. Bold is effective for highlighting but is occasionally hard to read depending on the font and font size used. A text-color change is effective.

If you abuse this potential for highlighting techniques, you could ruin your production. You must take care when using highlighting techniques. The following guidelines will help you highlight effectively:
• Use highlighting consistently to avoid confusing the learners.
• Generally, you only need one highlighting method to be effective.
   - If you must use more than one highlighting method, limit it to a maximum of two methods per screen.
   - More than two methods per screen can appear inelegant and even cause confusion as to what is important.
• Too much highlighting can de-emphasize important details.

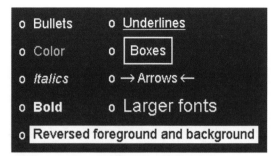

Figure 18.11 – Highlighting techniques

Practical Guideline:

Highlighting techniques should be consistent and used only to help learning.

18.7-2 Highlighting with Color

Use the following guidelines for highlighting with color:
- Yellow highlighting is excellent. Yellow seems to project out of the screen and is very effective for highlighting text.
- Highlighting with magenta or white is average.
- Highlighting with blue is poor. Since blue is a relaxing color, it tends to be ineffective for highlighting information.
- As discussed earlier, highlighting with red is poor.

18.7-3 Blinking

Blinking is when text or an object flashes on the screen. It is excellent for gaining attention but is extremely distracting when the learner is trying to concentrate on other things such as simply reading text. On the opposite extreme, blinking is sometimes missed if it is brief such as when there are two or three flashes. Blinking is best used at the end of a screen after students indicate that they are ready to continue. However, be aware that blinking can indicate a warning in some industries.

Practical Guideline:

Use blinking cautiously.

If your computer screen has animations or objects that turn on or off at the rate of four to fifty-nine flashes per second, where twenty flashes per second is the worst, you can trigger an epileptic seizure in people who have photosensitive epilepsy. As a minimum, allow learners to turn off the "flashing" component of the screen.

18.7-4 Switching Foreground and Background Colors

You can switch foreground and background colors to highlight non-critical information. However, use it with caution since it can sometimes de-emphasize information and be hard to read. Consider adding a space character before and after the text for esthetics as illustrated in figure 18.11.

18.7-5 Screen Transitions

You can use special transition routines, such as wipes and dissolves, to gradually reveal the following screen. Screen transition routines are common in many authoring tools. Screen transitions add variety and have initial appeal but can lose their appeal and become boring after a few are viewed.

Practical Guideline:

Screen transitions add variety but usually only have initial appeal.

The time needed for screen transitions can be significant by taking time away from learning. In general, if you use transitions, have the transitions take place in less than a quarter of a second. However, you may find longer screen transitions useful in computer-managed presentations because you can focus your thoughts during the time the transitions take place. As well, the time can be used by learners to mentally process the information you just presented. However, the best solution is if you avoid transitions and simply pause between slides in your presentation.

Summary

You can use color to gain attention, motivate learners, and help programs be user-friendly. However, care must be taken in choosing colors since some colors have associated meanings.

General guidelines you should follow for using colors include:
- Keep colors consistent.
- Use three or four text colors per screen.
- Use foreground and background colors with high contrast.
- Avoid backgrounds that highly vary in color and "picture" backgrounds when the text used for teaching will be placed directly over it.
- Use fully-saturated colors sparingly.
- Use system palette colors whenever possible to help ensure portability to other computer platforms.

There are many effective color combinations. If you use unproven colors, test them thoroughly. The following color recommendations work:
- On a dark-gray background, use a bright cyan (baby blue) for the main foreground text.
- On a dark-blue background, use a bright white for the main foreground text.
- Use bright yellow for orientation information and highlighting.
- On a dark-gray background, use white for prompt information.
- On a dark-blue background, use cyan for prompt information.
- Use bright yellow for highlighting correct answers and feedback.
- On a dark-gray background, use a medium-bright magenta for highlighting incorrect answers.
- On a dark-blue background, consider rose and medium-bright magenta colors for highlighting incorrect answers.
- Use light gray with black text for buttons.

You must take care when choosing colors since there are significant differences among different computer monitors and computer platforms.

Effective highlighting can help learning. When needed, you should highlight for emphasis, to show relationships, and to reduce the time needed to review. Consistently use the highlighting technique(s) you select. One highlighting method is usually adequate. The limit is two highlighting methods per screen.

In general, depending on what needs to be done, for highlighting:
- Bold is very effective.
- A color change such as yellow for text is effective.
- Blinking should be avoided.

Application Exercises

1) Color combinations to avoid include **red with green**, **blue with yellow**, **green with blue**, and **red with blue**.
   a) What is the highlighting problem in the above sentence?
   b) Rewrite the sentence so that highlighting is used effectively.
2) Instructional multimedia materials can include **text**, audio, visuals, and *video*.
   a) What is the highlighting problem in the above sentence?
   b) Rewrite the sentence so that highlighting is used effectively.
3) Which of the following statements is **false**?
   a) Color can be used to motivate learners.
   b) Colors have associated meanings that must be considered.
   c) The foreground and background colors should have high contrast.
   d) Variety in foreground text colors tends to add appeal to screens.
4) Which of the following statements is **false**?
   a) Blinking can be very distracting.
   b) Bold is a generally weak highlighting technique.
   c) Screen transitions can become boring.

Case Study

Six instructors were on a four-week professional development leave from their regular duties. During this time, the instructors participated in a workshop on creating instructional multimedia applications. One goal of the workshop was to create a small tutorial so that the instructors could apply what they learned.

The instructors had difficulties in deciding on which way to highlight text. Yellow text, which is very effective, could be easily inserted as the text was being created. However, due to authoring tool limitations, colors could not be quickly edited. Underlining could be easily edited but is not as effective for highlighting as a yellow color change. Bold text could also be easily edited and is very effective. However, bold text takes extra room on the screen. This room is sometimes needed.

Case Study Question

Given the same authoring tool, which highlighting method would you use? Justify your answer.

References

Alessi, S., & Trollip, S. (1991). Computer-based instruction: Methods and development (2nd ed.). Englewood Cliffs, NJ: Prentice-Hall, Inc.

Fenrich, P. (1993, August). [Interview with Dr. G. McKee, Optometrist.]

Fenrich, P. (1992). Screen design and user interface needs for successful multimedia applications. Proceedings of the Seventh Canadian Symposium on Instructional Technology.

Fenrich, P. (1991). The heart of multimedia design: An award-winning approach. Tenfold, 4(1), 10-11.

Garner, K. (1991, Summer/Fall). 20 rules for arranging text on a screen. <u>Emerging Technologies Bulletin</u>, 16, 2-4.

Treasury Board of Canada Secretariat (Government of Canada). (2004, March, 5). Common Look and Feel for the Internet. Retrieved January 30, 2005 from http://www.cio-dpi.gc.ca/clf-nsi/guide/guide_e.asp

Villarreal, K., & Oller, B. (1990). A graphic picture is worth... <u>Emerging Technologies Bulletin</u>, 14, 9-10.

Watzman, S. (1995). Information design principles for the interface designer. <u>Session Handout Book of the Performance Support '95 Conference, September 6-8, 1995, Washington, DC</u>.

Wood, E. (1993, October). A beginner's guide to multimedia. <u>Computer Graphics World</u>, <u>16</u>(10), 71-84.

Section 5: Final Steps

A final step in developing an instructional multimedia application is deciding how you should store and learners should retrieve the information. Since media can have enormous storage requirements, common methods of compressing and decompressing the data are first discussed. DVD-ROMs (Digital Video Disc Read Only Memory), CD-ROMs (Compact Disc Read Only Memory), intranets, and the Internet are compared with respect to retrieving program data. Details are also provided on how to produce DVD-ROMs and CD-ROMs.

Chapter 19:
Compression/Decompression

Learning Outcomes

After completing this chapter, you should be able to:
- describe how information is compressed
- describe lossless and lossy compression
- choose an appropriate compression/decompression technology

Introduction

Being fluent with the different compression/decompression techniques can help you choose the appropriate method for compressing and decompressing the vast amounts of multimedia data that you may require in your multimedia production. This chapter describes compression and decompression, states how compression is done, contrasts lossless and lossy compression, and states considerations for choosing compression/decompression formats.

19.1 Compression and Decompression

To calculate how much data a video clip requires:
Multiply the screen size by the number of frames (images) per second by the number of seconds of recording or playing time by the number of bits (which corresponds to the number of colors). Divide this by 8 bits per byte where a byte is the basic unit of computer data storage. If the compression ratio is 200:1 then divide the value just calculated by 200.

For example, if a video clip is captured at a screen size of 640 by 480 and 30 frames per second for 1 second with 24-bit color, the amount of uncompressed data required is:
640 x 480 x 30 x 1 x 24 ÷ 8 = 27,648,000 bytes
If a CD-ROM can hold 700,000,000 bytes of video data then it could hold:
700,000,000 ÷ 27,648,000 = 25.32 seconds of this video
If the video is compressed at a ratio of 100:1 then the amount of data per second equals:
27,648,000 ÷ 100 = 276,480 bytes
If a CD-ROM can hold 700,000,000 bytes of video data then it could hold:
700,000,000 ÷ 276,480 = 2,532 seconds of this compressed video

Obviously, compression is essential to reduce the large amount of storage space your multimedia data (e.g., video, visuals, animation, and audio) requires as well as to reduce the time needed to move data to and from the computer processor. The reduced time for data transfer can be important when your data is stored on slow technology like CD-ROMs. You can also transmit compressed information more quickly than uncompressed information. This is particularly important when using low-bandwidth connections.

Note that you must later decompress the compressed information to return it to a usable form. For practical reasons, such as image quality, decompression must be done at an acceptable rate on the target computers.

> **Practical Guideline:**
>
> Use compression to reduce the storage space your media requires.

Compression is often done by replacing redundant or repetitive pieces of information with simple codes. For example, redundant information occurs when parts of video images do not change between frames while repetitive information occurs when blocks of an image are the same color. Compression techniques are also based on predicting redundant information in future images and through detecting when entire objects move from frame to frame. Through compression, file sizes can be hundreds of times smaller. The numerous compression techniques can be categorized as lossless and lossy.

With lossless compression, all of the original information is retained. Consequently, lossless compression results in very low compression ratios - typically 2:1. You should use lossless compression when you must preserve all of the data. For example, this can be important if you must work with each individual image of a video clip.

If you use lossy compression, you will lose some data simply due to the compression algorithm. For video and visuals, this data loss results in a decrease in image quality. Video information can also be lost through reductions in frame rate, picture size, and color-palette size. Audio information loss often includes omitting frequencies beyond the normal human hearing range. The information loss is often necessary for you to fit larger amounts of data onto CD-ROM discs. Depending on your application this information loss can range from being significant (e.g., if details need to be seen) to insignificant (e.g., when watching people talk). The important criteria is how learners perceive the information rather than whether all of the information is present. Note that once you lose data in the compression process, the learners will never receive the lost information. Faster student-workstation computer speeds are irrelevant if the information no longer exists.

> **Practical Guideline:**
>
> Media quality that is deleted in the compression process will never be received by learners.

You can compress/decompress video and images with specialized hardware or software. Compared to software-only compression, hardware compression is faster. Nonetheless, software-only compression is adequate for most users.

Your video compression decisions should be based on the bandwidth you need. Bandwidth refers to a video signal's quality in practical terms of image size, number of colors, and frames per second - in other words the amount of information transmitted over a given time period. As the bandwidth increases, the amount of information that can be transmitted increases. There are many video and image compression/decompression techniques. Discussing each is beyond the scope of this book. However, from a practical perspective, you should consider:
- the quality of the final image when decompressed on the learner's computer
- the file size of the compressed video
- costs of purchasing the encoder
  - Note that many computers come loaded with consumer-level encoding software.
- whether the user's workstations can decode the video
  - If the decoding software must be loaded onto the learner's computer, it should preferably be transparent to the learner.
- whether there is a licensing fee for decoding the video
  - Licensing fees are more likely to be required for newer compression/decompression technologies as compared to old or obsolete technologies.
  - Licensing fees can be trivial, such as a few cents per disc.

In a similar way, audio compression/decompression techniques can also be important for your instructional multimedia applications since uncompressed audio requires a significant amount of storage space. You should consider the same factors for audio compression/decompression as listed above for video.

Although most do, be sure that your compression system simultaneously compresses both video and audio. It can be difficult, if not impossible depending on the tools you use, to synchronize separate video and audio clips during playback from a DVD-ROM or CD-ROM unit.

For instructional multimedia applications, you will usually want to store the compressed video as a series of short clips as specified in your storyboard. You can later access each file through your authoring tool.

19.2 Compressing/Decompressing Visuals

In general, different file formats are better for compressing/decompressing different types of images. For example, the JPEG (Joint Photographic Experts Group) standard compression technique can significantly reduce image storage requirements of photographs without noticeable degradation. The JPEG format can be inefficient for other types of images. Conversely, other file formats, such as the GIF file format, are excellent for compressing/decompressing graphic images such as line diagrams, graphs, and cartoons. The GIF file format is inefficient for compressing/decompressing photographs. You may want to compress a few sample visuals in a variety of formats to see what file type leads to the smallest file size.

19.3 Compressing/Decompressing Video

If you compress your video on a slow computer, your computer may drop frames as it tries to keep up. Since the data is not captured, learners will never see the missing frames. For this reason, you should compress video on fast computers. However, depending on the quality of video needed for the final product, this may or may not be significant. Note that if the playback computer cannot process the digital data fast enough, frames are simply dropped as the computer tries to keep up. Remember that a well-designed animation with an efficient runtime can be a substitute for some video sequences.

Summary

To calculate how much data a video clip requires:
Multiply the screen size by the number of frames per second by the number of seconds of time by the number of bits. Divide this by 8. If the video is compressed, divide the value just calculated by the proportional reduction.

You can use compression to reduce the amount of storage space your multimedia data requires. With lossless compression, all of the original information is retained. Consequently lossless compression only results in a very low compression ratio, typically 2:1. With lossy compression, some details are lost. Video information can also be lost through the frame rate, picture size, and color-palette size. Depending on your application, this information loss can range from being significant to insignificant. The important criteria is how learners perceive the information rather than whether all of the information is present. If you lose media quality in the compression process, the learners will never receive the lost information.

In general, different file formats are better for compressing/decompressing different types of images. For example, the JPEG standard compression technique can efficiently reduce image storage requirements of photographs. The GIF file format is excellent for compressing/decompressing graphic images.

If you compress or decompress video on a slow computer, the computer may drop frames as it tries to keep up. Depending on the quality of video needed, this may or may not be significant.

Application Exercises

1) Assume that you have a 20-second video clip that is 640 x 480, 32-bit color, and 30 frames per second.
   a) How many bytes of storage space does this require given one byte equals 8 bits?
   b) If the clip is reduced to a 320 x 240 screen size, how many bytes of storage space are required?
   c) If the clip is further reduced to 24-bit color, how many bytes of storage space are required?
   d) If the clip is further reduced to 15 frames per second, how many bytes of storage space are required?
2) Assume that you have a 10-second video clip that is 640 x 480, 32-bit color, and 30 frames per second.
   a) How much storage space does this require?
   b) If the clip is reduced to a 480 x 360 screen size, how many bytes of storage space are required?
   c) If the clip is further reduced to 16-bit color, how many bytes of storage space are required?
   d) If the clip is further reduced to 10 frames per second, how many bytes of storage space is required?
3) Assume a CD-ROM holds 700,000,000 bytes of video information, each uncompressed frame requires 250,000 bytes of storage, and the video plays at 30 frames per second.
   a) How many seconds of video does the disc store?
   b) How many seconds can be stored if the compression ratio is 100:1?
4) Assume a CD-ROM holds 640,000,000 bytes of video information, each uncompressed frame requires 560,000 bytes of storage, and the video plays at 30 frames per second.
   a) How many seconds of video does the disc store?
   b) How many seconds can be stored if the compression ratio is 8:1?

Case Study

Six instructors were on a four-week professional development leave from their regular duties. During this time, the instructors participated in a workshop on creating instructional multimedia applications. One goal of the workshop was to create a small tutorial so that the instructors could apply what they learned.

Assume the project required 30,000,000 bytes of compressed photographs, images, text, and programming code plus 250 video clips averaging 15 seconds each digitized at 30 frames per second with 32-bit color at a screen size of 320 by 240 pixels and compressed at a 100 to 1 ratio.

Case Study Question

In practical terms, could the tutorial be distributed on a 700 megabyte CD-ROM?

References

Harris, R. (2004, February). Affordable high-definition video. AV Video Multimedia Producer, 26(2), 10.

Magel, M. (1999, January). Dressed to compress: Choose your codecs wisely for smooth, high-res looks. AV Video Multimedia Producer, 21(1), 33, 152.

Chapter 20:   Storing Content

Learning Outcomes

After completing this chapter, you should be able to:
*   list characteristics of DVD-ROMs and CD-ROMs
*   choose between storing content on a DVD-ROM, CD-ROM, or a server for distribution on an intranet or the Internet

Introduction

Being fluent with digital video disc - read only memory (DVD-ROMs), compact disc - read only memory (CD-ROM) technology, intranets, and the Internet can help you choose the appropriate technology for storing and delivering multimedia applications. This chapter discusses characteristics of DVD-ROMs and CD-ROMs and presents factors to consider for choosing whether to deliver content on DVD-ROMs, CD-ROMs, an intranet, or the Internet.

20.1 Characteristics of DVD-ROMs and CD-ROMs

DVD-ROMs and CD-ROMs cost-effectively store vast amounts of physically encoded data with perfect accuracy. Their storage capacity is needed for the massive storage requirements your multimedia applications can require. The costs of publishing large quantities of DVD-ROMs and CD-ROMs are very low, especially when compared to traditional paper and tapes. Mass publication is easy and fast.

DVD-ROMs and CD-ROMs typically contain large amounts of multimedia content (up to about 4.7 Gigabytes and 700 Megabytes respectively), especially since digitized video and audio can quickly fill up a hard drive. A server can hold yet more data for intranet or Internet delivery.

> **Practical Guideline:**
>
> DVD-ROMs, CD-ROMs, and servers are excellent for storing and distributing large amounts of instructional multimedia data.

DVD-ROMs and CD-ROMs are a durable relatively permanent medium. Magnetic fields and viruses, assuming the data is stored free of viruses, do not affect them. Although lab tests suggest that data integrity should be at least 50 years, estimates of 100 years are reasonable. This makes DVD-ROMs and CD-ROMs safe for storing and retrieving data. Since the data is stored digitally (in the binary system of 1's and 0's used by computers), you can easily retrieve, manipulate, and distribute the data. However, CD-ROM technology is gradually being replaced by DVD-ROM technology. Most computer systems are now sold with DVD players that also read CD-ROMs.

New technologies and techniques will continue to be developed to increase the amount of data that can be stored as well as be quickly retrieved. When the current technology becomes obsolete, you will still have the content in a form that will be transferable to new technologies.

20.2 DVD-ROM / CD-ROM / Intranet / Internet

You will need to consider whether the students should retrieve the data from a DVD-ROM, a CD-ROM, an intranet, or the Internet. Table 20-1 summarizes differences between these data storage and retrieval options.

Table 20-1				
	DVD-ROM	**CD-ROM**	**Intranet**	**Internet**
Amount of data	Up to 4.7 gigabytes, enough for most applications	Up to 700 megabytes, enough for many applications	Limited by space on the host server. If needed, servers can be upgraded.	Limited by space on the host server. If needed, servers can be upgraded.
Learner access	Not found on old computers	Found on all but the oldest computers	Many organizations provide employees and/or students limited access to their intranet	Many learners are not connected but this number is decreasing yearly
Reliability	Very high	Very high	High but there are occasional system crashes	High but there are occasional system crashes
Bandwidth	Enough for most applications, faster than CD-ROMs	Enough for most applications, although high-quality video can push the limits	Enough for most applications although there can be problems with programs that are video intensive when there are numerous concurrent users	A high-bandwidth connection is preferred for most instructional multimedia applications, especially when quality video needs to be seen
Updating information	In general, this cannot be done unless combined with an intranet or Internet connection	In general, this cannot be done unless combined with an intranet or Internet connection	Can be done	Can be done
Developer costs	Copying and distribution costs	Copying and distribution costs	Need a server that can meet the demand	Need a server that can meet the demand
Student costs	One-time relatively low cost of the drive that is usually included when the computer is purchased	One-time relatively low cost of the drive although few computers are now sold with one	Usually none	Monthly fee that increases with the amount of bandwidth

Summary

DVD-ROMs and CD-ROMs cost-effectively store vast amounts of data. Their storage capacity is needed for the massive storage requirements your multimedia applications can require. It is inexpensive to publish large quantities of DVD-ROMs and CD-ROMs.

DVD-ROMs and CD-ROMs typically contain large amounts of multimedia content. CD-ROM technology is gradually being replaced by DVD-ROM technology. Most computer systems are now sold with DVD players that also play CD-ROMs.

When the current technology becomes obsolete, you will still have the content in a form that will be transferable to new technologies.

You will need to consider whether the students should retrieve the data from a DVD-ROM, a CD-ROM, an intranet, or the Internet.

Application Exercise

1) Your boss has decided that it would be better to deliver your multimedia tutorial on the Internet rather than on DVD-ROM. What would you say to debate the pros and cons of his or her decision?

Chapter 21:
Producing DVD-ROMs and CD-ROMs

Learning Outcomes

After completing this chapter, you should be able to:
- describe the steps for creating an instructional DVD-ROM and CD-ROM disc
- create instructional DVD-ROM and CD-ROM discs

Introduction

This chapter describes the basic steps you need to do to produce DVD-ROM and CD-ROM discs for instructional multimedia applications that are not going to be delivered on an intranet or through the Internet. Given the current state of the technology, this process is relatively simple and inexpensive.

Before producing an instructional multimedia DVD-ROM or CD-ROM disc, you should have already followed through the Instructional development cycle. In other words, you should be at the stage of having a thoroughly tested product that is ready to be transferred to DVD-ROM or CD-ROM and then tested further before final discs are pressed.

21.1 Basic Steps

The basic steps for producing a DVD-ROM or CD-ROM include:
- transferring data
- evaluating the check disc
- making copies
- packaging

Be sure that you budget for all of the steps.

21.1-1 Transferring Data

The data needs to be transferred from your hard drive or server to a DVD-ROM or CD-ROM disc. This process is done with a DVD or CD Recordable drive. These drives are affordable for most organizations and individuals and are typically included when you purchase a new computer system. Similarly, the needed and easy-to-use software is also supplied on new computer systems.

Your main task is to transfer the data or files from your hard drive or server to the recordable disc. The software program simply requires you to indicate which files and directories are to be copied. The DVD-ROM or CD-ROM recording unit automatically formats the discs to specifications that work on your computer platform. The initial disc that you make is called a check disc.

21.1-2 Evaluating the Check Disc

After the check disc is made, conduct a thorough evaluation. When evaluating the check disc, you should check for:
- content accuracy
  - This entails evaluating all of the text, video, and other media as well as the questions and detailed feedback for each answer choice.
  - Involve a subject-matter expert in this step.
- completeness
  - Was any content accidentally omitted?
- image quality
- computer programming errors
- its ability to run on a variety of hardware and software configurations
- viruses
  - Run a thorough virus check. Remember that viruses can be transferred with your data onto the check disc or the subsequent master disc. These viruses can then be transferred to the learner's computers. If you work with a manufacturer to make copies of the disc, they will automatically check for viruses.

After making revisions based on the evaluation, make a new check disc and, as a minimum, verify that all of the required changes have been made. Depending on the number and complexity of the revisions, a detailed evaluation may still be needed. You may need to make a few check discs before it is safe to make copies.

If you need many more copies, send your last check disc to the manufacturer for mastering and copying. Consider asking the manufacturer to make you a check disc with their equipment before letting them proceed with making copies. After you send the final check disc to the manufacturer, you can no longer make changes!

Practical Guideline:

After sending your final check disc to the manufacturer, remember that you can no longer make changes!

21.1-3 Making Copies

The disc you use for copying should be free of viruses and "finalized" so that more data cannot be copied onto the disc. Finalized discs are immune to viruses after production. A manufacturer will ensure that the disc is finalized. At this point, you can make as many copies of the check disc as you need. For convenience, it is generally wise to make more copies than you expect you will need.

You can have text, artwork, and/or logos added to the top or unused side of the disc. To avoid pressing delays, check with the manufacturer to find out whether you need to send "Camera ready" artwork and logos in advance of the check disc. Be sure to work with an artist who knows the exact specifications.

Copies are inexpensive but costs vary depending on the turnaround time and the number produced. As the quantity of discs copied increases, the average cost per disc decreases.

You will find that consumer-level recording systems can be cost-effective for creating small numbers of discs. However, remember that your time can be an expensive cost.

21.1-4 Packaging

Discs are tough and relatively immune to damage but consider providing a "jewel" case for protection.

Standard 2-color labels are a minimum. Special labels can be made from "camera ready" artwork. Similarly, jewel-case inserts can also be printed and inserted.

Packaging requirements become more critical if your product will be sold in retail stores. Base your retail-level packaging decisions on a market analysis. For example, consumers make assumptions about a product's quality based whether the package is fancy, big, and/or heavy. The outside artwork can also make a positive or negative first impression.

Summary

The basic steps for producing a DVD-ROM or CD-ROM include:
- Transferring data
- Evaluating the check disc
- Making copies
- Packaging

The data needs to be transferred from your hard drive or server to a DVD-ROM or CD-ROM disc. This process is done with a DVD or CD Recordable drive.

After the check disc is made, you should check for:
- content accuracy
- completeness
- image quality
- computer programming errors
- its ability to be run on a variety of hardware and software configurations
- viruses

At this point, you can make as many copies of the check disc as you need. You can have text, artwork, and/or logos added to the top or unused side of the disc.

Discs are tough and relatively immune to damage but consider providing a "jewel" case for protection. Packaging is also an option, especially if your product will be marketed.

References

Ashkinos, M. (2003, April). In the trenches: Replication. AV Video Multimedia Producer, 25(4), 73-74.

Kaplow, S. (2003, November). Disc duplication: Strategies for DVD do-it-yourselfers and outsourcers alike. AV Video Multimedia Producer, 25(11), 18, 22.

Conclusion

What will change in the future? Computers will become cheaper and faster. Hard drives and DVD-ROM drives or comparable technology will have much higher storage capacities and faster speeds. Many new technologies will evolve. Some of these will survive while many will fail. Some older technologies will co-exist with the new technologies while others will simply fade away. Computers will fully integrate multimedia in that they will have the built-in capacity for digitizing and editing high-quality video and the other media. Software and user-interfaces will become more powerful yet easier to use. None of this should come as a surprise to you. The technology has had these trends for years.

From a practical perspective, the important factor is how future changes will affect you. The answer is that many things will still be the same. You will still want to upgrade your hardware and software every few years. When you have the leading edge technology, you will still have to consider those who will want to run your products on old technology. You will still need to keep up-to-date with changes in technology.

Will what you have learned from this book be useless in a few years? The good news is that your knowledge will remain valuable. The principles and concepts you have learned will always be valid. You will always have to consider the costs and benefits of a multimedia production, follow the principles of instructional design, select media carefully, have the students actively participate in their learning, and follow the principles of good screen design.

Therefore, you can apply what you have learned both now and in the future.

Good luck with your instructional multimedia endeavors!

Appendix I:
Presentation Tips

Use the following tips to help make your instructional computer-managed presentations (CMP) successful:

- Fonts:
  - The text must be read from the back of the room.
  - Consider 44 point for headers and 36 point for the main text.
  - Vary the sizes for different rooms.
  - Arial/Helvetica are easy to read.
  - Test readability beforehand.
- Text
  - Use the 6 by 6 rule. This means that each full screen should have a maximum of 6 lines and 6 words per line. Some presenters follow a similar 5 by 5 rule. This rule is intended to be a guideline rather than a strict requirement. The key is to only provide enough text information to guide the audience through the presentation.
  - CMP are interesting if you elaborate on the points and provide valuable insights. If the screen provides all of the details then it is easier to simply provide a photocopy of your presentation.
  - It is generally wiser to have the presentation a bit short, where the audience wants more, rather than too long, which can leave the audience bored.
  - Only include the needed words.
  - Extra words crowd the screen.
  - Too much text makes you unneeded.
  - Too little text can frustrate participants.
  - Use simple words.
- Visuals:
  - Keep visuals simple.
  - Use graphs, bar charts, pie charts... to present data.
  - Simplify diagrams to the essential information.
  - Crop images to eliminate unnecessary details.
  - Use a series of diagrams rather than a single complicated diagram with all the details.
  - Add labels to diagrams to highlight key points.
  - Remove previous labels.
  - Horizontal labels are easy to read.
  - Store visuals and other media in standardized formats so that you can easily present them. You can retrieve media from hard drives or other storage devices.
- Projecting:
  - Different projectors have different image and sound quality.
  - Check image and audio quality well before you make your presentation. The audio volume must be loud enough for the audience and room. If the projection system does **not** have a built-in microphone and speakers, arrange to have them provided.
  - The projected image height should be at least 1/6 of the distance between the first and last seat.
  - Determine if the room be dark enough for the projection to be clearly seen. Most new projectors work well in both bright and dark rooms.
  - Consider whether the room will change for future presentations. This can affect the decisions you make.
- Clearly define the audience:
  - How many? This affects the room and consequently the font size as well as your choice of colors.
  - Who? Are they superiors, peers, and/or students?
  - What is their attitude toward the topic? Are they Interested, neutral, or hostile? How will you gain their attention and motivate them?
  - What is their level of expertise? You will need to talk at their level.

- What are their needs? You must make it worth their time.
- What are their expectations? Generally, give them what they want. What would be the consequence if you surprise or disappoint them?
- Based on the audience's needs and expectations, write learning outcomes. Learning outcomes are the foundation for your presentation! As you create the presentation, refer back to the learning outcomes.
- Presentation guidelines:
  - Include each event of instruction.
  - Logically sequence your main points and sub-points of the presentation. Each point should lead to the next point.
  - Use other media (e.g., visuals) to support text and to effectively make points, especially the important points. Note that if your presentation is too "flashy", your main points may not be noticed.
- Keep the presentation appealing.
  - Color can add appeal. Choose colors with high contrast. For well-lit rooms, use a bright foreground on a dark background. For darker rooms, use a dark foreground on a bright background.
  - You can provide some appeal by using text with drop shadows.
  - You can use transitions, such as wipes, dissolves, and special effects, between screens to maintain audience interest while you prepare for the following point or screen and to give learners a moment to catch up. Transitions do take time to occur and can become boring if overused. If you use transitions, use fast ones and use them consistently. However, it is debatably wisest to not use them. You are free to pause between points or screens.
  - Rehearse the presentation aloud a few times to help everything run smoothly. Leave enough time between the rehearsal and your presentation to make adjustments.
  - You should move around, use natural expressions and gestures, maintain direct eye contact, vary your voice, smile, and use humor.
- Use appropriate input devices.
  - You can control your computer-managed presentation with mouse input. However, it can also be useful to have:
  - a wireless pointing device to control the computer from any point in the room
  - a tungsten light to send a beam onto the screen to highlight a part of the projection
  - "digital chalk" that allows you or students to draw overtop of what is on the screen

References

3M. (1993). Brilliant meetings: The art of effective visual presentations. Austin, TX: 3M Austin Center.

Hofstetter, F.. (1994). Multimedia presentation technology. Belmont, CA: Wadsworth Publishing Company.

Pearlstein, R. (1993, November/December). Keep-your-distance learning. Performance and Instruction, 32(10), 8-9.

Appendix II:
Instructional Feature Checklist

To help enhance attention and motivation as well as ensure effective learning, your multimedia programs should have most, if not all, of the following features. (Each of these is covered in other chapters of this book.)

An Introduction

An introductory screen should relate the content to the overall course, clearly describe sections (e.g., "Computer animations" rather than "Module 2"), and help students become comfortable with what will be covered. An introduction should be brief.

Menus

Menus should be easy to read and help students locate information and organize their learning.

Goals

Goals are general skills that help students focus and orient their learning.

Learning Outcomes

Learning outcomes are specific skills that help students organize their studying.

Orientation Information

Orientation information, such as lesson names and page numbers, should be easy to find (i.e., on the top line of each screen). Orientation information helps prevent students from getting lost.

Clear, Accurate, and Concise Writing

Clear, accurate, and concise writing can reduce the learning time and the time the student is on the computer. This may require a professional writer.

Smooth and Logical Presentations

Smooth and logical presentations are particularly important since learners are often on their own.

Color

Color makes programs sight appealing and realistic and can increase attention and motivation.

Visuals

Visuals can greatly enhance learning over text alone and add variety to materials.

Variety in Activities and Question Types

Variety in activities and question types can reduce boredom and help reduce skewed results from students being particularly strong or weak at a particular strategy or question type.

Active Learning

Active learning is done effectively through frequently making students think. This is often done through asking questions. Active learning increases learning and retention as well as keeps students involved.

Immediate Feedback

Immediate feedback enhances learning and retention.

Summaries

Summaries help students study before exams and are fast checks for those who think they know the material well.

Tests

Tests provide students with information on how well they are doing. Tests must cover all of the learning outcomes, should contain a wide variety of question formats, should measure skills needed in "real" settings, and should provide results that give students feedback on which learning outcomes they still need to learn.

Learner Control With Guidance

Learner control with guidance is important since students like to have the freedom to choose their own learning paths. Learner control should usually be as flexible or complete as possible but can be a problem for younger or immature students who may need extra guidance.

Control Options

Control options allow students to move about the program. Control options should be easy to access (i.e., the same location, such as the bottom line, on every screen) and be available on every screen.

Help or Hints

Help or hints are used for clarifying or helping with the content by providing detailed descriptions, more sample problems or examples, diagrams, simpler explanations, references... Help or hints must be easy to access.

User Friendliness

User friendliness helps students stay motivated, prevent frustration, in gaining acceptance, and in quieting the critics.

Clear and Easy Instructions

Clear and easy instructions help keep the program flowing smoothly.

Clear Error Messages

Clear error messages help prevent frustration.

Consistency

Consistency helps prevent confusion and helps students find information quickly.

Resource Lists

Resource lists are for students who do not learn all of the material through the computer or want to learn more than what was presented. Resource lists provide a safety net for the students.

Appendix III:
Needs Assessment

A needs assessment can help you determine problems due to:
- a lack of skills or knowledge
- environmental or tool problems such as from a lack of equipment
- poor external incentives that can include achievements being ignored or leading to undesired consequences such as extra work, extra responsibilities, or a transfer to an unwanted location
- poor internal incentives stemming from poor motivation because of a combination of a low perceived value and low confidence in success
- motivational problems
- combinations of the above

This textbook focuses on providing instructional solutions for lack of skills or knowledge problems. The following notes offer you alternatives for solving lack of skills or knowledge problems as well as brief ideas for the other problem classifications.

Solving Lack of Skill or Knowledge Problems

Generally, you can solve a lack of skill or knowledge problem through:
- providing readily available information like a quick reference manual or on-line help
- providing job aids such as a page with a brief list of steps that need to be done for a specific task
- assigning other employees to the task
  - Consider the costs of re-assigning or overlooking employees. Employees can feel valuable if they receive training, feel unimportant if their enthusiasm for working on the project is ignored, or feel incompetent if they are removed from a project.
- coaching
- mentoring

Solving Environmental or Tool Problems

Generally, you can solve a faulty environmental or tools problem through:
- redesigning the job
- redesigning the work station
- providing technological solutions
- providing new tools or equipment
- creating new forms

Solving Incentive Problems

Generally, you can solve ineffective or absent incentives problems through:
- training managers and supervisors
  - Consider coaching programs.
- changing policies and recognition programs
- sharing profits
  - Consider sharing profits within teams.
- paying salaries based on performance

Solving Motivational Problems

Generally, you can solve weak motivation problems through:

- increasing confidence through providing:
  - opportunities for small challenges and successes
  - competent role models
  - a safe environment for setbacks or failure
- making the work more important by increasing value by:
  - clarifying the company's vision
  - increasing ownership such as through employee involvement
  - providing fair compensation
  - giving threats but only if absolutely necessary
- supporting the employee:
  - through providing education or training
  - with coaching, mentoring, or peers

References

Dick, W., & Carey, L. (1990). The systematic design of instruction (3rd ed.). Glenville, IL: Harper Collins Publishers.

Rossett, A. (1987). Training needs assessment. Englewood Cliffs, NJ: Educational Technology Publications.

Appendix IV:
Learning Outcomes

Introduction

Gagne and Briggs categorized learning outcomes into learning domains called verbal information, intellectual skills, cognitive strategies, psychomotor skills, and attitudes. By categorizing a learning outcome into a learning domain, you can facilitate the entire systematic instructional design process. Also, by classifying learning outcomes into learning domains, you can readily see the skill and thinking levels needed to accomplish the learning outcome. The subsequent questions or interactions you create should relate to the needed skill and thinking levels. As a rule, you should use a variety of different interactions or question types that test as many of the different learning levels as is appropriate to help students learn effectively. (See the Instructional Design chapter for more details.)

Bloom has different categories that indicate higher and lower learning levels. (See Appendix V for details on Bloom's taxonomy.) Gagne and Briggs' model more readily lends itself to instructional design than Bloom's taxonomy. For example, categorizing a learning outcome into a learning domain makes it easy to determine which appropriate subordinate skills analysis technique to use. However, Gagne and Briggs' model tends to be more difficult to learn than Bloom's taxonomy. Review both models and then choose one model with which to develop materials.

Verbal Information

Verbal information:
- usually has learning outcomes that require learners to give specific responses to specific stimuli
  - This often involves simply remembering and recalling information.
- typically has only one specific response for each question
  - For example, naming an object usually has one answer.
- usually has only one basic way to ask each question
  - For example, "This object is called a _____." Simple paraphrases of the question (e.g., "The name of this object is a _____.") are considered the same way of asking the question.
- usually does not involve symbolic manipulation
  - For example, there is no problem solving or applying rules.
- is often needed before higher-level skills can be learned
  - Imagine trying to master word processing skills without first knowing the keyboard keys.
- can be derived from experts

Examples: List Gagne and Briggs' learning domains.
               State which media is best for presenting numerous facts.

If there is a lot of verbal information to be presented then text is needed so that students can spend time memorizing the information. Audio and video are effective for teaching small numbers of facts.

Intellectual Skills

Intellectual skills:
- require learners to think
  - This is beyond simply remembering and recalling information.
- can have more than one way to answer a question
  - For example, when demonstrating effective screen designs, students could create a screen on the computer, draw a screen on paper, describe a screen in words, find an existing example...

- require symbolic manipulation
  - For example, algebraic problem solving involves symbolic manipulation.
- are further classified into one of six increasingly complex skill categories called discriminations, concrete concepts, defined concepts, rules, higher-order rules, and cognitive strategies (For simplicity, cognitive strategies have been combined with intellectual skills.)

Depending on the skill being taught, any media could be effective. Often a combination, such as text with audio, visuals, or video, is most effective.

Discriminations

Discriminations are relatively low-level skills where students simply note differences. Students do not have to explain the difference.

Examples: Discriminate between the letters "b" and "d".
             Given two notes played on a piano, state whether they are different.

Concrete Concepts

Concrete concepts are generally simple skills but are more advanced than discriminations. Concrete concepts may require students to note similarities and differences.

Examples: Identify, by pointing to the sample screen, five components of a computer-tutorial screen.
             Indicate which of two notes played on a piano is higher than the other.

Defined Concepts

Defined concepts require students to group or classify ideas and objects into specified categories. Defined concepts require higher-thinking levels than concrete concepts.

Examples: Classify a multimedia package as being a drill and practice, tutorial, simulation, or educational game.
             State the name of the note played on a piano.

Rules

Rules are combinations of concepts.

Examples: Demonstrate the effective use of background color in a multimedia package.
             Use the correct fingers to play the following notes on a piano.

Higher-Order Rules

Higher-order rules require the combination of more than one rule.

Example: Generate computer screens that incorporate principles of effective screen design.
             Use the correct fingers to play the following tune on a piano.

Cognitive Strategies

Cognitive strategies require learners to do something original or creative.
Examples: Design a multimedia simulation that...
             Create a set of standards that...

Write a melody for the piano that...
Judge the significance of...

Psychomotor Skills

Psychomotor skills require learners to use muscular actions to achieve something. These skills are more than a trivial task such as pushing a button. Psychomotor skills may require extensive mental activity as is needed for playing chess.

Examples: Given an edit decision list and editing software, make the video clips.
Using a graphics package, draw a blue circle with a 20-pixel vertical diameter.
Assemble the parts into a...
From behind the foul line, throw the ball into the hoop.
Play a melody on the piano.

Multimedia solutions for psychomotor skills often include video with audio and text.

Attitudes

Attitudes are tendencies people have to making particular decisions or choices under specific circumstances. For simplicity, interpersonal skills such as those involved in leadership and teamwork are included in this domain since they often have similar instructional solutions.

Attitudes can be hard to measure. After providing the instruction, it may not be possible for you to see whether the learners make those choices, such as not drinking alcohol and driving, in the "real" world. What you may see may be a measurable skill in another domain. For example, if a student chooses to wear safety equipment, what you may see (e.g., putting on safety equipment) is a psychomotor skill.

Examples: The learner will choose to follow the systematic instructional design process.
The learner will decide to adopt the "team approach" when creating multimedia products.
The student will encourage all group members to contribute in brainstorming activities.

Multimedia solutions for teaching attitudes and interpersonal skills often include video with audio. Video can show realistic consequences to choices. For example, a car crash can be shown if the learner chooses to drink alcohol and then drive.

Helpful Hints

Depending on how you use the verb, some verbs can occur in more than one type of learning domain. For example, indicating whether the two notes played on the piano are different is a discrimination skill while indicating which of the two notes played on the piano is higher is a concrete concept skill.

You may find that some of your programs only have learning outcomes that require the learner to simply recall information. This is fine when there is no requirement to test higher-learning levels. However, remember that research shows that moderate difficulty levels lead to faster, more accurate learning.

References

Gagne, R., Briggs, L., & Wager, W. (1988). Principles of instructional design (3rd ed.). New York, NY: Holt, Rinehart, and Winston.

Romiszowski, A. (1988). The selection and use of instructional media: For improved classroom teaching and for interactive, individual instruction (2nd ed.). New York, NY: Nichols Publishing.

Appendix V:
Bloom's Taxonomy

Introduction

Bloom classified learning outcomes into six taxonomies called knowledge, comprehension, application, analysis, synthesis, and evaluation. Similarly, Gagne and Briggs have categorized objectives into five learning domains. (See Appendix IV.) Compared to Gagne and Briggs' model, Bloom's taxonomy does not as readily lend itself to instructional design but tends to be easier to learn. Review both models and then choose one model with which to develop materials.

By classifying learning outcomes into taxonomies, you can readily see the skill and thinking levels needed to accomplish the learning outcome. The subsequent questions or interactions you provide should relate to the needed skill and thinking levels. As a rule, you should use a variety of different interactions or question types that test as many of the different learning levels as is needed to help students learn effectively.

Knowledge

Knowledge skills entail recalling information as it was presented.

Sample verbs: State, describe, label, list, name
Example: List the different types of media that learning packages can include.

Comprehension

Comprehension skills can include restating knowledge learned earlier in one's own terms, translating ideas and concepts, and recognizing inferences and assumptions. Comprehension skills can be different forms of questions and problems already seen.

Sample verbs: Convert, estimate, explain, summarize, locate
Example: Explain why multimedia applications should not necessarily include all types of media.

Application

With application skills, students apply knowledge to new situations. Students must decide which way to solve the problem. For application skills, you can use fictional situations, material students have not seen, or new slants on old problems.

Sample verbs: Relate, compute, change, apply
Example: Relate factors that increase a student's motivation to learn to successful performance.

Analysis

Analysis is breaking down existing knowledge into meaningful parts. Analysis can require students to detect relationships and draw conclusions. You can use experiments or supply data for analysis skills.

Sample verbs: Breakdown, differentiate, identify, relate, analyze
Example: Given a properly written objective, identify the objective's conditions, skill, and criteria.

Synthesis

Synthesis is combining parts to form a whole. Synthesis can take the form of a speech, proposal, project, or theory.

Sample verbs: Summarize, revise, compose, construct, create, synthesize
Example: Create a multimedia tutorial that includes all of the instructional events.

Evaluation

Evaluation entails using personal values to judge knowledge. Evaluations are hard to grade objectively.

Sample verbs: appraise, compare, conclude, criticize, assess, evaluate
Example: Evaluate whether a software package is user-friendly.

References

Bloom, B., Engelhart, M., Hill, W., Furst, E., & Krathwohl, D. (1956). Taxonomy of educational objectives, Handbook 1: The cognitive domain. New York, NY: David McKay Inc.

Butler, K. (1986). Learning and teaching style: In theory and practice. Columbia, CT: The Learner's Dimension.

Romiszowski, A. (1988). The selection and use of instructional media: For improved classroom teaching and for interactive, individual instruction (2nd ed.). New York, NY: Nichols Publishing.

Appendix VI:
Question Analysis

By analyzing questions, you can determine whether questions are effective or ineffective and obtain information for improving them. Improving poorly-written questions can help prevent student frustration. However, given a project's typical money and time constraints, you may choose to omit a question analysis. You should do an analysis when the formative evaluation indicates that many questions have problems or when a formal testing system has built-in analysis capabilities.

Determining Question and Test Effectiveness

Check five things to determine question and test effectiveness:

1) Does each question test a learning outcome?

   If not, then rewrite the question or eliminate it.

2) Is each question too hard or easy?

   Determine the degree of difficulty $= \dfrac{\text{number of correct answers}}{\text{total number of responses}}$

   The value should be between 0.2 and 0.8. Make the question easier if the value is less than 0.2 and harder if the value is greater than 0.8.

3) Does the test discriminate between strong and weak students?

   Use a computer to:
   a) mark the test
   b) rank the students
   c) select the top and bottom 25% of the students
   d) for each question, calculate the percent of top students who got the question right
   e) for each question, calculate the percent of bottom students who got the question wrong
   f) value of step "d" minus the value of step "e"
   g) convert the percent to a decimal

   Values between 0.1 and 1.0 are good (a value of 1.0 is the best). Rewrite or eliminate questions with a value less than 0.1.

4) Is each alternative or answer reasonable?

   If an answer is not selected at least 10% of the time, rewrite that answer or replace it with a different one. You may also choose to eliminate the answer choice.

5) Is the test reliable (i.e., the same result each time the student tries it)?

   Good analysis packages can determine test reliability. The result should be at least 0.6. Test reliability can be increased by asking more questions per learning outcome, by testing all of the learning outcomes, and by reducing the number of true-false questions.

Difficulties in Analyzing Questions and Tests

It may be hard for you to do an analysis because:
- Most authoring tools do not have a built-in internal question analysis tool.
  - It may be possible to create an analysis tool either internally with the authoring package or externally with a programming language. Technically this is not hard to do but it may be most efficient to hire a professional computer programmer to do this task. Once created, this tool could be used for other applications.
- There may not be enough students to attain statistical accuracy.
  - Statistical accuracy depends on the number of students who take the test and the number of questions on the test.
  - Providing more students and more questions per test gives higher accuracy. However, the value of the increased accuracy needs to be balanced with the increased costs of time and money.
  - Generally, 50 students is a minimum but over 100 students are preferred.
- There usually is not a budget for it.
  - Question analysis can take a lot of time.
- Part of the team may have already been dismantled.
- Money and/or time may have run out.
  - It is safest to specifically plan and budget for the analysis.

Reference

Mayer, M. (1988). Test item construction: A self-instructional manual. Victoria, British Columbia, Canada: Province of British Columbia, Ministry of Advanced Education and Job Training.

Application Exercises Solutions

1. Introduction to Instructional Multimedia

1) Textbooks are not considered multimedia products since, as defined, multimedia applications involve computer hardware and software.
3) To refute this claim say that the research states that students tend to prefer individualized lessons where they can:
   - set their own pace, proceed when they are ready, and review as often as they want
   - control their own learning path
   - experience an infinitely patient tutor
   - engage in programs that adapt to their abilities and backgrounds
   - have active involvement in their learning
   - have immediate feedback
   - be objectively evaluated
   - have privacy
   - learn when they want
5) 600 hours x $40 per hour = $24,000 development costs.
   $500 - $200 = $300 savings per employee
   $24,000 ÷ $300 = 80 employees

2. Team Approach

1) If a project manager has poor communication skills:
   - morale and motivation could be affected
   - cooperation could be reduced
   - team members may not be sure of their duties
   - timelines may not be met...
3) Some of the things you could say to justify the team approach include:
   - You do not have all of the necessary skills.
   - Teams usually produce better products than individuals.
   - The work will be done more efficiently by highly-qualified personnel.
   - The project will be done much more quickly with a team.
   - You do not have the time to do all of the tasks.
5) To help the team communicate effectively, you should be receptive and available, be involved, hold regular meetings, set standards for working as a team, delegate roles and responsibilities, make a timeline, write status reports, and create design documents.

3. Authoring Tools

1) This answer can also vary depending on the situation. For example, the decision can depend on whether any potential team member has experience working with C++. However, recommending an icon-based system or authoring system would likely be wise since these tools tend to be easier to learn and require less development time than C++.
3) As the capabilities of an authoring tool increases, the learning and authoring time tends to increase.
5 a) True
   b) True
   c) False
   d) False

4. Instructional Development Cycle

1) Errors may not be discovered until late in the project. Time and money is saved if errors can be detected early.

3) Your boss's plan may backfire. The time invested in the analysis phase tends to save more time throughout the rest of the process by preventing mistakes from occurring.

5. Instructional Design

1) a) Educational game
   b) Tutorial
   c) Simulation
3) Problems could be a result of a:
   a) lack of skills that may be solved through training and job aids
   b) ineffective or absent incentives that may be addressed through providing recognition or monetary rewards for learning the new system
   c) weak motivation that may be solved through increasing confidence (e.g., training) and value (e.g., clarifying how the new system will make their job easier)
5 a) This is poorly written since the verb "understand" is not measurable. A well-written objective could be: Students will be able to design multimedia tutorial screens that effectively use color.
   b) This is a well-written objective.
   c) This is probably poorly written since the accuracy would likely be important. A well-written objective could be: Using calipers, students will be able to measure the thickness of different objects to an accuracy of 0.2 millimeters.
   d) This is a well-written objective.
   e) This is poorly written since the verb "appreciate" is not measurable. A well-written objective could be: Students will be able to state three reasons why the precise accuracy that calipers can provide is important when measuring the thickness of certain objects.
7) Motivating a student on chemical safety could be achieved through:
   - gaining attention by showing injuries caused by chemicals
   - relating chemical safety to activities the student performs on the job
   - increasing confidence by asking questions most students can answer
   - increasing satisfaction through stating that the material will be challenging but fun and that passing the material is required for getting the job
9) If the target population has varied skill levels:
   - include a variety of instructional activities
   - ensure success by having the material proceed in small incremental steps and by providing frequent opportunities for practice and feedback
   - let students control the instruction's pace and sequence
   - include a workbook with summaries

6. Media Selection

1) For learning to occur, the message is more important than the medium. Media simply carry the message to the learner. For learning to occur, the message must be received and understood. This is independent of the media.
3) "D" is the best answer. Text is better than video when the topic is complex.
5) "D" is the best answer. Video is poor at providing details.

7. Text

1) Things, which could be improved, include:
   - Remove the bold (which does not highlight anything important).
   - Remove the italics (which are ineffective).
   - Correct the spelling (change "rite" to "write"...).
   - Correct the grammar (change "good" to "well"...).
   - Use the active voice (change "screens of computers" to "computer screens"...).
   - Use fewer words (change "features of text that are written well" to "features of well-written text"...).
   - Use point form.
   - Start each point with a bullet.

3   a) This sentence does not have a subject. The reader does not know what should have meaning.
    b) This sentence uses an unnecessarily complex vocabulary.
    c) This sentence is too wordy.
    d) This sentence should be written in the second person (you).
5) For learning to occur in a hypertext application, student learning should be specifically planned and guided. The principles of instructional design should be followed. You could do this by:
    • providing interaction that requires the students to think about the material
    • clearly indicating needed information
    • using a simple structure to organize the material
    • providing guidance in acquiring the needed knowledge
    • including clear orientation information on each page

8. Audio

1) A doctor's voice would provide credibility but would probably be less effective than a rock star's voice. Teenagers would likely be better able to relate to the rock star than to the doctor. Note that a combination of both could be more effective in reaching a wider range of students.
3) "A" is the best answer. A professional narrator can help in creating credibility. However, there is no guarantee of success. For example, if the narrator has an inappropriate accent or sounds too young or old then credibility can be lost.
5) 330,000 bytes.
    Use the formula:
    Number of seconds x (number of bits ÷ 8) x sample rate (Hz) x number of channels.
    15 seconds x (16/8) x 11,000 x 1 = 330,000 bytes.

9. Visuals

1) A videotape could be effective but a set of images would be easier to follow in a step-by-step procedure. A set of images would also be more portable than a videotape. Text-based explanations and a checklist would improve the package.
3) "C" is the best answer. On screens that build, you should remove all of the irrelevant information. This helps the student focus on the pertinent information and helps prevent the screen from becoming cluttered.
5   a) Each image requires 320 x 240 x 16 ÷ 8 = 153,600 bytes.
        600,000,000 ÷ 153,600 = 3,906 images.
    b) 600,000,000 ÷ 153,600 x 10= 39,062 images

10. Video

1) Some students would not be able to relate to the businessperson. This could have a negative impact on the student's motivation. (A peer would be more effective.)
3) "D" is the best answer. Video is poor at presenting large amounts of information since students tend to have difficulty recalling details. (To help facilitate recall, you should use short clips.)
5) To record high-quality video, you can:
    -   hire professional help
    -   use high-quality filming equipment and supplies
    -   work with a team

11. Animations

1) Since it is very difficult to concentrate on reading the text and viewing the animation at the same time, students will probably not fully understand the material.
3) If an animation is not self-explanatory, you could:
    -   direct a learner's attention
    -   add clarifying labels
    -   add supporting text
    -   consider redesigning the animation

5) If an animation is displaying too slowly, you could:
   - only run it on faster hardware platforms
   - reduce the number of colors (e.g., from 8-bit to 4-bit)
   - reduce the object's size
   - make it appear like the object is moving

12. Interactivity

1) Without interaction, the student would not learn as much and would probably be very bored.
3) Yes, the program is interactive as long as the students are actively involved and think about what they are doing. This kind of scenario could take place in a simulation or an educational game.

13. Input Devices

1) For most situations, touch or mouse input would be effective for students with weak keyboarding skills. Keyboard input would be required for teaching keyboarding, spelling... Some of these skills can be taught by having students click or touch the keys illustrated on a visual.
3) The difficulties you could have with the voice input system would revolve around training the system. The system would possibly have to be trained to handle different words, accents, and slang expressions.

14. Question Writing

1) The question can be rewritten as:
   Multiple-choice questions are very good for
   a) testing many facts in a short time
   b) measuring more than one objective at a time
   c) taking little screen room
   d) minimizing the guessing factor
   e) being easy to write
3) The question can be rewritten as:
   True or false? An important component of air is oxygen.
5) No, all questions must match a learning outcome. If the question does not match a learning outcome then the material should not have been covered. It is unfair to ask questions on material that has not been covered.

15. Feedback

1) The feedback could be:
   Correct, the reaction does release energy. Heat, light, sound, and mechanical energies were released.
3) The feedback could be:
   You are partly right. Beer is correct. Press Enter to try again.
5) Some research does support that some students should be able to choose the amount of feedback that they receive. However, for practical reasons it is better to automatically provide elaborative feedback because:
   - some learners will not make the right decision
   - most students prefer elaborative feedback
   - it adds a level of complexity to include this choice
   - students can simply choose to not read the feedback if they do not want it

16. Screen Design

1) Without orientation information, it would be easier to get "lost" and be harder to find reference points for later asking questions and returning to where you last finished.
3) If the control options are placed down the screen's left side, the students would not find the options in a logical place. When students finish reading the screen their eyes will be on the bottom right. It is then awkward for them to the search to the far left for the control options.

5)   If a menu had twenty selections, some of the selections should be placed into a submenu. As a rule, a menu should not contain more than nine selections.

17. User-friendliness

1)   There is no perfect answer for this question. Learner control can be appropriate if the students will follow the provided guidance. If there is doubt about the students' ability to effectively control their learning, then shared control between the learners and the program can be appropriate.

3)   If you provide learner control but do not spend the time to provide guidance, students may not proceed in the way that will most effectively help them learn or students may waste time figuring out the best way to proceed. Some students may wander through the program and learn virtually nothing.

5)   If the humor might be risky for a small part of the audience then you should **not** take the chance. It can be too difficult to undo any damage done.

18. Color and Highlighting

1   a)   Too many words are highlighted. Consequently, none of the words are emphasized.
    b)   The sentence could be rewritten as:
         Color combinations to **avoid** include red with green, blue with yellow, green with blue, and red with blue.

3)   "D" is the best answer. Screens should contain about three to four foreground text colors and these colors should be used consistently.

19. Compression/Decompression

1   a)   640 x 480 x 30 x 20 x 32 ÷ 8 = 737,280,000 bytes
    b)   320 x 240 x 30 x 20 x 32 ÷ 8 = 184,320,000 bytes
    c)   320 x 240 x 30 x 20 x 24 ÷ 8 = 138,240,000 bytes
    d)   320 x 240 x 15 x 20 x 24 ÷ 8 = 69,120,000 bytes
3   a)   700,000,000 bytes ÷ 250,000 bytes/frame ÷ 30 frames/second = 93.3 seconds
    b)   93.3 seconds x 100 = 9,330 seconds

20. Storing Content

1)   In comparing the distribution of content on DVD-ROM or the Internet, learners with older computers may not have a DVD-ROM drive, while some learners do not have Internet access. DVD-ROM drives are reliable while Internet access is not guaranteed as the system is sometimes "down". DVD-ROMs have pressing and distribution costs while Internet distribution is free assuming you already have and maintain a suitable server. However, learners will likely have monthly access costs for connecting to the Internet. DVD-ROM distribution is better for applications that need to show high-quality video.

References

3M. (1993). <u>Brilliant meetings: The art of effective visual presentations</u>. Austin, TX: 3M Austin Center.

Adams, N. (1993, May). CBT or not CBT. <u>Training, 30</u>(5), 73-75.

Agnew, B. (1994). Communication and the collaborative process. <u>Proceedings of the Multicomm '94 Conference on Multimedia Solutions for Business and Education</u>.

Alessi, S., & Trollip, S. (1991). <u>Computer-based instruction: Methods and development</u> (2nd ed.). Englewood Cliffs, NJ: Prentice-Hall, Inc.

Alten, S. (1990). <u>Audio in media</u> (3rd ed.). Belmont, CA: Wadsworth Publishing Company.

Armstrong, D., Denton, J., & Savage, T. (1978). <u>Instructional skills handbook</u>. Englewood Cliffs, NJ: Educational Technology Publications.

Ashkinos, M. (2003, April). In the trenches: Replication. <u>AV Video Multimedia Producer, 25</u>(4), 73-74.

Aspillaga, M. (1991). Screen design: Location of information and its effects on learning. <u>Journal of Computer-Based Instruction, 18</u>(3), 89-92.

Ayersman, D. (1993). <u>An overview of the research on learning styles and hypermedia environments</u>. Paper presented at the 1993 Annual Convention of the Eastern Educational Research Association, Clearwater Beach, Florida.

Baek, Y., & Layne, B. (1988). Color, graphics, and animation in a computer-assisted learning tutorial lesson. <u>Journal of Computer-Based Instruction, 15</u>(4), 131-135.

Bailey, J. (1992). Curriculum approaches in special education computing. <u>Journal of Computer-Based Instruction, 19</u>(1), 1-5.

Bastiaens, T., & Martens, R. (2000). Conditions for web-based learning with real events. In Abbey, B. (Ed.), <u>Instructional and cognitive impacts of web-based education</u>. (pp. 1-31). Hershey, PA: Idea Group Publishing.

Beach, B. (1993, October). Learning with Roger Schank. <u>Training & Development, 47</u>(10), 39-43.

Begley, S. (1993, May 31). Teaching minds to fly with discs and mice. <u>Newsweek, 121</u>(22), 45.

Bennett, G. (1994, June). More, More Morphing! <u>The Computer Paper, 7</u>(6), 24-29.

Benshoof, L., & Hooper, S. (1993, Autumn). The effects of single- and multiple-window presentation on achievement during computer-based instruction. <u>Journal of Computer-Based Instruction, 20</u>(4), 113-117.

Berge, Z., Collins, M., & Dougherty, K. (2000). Design guidelines for web-based courses. In Abbey, B. (Ed.), <u>Instructional and cognitive impacts of web-based education</u>. (pp. 32-40). Hershey, PA: Idea Group Publishing.

Berry, L. (2000). Cognitive effects of web page design. In Abbey, B. (Ed.), <u>Instructional and cognitive impacts of web-based education</u>. (pp. 41-55). Hershey, PA: Idea Group Publishing.

Billings, D., & Cobb, K. (1992). Effects of learning style preferences, attitude and GPA on learner achievement using computer assisted interactive videodisc instruction. <u>Journal of Computer-Based Instruction, 19</u>(1), 12-16.

Blaize, S. (1994, November). Who owns Rita Hayworth? Multimedia copyrights: Your rights and theirs. <u>Digital Video Magazine, 2</u>(10), 62-66.

Bloom, B., Engelhart, M., Hill, W., Furst, E., & Krathwohl, D. (1956). <u>Taxonomy of educational objectives, Handbook 1: The cognitive domain</u>. New York, NY: David McKay Inc.

Bonime, A. (1995, April). Menu metaphors and why I hate them. <u>CD-ROM Professional, 8</u>(4), 60-61.

Brush, T. (1998). Embedding cooperative learning into the design of integrated learning systems: Rationale and guidelines. <u>Educational Technology Research and Development, 46</u>(3), 5-18.

Butler, K. (1988). <u>It's all in your mind: A student's guide to learning style</u>. Columbia, CT: The Learner's Dimension.

Butler, K. (1986). <u>Learning and teaching style: In theory and practice</u>. Columbia, CT: The Learner's Dimension.

Card, D. (1992, April). Lotus Development v. Borland International. <u>Canadian Computer Law Reporter. 9</u>(4), 51-53.

Carlson, H. (1991). Learning style and program design in interactive multimedia. Educational Technology Research and Development, 39(3), 41-48.

Cavalier, J., & Klein, J. (1998). Effects of cooperative versus individual learning and orienting activities during computer-based instruction. Educational Technology Research and Development, 46(1), 5-17.

Cennamo, K. (1993). Learning from video: Factors influencing learners' preconceptions and invested mental effort. Educational Technology Research and Development, 41(3), 33-45.

Chun, D., & Plass, J. (1994). Assessing the effectiveness of multimedia in language learning software. Proceedings of the ED-MEDIA 94 World Conference on Educational Multimedia and Hypermedia.

Churach, D., & Fisher, D. (2001). Science students surf the web: Effects on constructivist classroom environments. Journal of Computers in Mathematics and Science Teaching, 20(2), 221-247.

Clariana, R. (1993, Summer). A review of multiple-try feedback in traditional and computer-based instruction. Journal of Computer-Based Instruction, 20(3), 67-74.

Clariana, R. (1993, Spring). The motivational effect of advisement on attendance and achievement in computer-based instruction. Journal of Computer-Based Instruction, 20(2), 47-51.

Colijn, B., & Petrick, J. (1987, June). Keep your wits about you: Humor in CBT. Data Training, 6(6), 38-41.

Conference Board of Canada. (1991). Employability skills profile: The critical skills required in the Canadian workforce. Ottawa, Ontario: The Conference Board of Canada.

Danielson, J., Lockee, B., & Burton, J. (2000). ID and HCI: A marriage of necessity. In Abbey, B. (Ed.), Instructional and cognitive impacts of web-based education. (pp. 118-128). Hershey, PA: Idea Group Publishing.

Dempsey, J., & Sales, G. (Eds). (1993). Interactive instruction and feedback. Englewood Cliffs, NJ: Prentice Hall.

Dick, W., & Carey, L. (1990). The systematic design of instruction (3rd ed.). Glenville, IL: Harper Collins Publishers.

Dunn, R., & Bruno, A. (1985, September). What does the research on learning styles have to do with Mario? The Clearing House, 59(1), 9-12.

Ellis, D., Ford, H., & Wood, F. (1993, February). Hypertext and learning styles. The Electronic Library, 11(1), 13-18.

Enochs, J., Handley, J., & Wollenberg, J. (1986). Relating learning style, reading vocabulary, reading comprehension, and aptitude for learning to achievement in the self-paced and computer-assisted instructional modes. Journal of Experimental Education, 54, 135-139.

Falk, D., & Carlson, H. (1995). Multimedia in higher education: A practical guide to new tools for interactive teaching and learning. Medford, NJ: Learned Information, Inc.

Feeley, J. (2005, February). HDV, film and me: Why HD makes film an undead medium. Studio/monthly, 27(2), 32.

Feifer, R., & Allender, L. (1994). It's not how multi the media, it's how the media is used. Proceedings of the ED-MEDIA 94 World Conference on Educational Multimedia and Hypermedia.

Fenrich, P. (2005). What can you do to virtually teach practical skills? The Journal of Issues in Informing Science and Information Technology, 2, 347-354.

Fenrich, P. (1993, August). [Interview with Dr. G. McKee, Optometrist.]

Fenrich, P. (1992). Screen design and user interface needs for successful multimedia applications. Proceedings of the Seventh Canadian Symposium on Instructional Technology.

Fenrich, P. (1991). The heart of multimedia design: An award-winning approach. Tenfold, 4(1), 10-11.

Ference, P., & Vockell, E. (1994, July-August). Adult learning characteristics and effective software instruction. Educational Technology, 34(6), 25-31.

Friend, C., & Cole, C. (1990). Learner control in computer-based instruction: A current literature review. Educational Technology, 30(11), 47-49.

Gagne, R., Briggs, L., & Wager, W. (1988). Principles of instructional design (3rd ed.). New York, NY: Holt, Rinehart, and Winston.

Gagne, R., & Driscoll, M. (1988). Essentials of learning for instruction (2nd ed.). Englewood Cliffs, NJ: Prentice Hall.

Gagnon, D. (1986). Interactive television: The influence of user control and interactive structure. Paper presented at the International Television Studies Conference.

Garner, K. (1991, Summer/Fall). 20 rules for arranging text on a screen. Emerging Technologies Bulletin, 16, 2-4.

Gillingham, M. (1988). Text in computer-based instruction: What the research says. Journal of Computer-Based Instruction, 15(1), 1-6.

Grabinger, R. (1993). Computer screen designs: Viewer judgments. Educational Technology Research and Development, 41(3), 35-73.

Gray, S. (1988). Sequence control menus and CAI: A follow-up study. Journal of Computer-Based Instruction, 15(2), 57-60.

Grimes, T. (1990). Audio-video correspondence and its role in attention and memory. Educational Technology Research and Development, 38(3), 15-25.

Guild, P., & Garger, S. (1985). Marching to different drummers. Alexandria, VA: Association for Supervision and Curriculum Development.

Gustafson, K. (1981). A survey of instructional development models. (ERIC Document Reproduction Service No. ED 305 921)

Habstritt, G. (2000, February). Sounds important: Spreading the word about new media audio. newmedia.pro, 3(1), 9-13.

Hammond-Kaarremaa, L. (1992, April). Issues affecting the implementation and use of educational technology. Victoria, British Columbia, Canada: Standing Committee on Educational Technology.

Hannafin, M., Dalton, D., & Hooper, S. (1987, October). Computers in education: Ten myths and ten needs. Educational Technology, 27(10), 8-14.

Hannafin, R., & Sullivan, H. (1995). Learner control in full and lean CAI programs. Educational Technology Research and Development, 43(1), 19-30.

Harris, R. (2004, February). Affordable high-definition video. AV Video Multimedia Producer, 26(2), 10.

Hartley, J. (1985). Designing instructional text. New York, NY: Kogan Page.

Hedgecoe, J. (1989). John Hedgecoe's complete video course: A step-by-Step, self-instruction guide to making great videos. London, Great Britain: Octopus Publishing Group.

Hirai, S. (1994, January). A few words on type. The Computer Paper, 7(1), 94-98.

Hoffman, J., & Waters, K. (1982, March). Some effects of student personality on success with computer-assisted instruction. Educational Technology, 22(3), 8-14.

Hofstetter, F. (1994). Multimedia presentation technology. Belmont, CA: Wadsworth Publishing Company.

Holsinger, E. (2005, February). Sony HVR-Z1U and HDR-FX1 HDV Camcorders. Studio/monthly, 27(2), 12-14.

Huntley, J., & Easley, G. (1994). The brown book of multimedia. Dubuque, IA: Wm. C. Brown Communications.

Ives, B., & Forman, D. (1991). Calculating competitive advantage. Multimedia Solutions, 1(6), 32-37.

Jamieson, J., & Chapelle, C. (1988). Using CALL effectively: What do we need to know about students? System, 16(2), 151-162.

Janniro, M. (1993, Spring). Effects of computer-based instruction on student learning of psychophysiological detection of deception test question formulation. Journal of Computer-Based Instruction, 20(2), 58-62.

Jin, H., & Reeves, T. (1992). Mental models: A research focus for interactive learning systems. Educational Technology Research and Development, 40(3), 39-53.

Johnson, D. (2005, March). Lighting a Video Interview With Arri Fresnels. Studio/monthly, 27(3), 30-31.

Johnson, D. (2005, March). Take Control of Your Lighting. Studio/monthly, 27(3), 44-46.

Jonassen, D., & Wang, S. (1993, Winter). Acquiring structural knowledge from semantically structured hypertext. Journal of Computer-Based Instruction, 20(1), 1-8.

Jonassen, D., & Hannum, W. (1991). Analysis of task analysis procedures. In G. Anglin (Ed.), Instructional technology: Past, present, and future (pp. 170-187). Englewood, CO: Libraries Unlimited.

Joss, M. (1996, January). Multimedia presents! A look at high-powered interactive presentation software. CD-ROM Professional, 9(1), 62-72.

Kaplow, S. (2003, November). Disc duplication: Strategies for DVD do-it-yourselfers and outsourcers alike. AV Video Multimedia Producer, 25(11), 18, 22.

Kaplow, S. (2002, June). The streamy underbelly: How to avoid pitfalls in producing and delivering web video. AV Video Multimedia Producer, 24(6), 21, 72.

Karon, P. (1996, January, 22). Multimedia for the masses. Infoworld, 18(4), 64-79.

Keller, J. (1987). Strategies for stimulating the motivation to learn. Performance and Instruction, 26(8), 1-7.

Kouzes, J., & Posner, B. (1987). The leadership challenge: How to get extraordinary things done in an organization. San Francisco, CA: Jossey-Bass Publishers.

Kozma, R. (1991, Summer) Learning with media. Review of Educational Research, 61(2), 179-211.

Leflore, D. (2000). Theory supporting design guidelines for web-based instruction. In Abbey, B. (Ed.), Instructional and cognitive impacts of web-based education. (pp. 102-117). Hershey, PA: Idea Group Publishing.

Li, R. (1993, May). Creating interactive CBT lessons without video. Educational Technology, 33(5), 20-26.

Livingston, D. (1994, January). Choosing an authoring system: Tips to guide your selection. CD-ROM Professional, 7(1), 83-90.

Macromedia. (1994). Multimedia essentials for windows. San Francisco, CA: Macromedia, Inc.

Maddux, C. (1994, September). The Internet: Educational prospects and problems. Educational Technology, 34(7), 37-42.

Magel, M. (1999, January). Dressed to compress: Choose your codecs wisely for smooth, high-res looks. AV Video Multimedia Producer, 21(1), 33, 152.

Magel, M. (1998, June). Splat! There's more than one way to debug a project. AV Video Multimedia Producer, 20(6), 39, 41.

Mager, R. (1962). Preparing instructional objectives. Belmont, CA: Fearon Publishers.

Main, R. (1993, December). Integrating motivation into the instructional design process. Educational Technology, 33(12), 37-41.

Mayer, M. (1988). Test item construction: A self-instructional manual. Victoria, British Columbia, Canada: Province of British Columbia, Ministry of Advanced Education and Job Training.

McCarthy, B. (1987). The 4MAT system: Teaching to learning styles with right/left mode techniques. Barrington, IL: Excel, Inc.

McFarlane, A., Sparrowhawk, A., & Heald, Y. (2002). Report on the educational use of games. Teachers Evaluating Educational Multimedia (TEEM), Cambridge, UK. Retrieved November 12, 2004 from http://www.teem.org.uk/publications/teem_gamesined_full.pdf.

Meyer, T. (1998, February). The pixel formerly known as square. DV, 6(2), 82, 84.

Milheim, W., & Martin, B. (1991). Theoretical bases for the use of learner control: Three different perspectives. Journal of Computer-Based Instruction, 18(3), 99-105.

Miller, S., & Miller, K. (2000). Theoretical and practical considerations in the design of web-based instruction. In Abbey, B. (Ed.), Instructional and cognitive impacts of web-based education. (pp. 156-177). Hershey, PA: Idea Group Publishing.

Murphy, M., & Davidson, G. (1991, Spring). Computer-based adaptive instruction: Effects of learner control on concept learning. Journal of Computer-Based Instruction, 18(2), 51-56.

Newby, T., Ertmer, P., & Stepich, D. (1995). Instructional analogies and the learning of concepts. Educational Technology Research and Development, 43(1), 5-18.

Orey, M., & Nelson, W. (1993). Development principles for intelligent tutoring systems: Integrating cognitive theory into the development of computer-based instruction. Educational Technology Research and Development, 41(1), 59-72.

Ormrod, J. (1990). Human learning: Theories, principles, and educational applications. New York, NY: Merrill Publishing Company.

Orr, J. (1994, Spring). Light from shadow: The virtues of virtual reality. The Human Interface Technology Lab Review. 4, 21.

Park, O. (1998). Visual displays and contextual presentations in computer-based instruction. Educational Technology Research and Development, 46(3), 37-50.

Park, O. (1994, April). Dynamic visual displays in media-based instruction. Educational Technology, 34(4), 21-25.

Park, O., & Gittelman, S. (1992). Selective use of animation and feedback in computer-based instruction. Educational Technology Research and Development, 40(4), 27-38.

Pearlstein, R. (1993, November/December). Keep-your-distance learning. Performance and Instruction, 32(10), 8-9.

Rambally, G., & Rambally, R. (1987). Human factors in CAI design. Computers & Education, 11(2), 149-153.

Reiser, R., & Dick, W. (1990). Evaluating instructional software. Educational Technology Research and Development, 38(3), 43-55.

Reiser, R., & Gagne, R. (1983). Selecting media for instruction. Englewood Cliffs, NJ: Educational Technology Publications.

Reizner, D. (1997, October). Tips to clip. AV Video & Multimedia Producer, 19(10), 29.

Riding, R., & Sadler, S. (1992, October). Type of instructional material, cognitive style, and learning performance. Educational Studies, 18(3), 323-339.

Rieber, L., & Kini, A. (1991). Theoretical foundations of instructional applications of computer-generated animated visuals. Journal of Computer-Based Instruction, 18(3), 83-88.

Rieber, L. (1990). Animation in computer-based instruction. Educational Technology Research and Development, 38(1), 77-86.

Romiszowski, A. (1988). The selection and use of instructional media: For improved classroom teaching and for interactive, individual instruction (2nd ed.). New York, NY: Nichols Publishing.

Rose, J. (2000, March). Boom Mic Basics. DV, 8(3), 38-44.

Rose, J. (1998, May). Cutting remarks. DV, 6(5), 98, 100.

Rose, J. (1997, May). You can't always fix in the mix. DV, 5(5), 86-87.

Rosebush, J. (1995, July). A guide to multimedia production staffing. CD-ROM Professional, 8(7), 32-43.

Rosenborg, V., Green, B., Hester, J., Knowles, W., & Wirsching, M. (1993). A guide to multimedia. Carmel, IN: New Riders Publishing.

Rossett, A. (1987). Training needs assessment. Englewood Cliffs, NJ: Educational Technology Publications.

Sales, G., & Williams, M. (1988, Fall). The effect of adaptive control of feedback in computer-based instruction. Journal of Research on Computing in Education, 21(1), 97-111.

Salisbury, D. (1990). Cognitive psychology and its implications for designing drill and practice programs for computers. Journal of Computer-Based Instruction, 17(1), 23-30.

Sawyer, T. (1985). Human factors considerations in computer-assisted instruction. Journal of Computer-Based Instruction, 12(1), 17-20.

Schwier, R. (1994). Multimedia design principles for constructing prescriptive, democratic and cybernetic learning environments. Proceedings of the ED-MEDIA 94 World Conference on Educational Multimedia and Hypermedia.

Schwier, R., & Misanchuk, E. (1993). Interactive multimedia instruction. Englewood Cliffs, NJ: Educational Technology Publications.

Sherman, G., & Klein, J. (1995). The effects of cued interaction and ability grouping during cooperative computer-based science instruction. Educational Technology Research and Development, 43(4), 5-24.

Shi, L., Kinshuk, Lin, T., & Patel, A. (2004). High level intelligence through horizontal and vertical networking of tutoring applications. Proceedings of the Third Pan-Commonwealth Forum on Open Learning.

Siegel, M., & Sousa, G. (1994, September). Inventing the virtual textbook: Changing the nature of schooling. Educational Technology, 34(7), 49-54.

Smith, C. (1990). Mastering television technology: A cure for the common video. Richardson, TX: Newman-Smith Publishing Company.

Smith, L., & Renzulli, J. (1984, Winter). Learning style preferences: A practical approach for classroom teachers. Theory Into Practice, 23(1), 44-50.

Spitzer, D. (1991). Introduction to instructional technology (2nd ed.). Boise, ID: Boise State University.

Stamberg, R. (2004, June). Sound design: Creating big impact with a small budget. AV Video Multimedia Producer, 26(6), 10.

Standing Committee on Educational Technology. (1993, June). Educational technology: A building block for the future. Victoria, British Columbia, Canada: Standing Committee on Educational Technology.

Staninger, S. (1994, July-August). Hypertext technology: Educational consequences. Educational Technology, 34(6), 51-53.

Strauss, R. (1995, February). The development tool fandango: Deciding the authoring system versus programming language question. CD-ROM Professional, 8(2), 47-55.

Sukhoo, A., Barnard, A., Eloff, M., Van der Poll, J., & Motah, M. (2005). Accommodating soft skills in software project management. The Journal of Issues in Informing Science and Information Technology, 2, 691-703.

Terwilliger, C. (2004, October). Voiceover 101: How to hire, direct and format scripts to get the most out of your talent in the studio. AV Video Multimedia Producer, 26(10), 20, 22.

Thurman, R., & Mattoon, J. (1994, October). Virtual reality: Toward fundamental improvements in simulation-based training. Educational Technology, 34(8), 56-64.

Thurman, R. (1993). Instructional simulation from a cognitive psychology viewpoint. Educational Technology Research and Development, 41(4), 75-89.

Treasury Board of Canada Secretariat (Government of Canada). (2004, March, 5). Common Look and Feel for the Internet. Retrieved January 30, 2005 from http://www.cio-dpi.gc.ca/clf-nsi/guide/guide_e.asp

Tuck, J. (1988, September). Professional development through learning centers. Training & Development Journal, 42(9), 76-79.

Vaughan, T. (1993). Multimedia: Making it work. Berkeley, CA: Osborne McGraw-Hill.

Villarreal, K., & Oller, B. (1990). A graphic picture is worth... Emerging Technologies Bulletin, 14, 9-10.

Vockell, E. (1990, August/September). Instructional principles behind computer use. The Computing Teacher, 18(1), 10-15.

von Wodtke, M. (1993). Mind over media: Creative thinking skills for electronic media. New York, NY: McGraw-Hill.

Wager, W., Polkinghorne, S., & Powley, R. (1992). Simulations: Selection and development. Performance Improvement Quarterly, 5(2), 47-64.

Watzman, S. (1995). Information design principles for the interface designer. Session Handout Book of the Performance Support '95 Conference, September 6-8, 1995, Washington, DC.

Wheelwright, G. (1993, December). The talkin' listenin' PC. The Computer Paper, 6(12), 58-61.

Williams, R., & Dreher, H. (2004). Automatically grading essays with Markit©. Proceedings of the 2004 Informing Science and IT Education Joint Conference.

Williams, R., & Dreher, H. (2005). Formative Assessment Visual Feedback in Computer-Graded Essays. The Journal of Issues in Informing Science and Information Technology, 2, 23-32.

Winn, W. (1994). Designing and using virtual environments: The advantage of immersion. Proceedings of the ED-MEDIA 94 World Conference on Educational Multimedia and Hypermedia.

Wlodkowski, R. (1985). Enhancing adult motivation to learn. San Francisco, CA: Jossey-Bass Publishers.

Wodaski, R. (1994). Multimedia madness. Indianapolis, IN: Sams Publishing.

Wood, E. (1993, October). A beginner's guide to multimedia. Computer Graphics World, 16(10), 71-84.

Wunderlich, K., Bell, A., & Ford, L. (2005, January). Improving Learning Through Understanding of Brain Science Research. Retrieved Mar. 31, 2005 from http://www.league.org/publication/abstracts/learning/lelabs200501.html

Xerox Corporation. (1988). <u>Xerox publication standards: A manual of style and design</u>. New York, NY: Watson-Guptill Publications.

Yung-Bin, B. (1992). Effects of learning style in a hypermedia instructional system. <u>Proceedings of Selected Research and Development Presentations at the Convention of the Association for Educational Communications and Technology</u>, pp. 506-508.

Glossary

AIF or **AIFF** (audio interchange file format) is an audio standard for PC and Macintosh® computers.

Analog refers to data stored as natural waveforms. Contrast this with digital data.

ARCS refers to the attributes called attention, relevance, confidence, and satisfaction. The ARCS model promotes addressing these attributes to motivate students.

Attitudes are tendencies people have to making particular decisions or choices under specific circumstances.

Attract sequences are devices, such as interesting animations and video clips, designed to capture a student's attention.

AU refers to an audio standard.

Authoring is the process of issuing, testing, and revising instructions for presenting materials on a computer system.

Authoring systems tend to be menu-driven authoring tools that guide the production of computer-based instructional materials.

Authoring tools are software products designed to make authoring efficient.

AVI (audio-video interleave) is a software-based compression/decompression standard for digitally storing video and audio.

Bandwidth refers to the amount of information that can be transmitted over a given time period.

Betacam SP is a high-end, professional-level analog video standard.

Bits represent 1's or O's, the smallest amount of computer data. There are 8 bits in a byte.

Black striping is a way to put continuous time code onto a video tape. You can do this by recording video over the entire tape with the camera's shutter closed.

BMP (bitmap) is a standard graphics file format.

Book marking is a navigation feature for restarting students where they left off in the previous session.

Bytes are the basic storage units of computer data. There are 8 bits in a byte.

Check discs are initial versions of discs created for proofing materials.

Cluster analysis is used to organize verbal information into logical groupings that are small enough to be learned successfully.

Computer-managed presentations are used to control the display of digital text, audio, graphics, animations, video, and special effects, such as dissolves and wipes, to audiences. In computer-managed presentations, instructors retain the responsibility for teaching.

Control options are navigation tools that allow users to control their own learning paths.

Copyright is the exclusive privilege that only allows authors or assignees the right to copy, sell, and/or transmit their own original work.

Criterion-referenced tests explicitly measure the determined learning outcomes. Student success is based on the number of learning outcomes passed.

Cross-platform refers to the portability of a program or code between different computer platforms.

DAT (digital audio tape) is a system for recording audio in a digital format.

Digital refers to data stored as 1's and O's that computers can interpret. Contrast this with analog data.

Digital cameras can digitally record quality images that can be downloaded to a computer.

Digital chalk is a tool that lets you write on top of a computer display.

Dithering is a process that changes the color value of every pixel to the closest matching color value in the target palette. Dithering can make it appear as though there are more colors than are actually present.

Drill and practice is a type of instructional multimedia that provides repeated activity (drill) and opportunities (practice) to try skills or concepts learned elsewhere.

Dubs are copies of tapes.

DV is short for digital video.

Educational games are usually decision-making activities that can include rules, a goal, conditions or constraints, competition, challenge, strategies, and feedback.

8 mm is a consumer-level video standard.

Elaborative or informational feedback typically takes the form of corrective statements and elaborations or guidance in how to attain the stated learning outcome.

Feedback is any message or display that you give to a learner based on his or her input.

Fixed spacing is present when the spacing between letters is constant. Fixed spacing requires more space than variable spacing.

FLC is an animation file format.

FLI is an animation file format.

Formative evaluation is the collection of data and information, throughout the instructional development process, that is analyzed and used to improve the instructional effectiveness of the application.

Frames are single video images. In North America, there are usually 30 frames or images per second of video.

GIF (graphics interface format) is a standard graphics file format.

Goal analysis is the process for providing a general but exact visual statement of what the learner will be able to do.

Hi8 is a consumer-level video standard.

Hierarchical analysis is used to determine the subordinate skills required to learn each intellectual skill.

Hot words are highlighted words that indicate active links to other material.

Hue is a tint or color.

Hypermedia is media that is indexed and linked in a logical manner to other information.

Hypertext is text that is indexed and linked in a logical manner to other information.

Icons are graphic or symbolic representations of objects or processes.

Instructional design is the specific systematic, repetitive process of activities aimed at creating a solution for an instructional problem.

Instructional development cycle is the overall systematic, repetitive process made up of essential activities to solve an instructional problem.

Instructional events represent what should be done to ensure that learning occurs. These events include gaining attention, informing the learner of the learning outcome, stimulating recall of prerequisites, presenting the material, providing learning guidance, eliciting the performance, providing feedback, assessing performance, and enhancing retention and transfer.

Instructional goals are general skills that will be further defined into specific learning outcomes.

Instructional strategies describe components of a set of instructional materials and the activities that the students must do to achieve the learning outcomes.

Intellectual skills are those that require learners to think (rather than simply memorizing and recalling information).

Intelligent tutoring systems are computer programs that attempt to mimic perfect instructors.

Interactivity is active learner participation in the learning process.

JPEG (joint photographic experts groups) is a hardware-based international compression/decompression standard for digitally storing visuals. Photographs are often stored in the JPEG format.

Learner analysis determines information about the student's abilities, language capabilities, motivation, interests, human factors, and learning styles.

Learning outcomes or objectives are specific measurable skills.

Learning styles are characteristic behaviors that indicate how students prefer to learn. They are also known as cognitive styles or learning preferences.

Lossless compression reduces the storage requirements of data while retaining all of the original information.

Lossy compression reduces the storage requirements of data with the loss of some of the original information (e.g., through the frame rate, picture size, and color palette size).

Luminance is the overall brightness of an image.

Master discs are final versions of discs from which copies are made.

Media mix is the combination of media used to ensure learning.

Menu metaphors are graphical representations of menu items.

Metafiles are graphics stored as a set of mathematical instructions.

MIDI (musical instrument digital interface) is a standard that allows personal computers, synthesizers, sequencers, keyboards, drum machines, and so forth to interface with each other.

Mini-DV is a quality video standard.

Morphing is changing one image into another. Morphing can also produce special effects such as stretching, compressing, distorting, or transforming images.

MPEG (moving picture experts groups) is an international compression/decompression standard for digitally storing video and audio. There are a variety of standards including MPEG-1, MPEG-2, and MPEG-4. Each standard is compressed for a different purpose ranging from DVD storage to Internet streaming.

MP3 refers to an audio standard.

Multimedia is the combination of hardware and software that allows you to integrate different media such as video, animation, audio, graphics, and text on an affordable computer.

Natural language interface refers to interacting with a computer through verbal communication.

Needs assessment is a method of gathering information for determining the actual problem.

Normative-referenced tests compare students to each other. Student success depends on how well other students perform.

Object-based systems are a classification of authoring tools containing predefined objects that can be programmed to do things.

Optical character readers convert text images into a digitally equivalent form that can be edited with word processors.

PIC is an animation file format.

Post-tests are tests given after the material is presented.

Pre-tests are tests given before instruction is presented.

Procedural analysis is used to derive subordinate psychomotor skills.

Programming languages are general software tools that have an extensive command set available for creating computer programs.

Prototypes are original models used to test whether an idea will work before significant development takes place.

Psychomotor skills are those that require learners to carry out muscular actions.

QuickTime is a software-based compression/decompression standard for digitally storing video and audio.

Red book standard is an international storage standard for digital audio that allows you to address audio by minutes, seconds, and frames.

Rendering is a process of converting computer data into an animation or video clip.

Resolution refers to the number of dots (or pixels) per inch.

RTF (rich text format) is a text storage standard that retains attributes like bold and underlining.

S-VHS is a consumer-level video standard.

Sampling rates indicate how often data is recorded.

Saturation is the intensity of a color.

Scanning is a method of digitizing images into data that can be accessed by computers.

Screen capture utilities allow you do digitize any image on the screen.

Screen design determines how each screen will appear to learners and how the learners will interact with the computer.

Screen size refers to the number of pixels (or dots) on a screen or a portion of the screen.

Screen transitions are routines, such as wipes and dissolves, that gradually reveal the following screen.

Scripts are text copies of narrations or dialogues.

Scrolling is a process for displaying more text than a screen can display by adding new text lines to the bottom of the display while the top lines disappear.

Simulations present or model the essential elements of real or imaginary situations.

SND refers to an audio standard for Macintosh® computers.

Storyboards are paper-based scale replica drafts of each screen that will appear on the computer.

Subordinate skills analysis is a process for determining the skills that must be learned before performing a step.

Task analysis is a complete step-by-step breakdown of the duties needed to perform a task.

TelePrompTers are devices that show scripts for those who have not memorized their lines.

3/4 inch is a good-quality, professional-level analog video standard.

TIF or TIFF (tagged image file format) is a standard graphics file format.

Time codes are a numbering scheme recorded in sequence onto videotape. Time codes are used to reference each frame.

Tutorials are computer programs that imitate a human tutor.

User-interfaces are how the user communicates and interacts with the computer.

Variable spacing is present when the spacing between letters is reduced. Variable spacing requires less space than fixed spacing.

Vector graphics are graphics stored as a set of mathematical instructions.

Verbal information is material, such as names of objects, that students simply have to memorize and recall.

Verification feedback often only states that an answer is correct or incorrect but can take the form of praise, animations, and sound effects.

VHS is a consumer-level video standard.

Virtual reality is a type of computer program that allows people to be totally immersed in an artificial or simulated environment yet retain the feeling that the environment is real.

WAV refers to an audio standard for PC computers.

WMV is a software-based compression/decompression standard for digitally storing video and audio.

Index

- Computer-managed presentations. 1956
- what are learning paths? — pg 64
- rationale for using multiple media — pg 98 (sus)
  (multi-sensory learning)

- types of questions / tests → connected to the
  learning strategies used → pg 172